COX'S COMPANY

Phil Arnold

Order this book online at www.trafford.com
or email orders@trafford.com

Most Trafford titles are also available at major online book retailers.

Printed in Victoria, BC, Canada.

ISBN: 978-1-4251-9135-1 (sc)
ISBN: 978-1-4251-9136-8 (dj)
ISBN: 978-1-4251-9137-5 (e-book)

*Our mission is to efficiently provide the world's finest, most comprehensive
book publishing service, enabling every author to experience success.
To find out how to publish your book, your way, and have it available
worldwide, visit us online at www.trafford.com*

Trafford rev. 1/28/2010

www.trafford.com

North America & international
toll-free: 1 888 232 4444 (USA & Canada)
phone: 250 383 6864 ✦ fax: 812 355 4082

1

How he got the name of Cox's Company Sergeant was when he drilled the company and it received a citation for the smartest company in the regiment. He represented a body of men who were the smartest, cleanest, most eager and keen set of soldiers in the annals of the regiment's history.

He did not push them with threats or the promise of reward at the end of square bashing. He did not punish them by giving them hours of extra duty or detailing someone to watch them while they did it. He let them do the spit and polish without even keeping a watch on them, merely allowing them to do their own thing; letting them keep to their own rules without supervision. That way he got the reputation of expecting their all and nothing else.

He was referred to as Cox of Cox's Company. This was shortened to Cox's men or Cox's Company.

Sergeant Christopher Cox, or to his friends, 'Coxey', for short, was the drill sergeant for the company of men known as the Ninety-ninth Regiment of Foot, or the 'one short', owing to the one short of a hundred. With a major to command them, a captain as his adjutant and three or four junior officers to help a dozen or so NCOs it was considered a happy company.

When he was referred to as Sergeant Cox, they at once called him Coxey, a name that stuck to him, especially when he was addressed by his fellow NCOs. Privately, even the junior officers referred to him as Coxey, although it was frowned on by the senior officers.

Now the rest of the regiment was posted to France for the duration of the war against the German armies. It was 1915 and the war had been on for over a year.

The British army was suffering casualties in the field and the company of foot was called to the front line. They filed aboard the ship that was designated their troop ship and within hours were lining up on the crowded French quay.

For ninety per cent of the men a foreign port was a novelty. Of course, the local whores made it a field day. For a time they flocked around the foreign soldiers until their money ran out. The ladies then went back to their normal boyfriends.

"Typical," snorted Private Smithers in derision to his mate. "When they see you have spent your money and you have an empty pocket, they don't want to know you. It's the same the whole world over. When they've had your money they don't want to know you."

Neil Hartley, or Ginger to his friends, fingered a couple of French coins and mentally calculated what they were worth in drinks.

"I've got enough for a couple of beers. How much you got?"

Smithers rattled a few sous in his pocket and shook his head.

"About two more, then *finito*." He espied a corporal going into a bar. "If I was a sergeant or a corporal I'd be roaring pissed by now, what with all the pay they get," he muttered, shaking his head.

Hartley nodded in sympathy and pointed to a dingy bar.

"Let's try this one," he said, pushing on a paint-peeled door and stepping into a dark and oppressive barroom.

As they entered they counted up the value of the coins and added them together to produce the total of two francs and two centimes. Smithers tossed the coins into the air and expertly caught them, eyeing the Frenchman who was following their flight from behind the bar.

"Two beers," said a grinning Smithers, putting his elbow into a pool of stale beer and wiping his khaki sleeve on a slop rag that was left on the bar counter.

"Two beers coming up," said the barman in broken English. He scooped the coins into a drawer behind the bar. "You like French beer?"

Neil sniffed in the aroma of cooking cabbage and smiled.

"Smells like you're cooking your dinner," he said. "What you got, roast beef and Yorkshire pudding?"

The Frenchman shook his head and put two more glasses on the counter to indicate he did not understand then went back to his work under his counter. They sipped the amber liquid slowly to make it last. Smithers looked all around.

"This place is empty," he said ruefully, "where's all the birds gone?"

"Same place as our money - gone with the drifting wind."

Smithers sipped the top off the flat ale and grinned wryly.

"Serves you right, you shouldn't have joined."

Hartley licked the surface with the tip of his tongue and gazed at the wall of the barroom. He noted the cracked and crinkled wallpaper, and the smudges of long gone names that still decorated the brown and yellow paper. His eyes dropped to his battered tobacco tin resting on the thickly marked counter, and he deftly rolled a thin sliver of a cigarette. He gave it to Smithers, and watched as he lit it and inhaled the blue smoke.

"Roll on pay day," he said.

He rolled another and coughed as he deeply inhaled the biting smoke. Talking as well as smoking caused him to cough and he held the roll with the strength of his lips, speaking through the haze.

"If the sergeants or the corporals had to exist on our pay they would know what we are going through."

Smithers nodded, drew in a great gasp of smoke and blew it out in a huge cloud.

"They couldn't manage it," he grated, taking a drink of the beer and looking into the drink with a corrugation of his drawn brows. "Five bob is all I get every pay day, five measly bob and my keep. Can you imagine *them* living on that for a week?"

Hartley shook his head and shifted on the hard chair.

"It might be more if you had a stripe," he suggested. "If you were a lance corporal or even a full corporal you would be on twelve bob per week."

Smithers sniffed and sipped the beer.

"I won't be in it till then. I want to get out when the war is over, get a normal job and make a living wage. My dad said there's a lot of unemployment; he's on the dole," he said, eyeing a trail of smoke as it drifted up towards the ceiling. He inhaled and watched the lungful of smoke as it joined the rest of the cloud curling across the cracked ceiling. "They are all on the dole, the whole of the working class," he said, grimacing at Hartley, "but when we get out it might be different."

"I might sign on for another few years till I make corporal," Hartley said through the tobacco fumes. "If it means no work outside we might have to stay in the army."

Smithers turned to regard his mate and spoke in a quiet voice.

"You might get killed or wounded, you ever considered that?"

Hartley slewed around on his chair and grinned.

"There is that eventuality. We both have the same sort of risk, you stand the same chance I do."

Smithers hunched his shoulders to indicate that what will be, will be.

"If that is the case then I won't need a job," he replied.

They both laughed in unison and drained their glasses. They ordered another beer each and watched the Frenchman flick the small coins into the drawer with a quick flourish.

Within the course of an hour the beer slowly disappeared at a leisurely pace and time elapsed with it. Not a fresh soul joined them in the barroom then the owner looked at the big clock ticking on the wall.

"Time to close up," he announced.

He hung a soiled towel over the beer tap and mopped up the beer residue coating the tiny bar. Within a short while they emptied their glasses and said goodnight in faltering French. He just nodded in reply and slammed the door behind them as they exited. After he shot the bolt on the door they heard another door slam on the inside - then silence.

"Gawd, I'm starving," complained Smithers, "wonder what's for supper?"

Neil Hartley looked at the town hall clock.

"It's well past supper time, you'll have to wait until breakfast," he declared.

Smithers groaned in mock agony.

"*Breakfast*, I'll never last until breakfast time, I'm starving *now*."

The two soldiers tiptoed past the guardroom after removing their boots. When they were safely past, they tied them back on as the guardroom vanished into the gloom of the rainy night. The lights of the barracks lit their way into the huge building and momentarily blinded them as they swung the door open.

They passed rows of sleeping forms huddled beneath brown blankets and tiptoed into the room amid heavy snores and heavy breathing. Smithers found his bed space and flopped onto the straw mattress. The next man, hunched beneath his blanket, snored away happily and emitted a soft whistle as he breathed out.

Smithers, although suffering the pangs of hunger, had to be content with his previous meal and soon fell into a dreamless sleep.

Someone must have switched off the lights because in the morning at six they were awakened by the calling of Corporal Gunn, who stumped into the room blaring:

"Rise and shine, on with socks etc."

Groans met this daily ritual and the men spilled from their warm beds into the cold light of day, with spoons and other implements rattling in the metal mess tins.

Sergeant Cox strode to the centre of the group of men and addressed the lines of waiting troops.

"All right, you know where we are and what we are doing here. Our allies need our help on the western front and they have called for us to give it to them. I will call on Corporal Gunn to put you right if you need help, and he will listen to your complaints." He pulled himself up to his full height of five feet ten inches and bellowed. "Let's make one thing crystal clear. You are highly trained men of the foot regiment. You know what is expected of a soldier and will act as a soldier, or I will know the reason why."

He called for Corporal Gunn to take over and watched as the corporal called the men to order. The lines of khaki-clad men snapped to attention at his command and stood stiffly straight as Gunn walked through their midst, inspecting their equipment.

"Smithers, not you *again*," he said, pulling the rucksack to the right order by tightening the buckle. "You slovenly soldier, Smithers, you would get two weeks confined to barracks if we were back home in Blighty." He marched to the front and shouted. "I want nothing but discipline if you want to be in my company. I don't want slackers of any kind, barracks room lawyers, jumped up heroes or mamas' boys. Now it must cease or I will know the reason why." He walked through the entire line of men then came to a halt at the end of the parade. He retraced his steps and yelled at the assembly. "Those rifles are a disgrace; the pull-throughs are not being greased. They must be sparkling clean every day after a complete clean of the barrel and the firing mechanism. I am Corporal Gunn and I am clean, like I expect your rifles to be clean."

He spun around to gaze at the sergeant. "I want Sergeant Cox to be proud of his company as is his due. He won't be proud of a bunch of men who can't find their arses from their elbows when it comes to cleaning their rifles like they're supposed to do. This is *with* your usual duties, not *instead of.*" He stiffened to attention and addressed them again. "You will march away in fours to the barracks wot has been assigned to you. It's a French barracks, so don't be surprised to hear other soldiers of other countries in there." He addressed the sergeant again. "Company at the attention and ready to march away, Sergeant Cox."

His place was taken by the sergeant.

"You've heard Corporal Gunn, now it's up to you to fit the bill and fall in with our wishes," he shouted. "If you do you will all get a pass till midnight to see all the local Judies. If you do not, I'll make you wish you had never been born..." He paused and added, "I want a company I can be proud of. It can't be assumed, but it can be earned. In the next few weeks we will weed out the slackers and reward the triers. I want no lawyers or complainers. I want men who ignore them and do what the British soldier is best at - fighting the enemy. I want no trouble, only to the opposition, not amongst yourselves or with yourself. You be true to me and I will be the same to you. You be smart to me and I will be extra smart to you."

Cox gave a cough to indicate he was at the end of his narrative. He straightened to his full height and pushed out his chest.

"You will get the passes if you have earned them. In the past I have not pushed you to do anything, but have left it to your conscience to do what is required. In your past record you have shown that you are trusted to do this, so I will not waste my time or breath in repeating it." He paused to regain his breath. He looked all around the ranks and eyed them with serious eyes. He came to attention and snapped, "Company, company attention."

The boots of the massed ranks came together as one and echoed around the parade ground. As they marched away, Cox shifted the chinstrap of his cap and watched them go. He had a slight smile on his face that changed as he saw the misfit, Smithers, edging his pack higher up his back.

"Smithers, you bloody idiot," he muttered to himself, "when will you ever learn?"

Although a strict disciplinarian, Corporal Gunn had a different face when he was sampling a pint of his favourite mild beer. His cares seemed to fade away when he quaffed the liquid and gazed at the love of his life, Freda.

She was a slightly overweight woman of forty with a bunch of mousey hair that ended with a fringe just above her nose; a thin-lipped woman who applied her red lipstick, which was inclined to smudge, with a liberal hand.

Gunn watched her pull a pint with the finesse of a woman used to the work and who loved every minute of it. She pulled the handle and as he watched her ample breasts heaving with the work, he licked his lips, thinking of what he would be doing with them that evening.

She twinkled a smile to him and nodded to the rain dripping down from the edge of the wooden window frame.

"All right for ducks," she said, adding a little drop more with a final squeeze of the pump handle, "but not those like me who can't swim."

Gunn shifted his gaze from the delicious breasts and smiled. His mind was on the night before when he had made lingering love to the woman.

"Me neither," he said, dropping his eyes to his pint. "I couldn't swim a stroke even if my life depended on it."

Freda handed a brimming glass to another soldier and dropped the coins into a wooden drawer. In the call for women to aid the men she had replied to the summons and volunteered for duty in the catering arm of the British Army. As she was already working as a barmaid she was accepted into the service as such and was posted to the area of Calais in one of the British pubs meant for army servicemen.

The hope of steady employment was gradually eased as the onset of the war continued. Freda Harcourt was another victim of the restless divorce rate, and parted from her violent husband after three stormy years of unsuitable marriage. Surprisingly she met up with him in one of the catering pubs, but he still maintained his indifferent ways. She just forgot her previous life with him and started another with the army.

Although there was a shortage of suitable barmaids and she was spoilt for choice, she still preferred Gunn. He was not bad looking, had a pleasant nature and a smile that made her heart cave in. His pay as a corporal is an added factor, she mused to herself, but the money meant little to her. I have plenty of money to pay my way in this world, she thought.

She had a secret wish to be famous though, and dreamed of having a voice like other renowned singers, but even if she had the gift of a lovely voice she doubted whether she would have the guts to do anything about it anyway. She knew she lacked spirit, but it did not bother her. She enjoyed life, and other unobtainable things were just pipe dreams.

2

Gᴜɴɴ ᴀᴅᴍɪʀᴇᴅ Sᴇʀɢᴇᴀɴᴛ Cox. Not because he held the rest of the men with his rank, but as a man who held his respect with dignity. Of course he envied the sergeant his stripes and envisioned another stripe to go with his own two. He smiled to himself and fondled his arm.

"Sergeant Gunn," he whispered to himself.

It has a certain ring to it, he thought, running the name through his mind - a certain consistency about it.

"What did you say?" commented Freda, coughing with the cloud of cigarette smoke that wreathed about them.

"Nothing," he said, over the top of the glass, "just talking to myself."

"You get put away for doing that, sunshine," she sparkled, showing her teeth in a big smile.

She had stopped serving the customers in the lull that came after several rowdy soldiers had left.

"Have you thought over what I asked you last night?"

"About what?"

"Don't say you've forgotten what I said to you?"

His face was a picture.

A man, dressed in the regulation uniform of khaki tunic and trousers gathered at the knees with puttees wound tightly around his legs, which stopped short at a pair of muddy boots that trailed rainwater, appeared in the doorway. He stamped his boots a few times to rid them of the clinging mud and wiped them on the wire mud remover.

"Hello, you two," he called, "all right for you two getting excused duties with your injuries you got when the shell landed in the trench."

Hartley rubbed the soreness in his wrist and started to complain.

"We both got injuries, me with my wrist and Smithers his finger. It was one of them ones that landed on a side trench, we were lucky to have only got slight injuries. The explosion dislodged a stone that caught the pair of us together, Steve."

Steve Willcox gave a loud laugh.

"You just missed the charge and got the slack, shame, you might have got a medal and a Blighty wound. You might have been going home if it was any worse."

"Fat chance," said Hartley, looking at his wrist and shaking it to settle it down. "I'd like to get something to get into hospital - nothing serious though, just a cut finger on the barbed wire."

"You're not getting the chance to go home," piped up Smithers, pinching out his fag end. "If *I* don't get nothing then *you* don't get nothing, I'll see to that."

"What're you going to do, Smithers?" Hartley chaffed, exercising his arm with turning motions of his wrist. "Tell Gunn to put me on light duties?"

Smithers laughed off the notion then suddenly sprang to his feet hissing:

"Here he comes himself, Gunn."

The door opened to admit the corporal, who entered the dugout with a sweep of rain that had the latest man, Steve Willcox, dodging the rain spots from the NCO's raincoat.

"Aha, so *this* is where you are all hiding," Gunn said, shaking his hair free of the rain. "I'd put you on guard duties if it you weren't on light duties, Hartley."

The three stiff men looked at the corporal and Smithers.

"Aw, have a heart, Corp," said Smithers.

"Have a heart, Corporal, indeed," mimicked Gunn in a voice that was trying to ape the young soldier. "You ask me to have a heart when you do other things to annoy me, like keeping this dugout like a shit house like you do." He looked all around the room with obvious displeasure and eyed them, one after the other, with his face frowning and troubled. "Look at them beds all haphazard and crooked. Those packs at the end of your bed should be square and lined up with the end of your bed." He strode forwards with measured tread and stopped at the bunk farthest from the door. "Look at the mud on the floor. Don't you use the scraper outside? Don't you wipe your boots before you come off watch? I know we are in the front line and ready to die at any moment, but that's no excuse to let standards slip." He ended his tirade with a warning. "If you all don't buck up your ideas, and soon, you will be on a charge, no matter where we are, on the parade ground or in the centre of no-man's-land, do I make myself clear?"

No one uttered a single word as he opened the door to go out. He stood at the entrance.

"I'll give you just twenty-four hours to get this dugout right, after that all hell will break loose."

After he had left they relaxed as one and fell into the same mode of movement they had done before.

"Well, you look at *that* now," said Smithers, fishing in his pocket to find the cigarette end and lighting it with eyes that reflected the match light. "He talks about cleaning the dugout when we all know he gets his cleaning done for him."

"Yeah, but he is in charge," Willcox said with a trace of irony in his voice. "When you are in charge even though all these duties are done for you, *he* calls the tune."

"Well, it is a bit manky-like," commented Hartley, dropping onto his bunk and sitting cross-legged on the side. "Look at the mud on the floor, it's a wonder we don't get any rats in here."

Later on they made a start on the floor, which was lined with old oilcloth and pieces of coconut matting.

"That's all we can do under these conditions," said Hartley with a sniff. "Anyway, it's 'Smoke ho' time for a cup of tea."

It was at this precise time that a small shell hit the dugout and half-demolished it with an enormous bang. Smithers was half-buried under mud and other indefinable objects that all missed giving him a serious wound. The others all escaped harm except for mild cuts and bruises.

3

THEY WERE ASTOUNDED AND surprised by the sudden force, and for a moment they were disorientated.

Hartley and Willcox shook themselves free of the encumbrances and mud-encrusted items, and straightened up from the remains of the dugout.

"Where's Smithers?" Hartley asked in alarm, searching for his mate.

A hollow moan then sounded through the debris, and one arm broke through the surface of the soil, showing them where he was. The two soldiers dug down into the earth and managed to free the face of the buried soldier. They heaved and pulled the struggling form of the unfortunate Smithers from the muddy floor and rubble surrounding him.

"Gawd!" exclaimed Smithers through a mouthful of dust and mud. "What happened? One minute I was lying on me bunk smoking a fag the next minute I was buried under a bloody great big shower of sticky mud." He spat the remains of the mud from his teeth and groaned. "It tastes awful, just like shit."

He held on to the remains of his bunk and levered himself upwards.

"I was wondering where you went to," laughed his mate. "We thought you were a gonner under that great pile of mud and other things."

Smithers staggered to the centre of the destroyed dugout, and up-righted a partially buried wooden chair. He scraped the mud from the seat and with a heavy sigh plonked his buttocks onto the thin plate of wooden seating.

"I didn't hear anything at all," Willcox concluded, treating the heap of earth and broken woodwork to a look of extreme agony. "We usually hear something of a warning like a howl, but there was nothing to indicate it was coming. One minute it was normal, then *bang* - this."

"Looks like we will be shifting our digs in the near future," said Hartley, pulling the mud-encrusted butt of his rifle from the slimy embrace of the mud pile.

"Oh no, here comes trouble," groaned Smithers as he espied the shape of Gunn.

Corporal Gunn appeared from the broken doorway with a wide grin on his face.

"Now, wasn't that nice of them to wait until I was out of the way? They must have
    known I was about and hung back just to please me."

Smithers gave a sickly grin in reply to the corporal's remark and, bending down, retrieved his rifle.

"Now, after you get another dugout you can clean it up seeing you ain't got nothing to do for the rest of the day," Gunn remarked, looking at Smithers and eyeing his rifle.

Smithers spat out the rest of the mud crunching between his teeth.

"I think I have been wounded, Corp," said the NCO, holding his arm at the elbow.

"You ain't hurt, Smithers," Gunn insisted, looking at him with a suspicious stare that spoke of him trying something on. "You ain't got no injury, you're trying to con me."

"No, Corp, my arm feels numb and lifeless."

"Lifeless like you are, Smithers. You use it a bit more often to get the pull-through in the barrel of your rifle and you might ease the pain of numbness."

After queuing for the daily rations, they opened the large tin of bully beef with a bayonet, and emptied it into their mess tins. The hard tack biscuit was softened with a little tea before being mixed with the hardness of the bully beef.

The men were cleaned up to the corporal's liking and, after changing their wrecked dugout for a different one, were ready for grub up.

"Don't we ever get nothing but bully beef?" complained Smithers, pulling his greatcoat around his ears. "Gawd, it's bloody cold as well. Oh, for some sunshine in this godforsaken country."

"It's going to rain again soon," said Hartley looking at the sky.

Smithers' moaning was as natural as the weather - and that was what it did. It started to rain soon after Hartley had mentioned it.

"You some sort of Jonah?" asked Willcox, when he felt the pitter-patter of falling raindrops on his helmet.

"I ain't no Jonah," insisted Hartley, swallowing a big slice of the tinned meat.

"Well, you just said about the rain and that it looks like it is coming," said Willcox, who was standing at the side of the trench. "You must be a bleeding Jonah or something."

"I tell you I'm not a Jonah," insisted Hartley, going red with anger.

"All right, all right," said Willcox, punching a hole in a tin of soup and tipping it into his mouth with a slight gulp. "I was only fooling with you, can't you take a joke?"

Hartley just ate in silence, but he was annoyed with the other trooper.

Along the trench a man was wounded when he popped his head above the sandbag line of the trench head. He just sustained a crease mark of the bullet as it struck his steel helmet. He was lying on a wooden stretcher at the foot of the trench, and was bleeding slightly from the wound. A khaki-clad figure with a red cross on his armband was bending over his prostrate body.

Later the rain eased off and the stars were just emerging when the day was drawing to a close.

Smithers took the first watch, the twelve to four. He leaned against the trench sides until it was the turn of Hartley to stand there with his rifle loaded and his bayonet fixed.

The night passed and with the return of daylight Corporal Gunn, with Sergeant Cox in attendance, trudged up and down the lines of men as they waited for the order to stand-to. Slowly, but deliberately, the junior officers and NCOs were assembled into a wall of men who laid the wooden steps of the assault ladders against the trench sides, ready for the expected charge.

Smithers and Hartley, with Willcox flanking them, waited, hearts pounding against tight breasts and senses alert with anxiety.

The order came with the men to make ready, with the first man lifting his boot to the bottom rung of the ladder. The order came from one mouth to another.

"*Stand-to.*"

The men waited, strained, ready for the order to be given with a blast on the officer's whistle.

Smithers pressed his forehead against the cold dampness of the trench walls. He had tipped the steel helmet backwards on the crown of his head to lessen the tightness of the chinstraps. His actions were automatic now; he clipped the long steel bayonet to the end of the barrel and heard it click home. He was third in line of the waiting men and he heard the deep gasp for air as each man clutched for the foul atmosphere that seemed to attach to the lines of waiting troopers. Others, all standing still on the muddy floor of the trench, muttered prayers from tight lips, or closed their eyes in preparation for the harrowing event.

The Germans seemed to sense what was happening in the British lines. Their machine-gunners seemed to know what was going on in the trenches opposite.

Smithers, his pulses racing, closed his eyes and felt for the St Christopher around his sallow neck. He had a dry cough that seemed to come when he was worried - like now.

Right down the line whistles shrilled and the columns of waiting soldiers jumped onto the ladders and began to climb the rungs to the edge of the trench overhead. The whine of a mortar bomb swished above and exploded in the rear. Bullets beat a rapid tattoo on anything that stood in the way or became buried in the soft soil of the trench sides.

Smithers felt himself being pushed up the ladder and over the top of the sandbags that were filled with black earth. A burly man he knew as 'Geordie' fell past him as he crouched down in the rain of slugs that whizzed by them. Frantically he dived for cover and slid down into a deep shell hole. As he wriggled lower over the rim he put his feet to the bottom of the pit and felt cold water seep into his boots and socks.

Above him, all hell was breaking loose as the flying bullets whizzed and pinged off any stationary object. He stretched out his hand and felt for his rifle he had left in his sudden dive for cover. With easy movements he pulled the rifle to his body and felt the welcoming hardness of the barrel come into contact with his left cheek.

A whiz-bang shell, fizzing and gyrating as it tore through the air, exploded with a terrific roar somewhere near. He didn't dare look up - machine guns were blazing away, ricocheting off anything and everything.

Less than fifty yards away Hartley was doing the same thing, but as the hail of lead marched across the battlefield unhindered, he dared to peep over the top of the shell hole to have a look for the rest of the company.

As the firing eased and tailed off he had a chance to see where Smithers had gone and how he had fared. As far as he was aware the rest of the company had done almost the same sort of thing as himself, although there were a few casualties lying motionless in the mud of the battlefield.

Knowing how Smithers' mind worked, he shouted in a hoarse voice across the pockmarked terrain. Back came an equally hoarse voice from a matter of a dozen or so more yards away.

"What're you doing?" Smithers asked, trying to keep his voice in a low register.

"Same as you are; hiding in a shell hole till it's all over."

"We have to get back to our own lines," Smithers said hoarsely.

"I know that, but how do we do it?" came the reply from Hartley.

"We might have to stay here for a few hours."

"I know that," whispered Hartley. "It's bloody freezing; I am sitting in a pool of cold water." He heard a rustling noise. "What's that in the shell hole with me?"

"Most likely rats," Smithers said croakily.

"I hate rats," Hartley said quietly.

"So do I."

"They eat dead bodies," remarked Hartley, in a quiet voice.

The guns started up again and ended the conversation.

A man suddenly jumped down into Smithers' hole and soon the caustic tones of Corporal Gunn were heard reproaching the soldier.

"Not you again, Smithers," he said in a cold voice.

"Corporal Gunn, I think I want to report sick with my arm," he said in his usual way. "It is paining me a lot."

"You and your bloody arm," exploded Gunn, "did you ever think about getting back to our line?"

"I'm staying right here," Smithers said under his breath.

"I heard that, Private Smithers," the corporal said. "I could have you on a charge for insubordination, you know that?"

In a bid to change the subject, Smithers tried another tactic.

"You think we will get back, Corp?"

"Not before nightfall. Who was that you were talking to just now?"

"546 Hartley, Corp, he's in the other shell hole close by."

"I might have known it was him," the corporal remarked with a sneer. "Where Smithers goes so does his mate. I have a good mind to put you both on a charge when we get back."

"*If* we get back," muttered Hartley, in a voice that floated over the noise of the guns.

"We'll have to wait till it's dark," Gunn said. "If we try now we will be cut to pieces before we get a dozen yards."

"I was just thinking that, Corp," said Hartley, trying to talk above the chattering of the machine guns, and raising his voice a couple of octaves higher.

"We could try it by keeping low," Smithers shouted. "All we have to do is bend down low. We ain't reached the barbed wire, so we don't have that to climb over."

"We could try," the corporal said, poking his head over the rim of the hole.

"Anything's better than sitting in this freezing cold water," Hartley said, his teeth chattering with the cold.

They gingerly climbed up the sides of the shell holes and, keeping a low profile, wriggled their way across the battlefield. The going was rough and they fell into a few holes as they squirmed over the rock-strewn ground near the start of no-man's-land. They had to crawl into other shell holes for cover as the machine guns started up again. One minute they were crawling together the next they were separated by another shell hole.

It took all of an hour to crawl the distance to the friendly lines, testament to the mad run outwards that had them dodging the initial rush to avoid the start of the attack. Others with the same thing in mind were slithering back to the comparative safety of the trenches. They risked life and limb to do it more quickly by crouching down instead of sliding on their bellies like the others. In many cases they received a bullet that ended their short life on the Somme battlefield.

"Keep down," Gunn whispered to Smithers as he turned to look for the others, "you want to cop one?"

Bit by bit they slid through the mud of the line trench tops, eventually gratefully edging over the lip of the trench into the welcoming arms of the other troopers. They were plastered from head to foot with the mud of the battlefield and, although they were covered with slime and filth, they had still managed to hold on to their rifles.

Others of the failed attempt to take the lines of the Huns reached their own British trenches by trickling slowly back to safety. Many were missing when the final register of returns was noted.

After cleaning themselves up and scraping the mud from their equipment they set out to satisfy their other wants, like food.

"I'm famished," complained Smithers to the others as he flopped down on his bunk. "I could eat a horse and come back for the bones."

"It will more than likely be a horse," commented Hartley to a new man who had been billeted with them in place of Willcox, who had been shifted by Sergeant Cox.

The newcomer, Den Horsefield or 'Horsy' for short, was pulling through the lanyard string of the rifle pull-through and eyeing the barrel for shininess. He tipped up the rifle and, after pulling the breech open, turned around to regard Hartley.

"Could very well be," he was saying, greasing the lock of the gun and running his thumb through the bolt action of the mechanism. "After that balls up what we did, it's no wonder we are still here - to enjoy this wonderful repast of stew and tinned soup."

"Well, Horsy, we made it on our first 'do'. The main thing is we returned to tell the tale," Hartley announced, borrowing the pull-through and threading the metal end of the string through the muzzle of his rifle.

He copied Horsy's example and eyed the barrel for dirt and rust.

It was the morning after the abortive attempt into enemy territory and it was Smithers' turn to cook the breakfast. He was cooking bully beef in a frying pan over an open fire in the dugout. He added a sausage to the mixture and stirred it up to let them cook together. He stirred the tea leaves into an open saucepan and added a heaped spoonful of sugar to the brown liquid.

"Come and get it," he yelled, slightly burning his thumb on the hot ring of the coal fire.

The others stood around the stove warming their hands and taking the hot food as it was dished up onto cracked plates.

"Somebody else's turn to cook the grub for supper tonight," he declared as he licked his thumb with the end of his pink tongue, "and that means washing up as well."

Horsy burped loudly after eating his meal sitting on the side of his bunk.

"I'm known as something of a cook, so it will be my turn to cook the next meal. I will be on watch this evening though, so I can't do it this evening."

"Then you can cook the breakfast when you come off watch," Smithers said.

"So, that's settled then," Hartley announced with a sigh.

Smithers just sat on the side of his bunk sucking his thumb.

That evening when the light was fading fast, Smithers was on watch when the Huns made a surprise attack on the trench he was guarding.

A big burly German bore down on him with his bayonet outstretched, ready to spear him on its point...

4

SMITHERS IMMEDIATELY SHOT HIM and, turning around to do the same thing to the other Huns who might be near, faced his attacker with his rifle pointing at the downed German soldier. Cox then appeared on the scene and stood over the Hun with his bayonet poised.

"It looks like he is a gonner," he rasped, standing his firearm against the trench wall. "Good work, Smithers."

All inhabitants of the dugout heard of his exploits, and when he eventually came off watch and the German thrust was repelled, his mate was the first to congratulate him on his good fortune.

"You are very lucky to be here with us," said Hartley, helping him with his pack and other equipment.

Smithers frowned and lit another fag.

"It was either him or me," he announced with a visibly deepening frown.

"Does it bother you, Smithers?" Hartley asked, when the bayonet and the scabbard were lying on his bunk.

"Not really, Hartley," he said, drawing on the cigarette and coughing on the smoke, "but it shook me up a little while it lasted."

The subject fizzled out after a while and soon they were back to normal.

Later on, in one of the quiet times that came periodically, Horsy produced a grubby pack of cards and they sat on a makeshift group of rickety chairs and played rummy. After a while they took out a board and played draughts. They eventually got fed up with the game, lay down on their bunks and tried to sleep.

It was one of those nights with the guns thudding in the background and an unusual quiet in the trenches.

"Bit unearthly," maintained Horsy, with widened eyes.

He wore glasses that magnified his eyes to twice their normal size.

The pilot of the downed aircraft looked at the smoke trailing off into the sky and gave a long sigh. His gaze dropped to his leg, which was issuing blood. He had managed to crawl over from the blazing aircraft and sit on a small rock, which is where he was at that moment. His gaze shifted over to the smoke, which was starting to ease. There was not much left of the Sopwith Pup aircraft when the fire took hold of the single-seater fighter, and now it was a smouldering wreck.

He shifted his legs on the piece of rock, so that he could see the Vickers machine gun atop the fuselage, enveloped in smoke and flame. He heard the muffled reports of the ammunition as it exploded, and watched a tongue of red flame as each cartridge uttered a small bang. He shifted his injured leg and, parting the fabric of his flying suit, examined his shattered leg. The bullet that had caught his kneecap was lodged close to surface after it had ricocheted off a metal spar of the aircraft. He could see it just below the skin and as he felt it, could almost touch its roughness beneath his flesh.

The lesion was sore to the touch and painful. He pulled the leg straight with great difficulty and, after blowing with the effort and the pain, pulled the torn flying suit apart a little farther. The pain knifed through the fractured knee and caused him to grit his teeth against the agony. The leg was still bleeding, although it was beginning to clot on the extreme edges of the wound with less blood coming from it. He used his white scarf to dab it and gently wipe the blood away. As the blood coagulated on the whiteness of the scarf he turned it over to use the fresh side. Gradually he stopped the bleeding and ended up by tying the scarf twice around the wound and knotting it behind the angle of his knee.

The aircraft was intermittently giving off a puff of oily smoke that slowly drifted up into the grey of the morning sky. Away in the distance he saw a movement of figures in the smoke, who were in the process of investigating the cause of the fire. His hand fell to the holster of the .38 strapped to his waistband and he pulled out the revolver in case it was the enemy advancing. He broke open the breech of the gun and looked at the six bullets. It was then he resolved to fight and sell his life dear if it was the enemy.

The figures got nearer and he was able to glimpse the welcoming sight of a flash of khaki amongst the moving men. His heart gave a leap as the soldiers got closer. They saw the figure of the pilot sitting on the rock at the same time he saw them, and to cap his good luck he saw the welcoming sight of a red cross on the arm of one of the troopers.

A trooper with a red cross immediately came across to the inured pilot and inspected the damage to his knee, while the corporal in charge of the platoon oversaw the blaze of the fallen plane. The corporal and the rest of the platoon beat out the flames with fallen leaves and twigs left by the crash, to stop broadcasting that one of their aircraft had been shot down.

They fashioned a stretcher out of greatcoats and a couple of branches. Two brawny troopers carried him over to the improvised stretcher and helped him onto it.

His final glimpse of the plane was when he twisted around to see it covered in a curtain of greenery.

The platoon detoured around a larger force of grey-clad Huns and watched them whipping their horses into a frenzy, pulling huge guns and ammunition limbers. The Germans were in the process of adding to the enemy ordinance and were treating the animals pulling the heavy guns abominably. The procession passed by only a few hundred yards away, and the watchers saw foam-flecked lips below wild and staring eyes as they hid behind a host of silver birch trees and wild hawthorn bushes. The guns and limbers passed and the area was quiet once more. What birds there were in the grey of the morning, returned to the safety of the forest and the outlying shrubs.

Once more they proceeded now the disturbance was over, and made a wide circle of the German lines and the area of the Somme. In the distance the flashes of the guns could be seen and the roar of the echoing shells could be heard after they landed on the ground between the two opposing forces locked in mortal, death-defying combat.

Above them as they walked, a solitary plane flew through the cloud-bedecked sky and was gradually disappearing in the mist of the daytime haze of rain.

Sergeant Cox was in a jovial mood. He was looking at a photograph of a group of old war veterans, and he laughed at the change of the redcoat of old and the advances of British uniform with the advent of khaki in the present. He pointed out the red colour of the old uniform, and the difference it made on the battlefield.

"It stands out like a sore thumb," he maintained. "I know it was meant to avoid panic at the sight of blood. The red uniform was supposed to waylay the effects of seeing blood against a red background.

I prefer our khaki uniform of the present. It offers better protection for the soldier as he attacks the enemy."

He was talking to Corporal Gunn and other members of the NCO fraternity, who were gathered around a red hot, pot-bellied stove that stood in the corner of the hut.

"But I ask you, would you stand a chance in these colours now? They would see you a mile away; that red uniform and especially the white hat. They wouldn't need a telescope to see you on no-man's-land; the brown mud would show you up for all sides to see."

Regimental Sergeant Major Briss gave a great guffaw at the comparison and at the picture he had taken from Cox.

"I can see why you had some difficulty with the Boers when you were fighting them in South Africa; they just had to point their rifles at the red coat and just blaze away."

The laughter of the NCOs trilled around the small dugout. A small moustached batman stood to one side, dangling a wooden tray to his knees. He stood beside a damaged bureau that had the NCOs' drinks spread about on the top. Cox signalled for another drink and held out a battered tin mug as the orderly refilled it.

Another NCO with the three stripes and a crown on his arm, took the photo from Briss and chortled at the picture. This NCO, Regimental Sergeant Harry Bliss, cigarette clenched firmly between two overfull lips, coughed and laughed at the comic comparison between the two sides.

The orderly shifted the red hot damper of the stove and raked the bars with an iron rake, clutching the hot iron between two hands wrapped in a newspaper glove.

"Wonder what's on for tonight?" said Cox, putting the photo down onto the floor and changing the subject. "It's so unusually quiet."

"It might be because there is a full moon outside," said Bliss, "nothing like a full moon to dissuade the Germans from starting trouble. Their grey trousers show up like dirty washing on an old maid's kitchen line!"

Outside, Smithers shivered in the chill wind that seemed to sweep along the mud-encrusted wooden slats that made up the bottom of the slimy trench. He had lost count of the many times he had patrolled that section of his nightly walk.

He marched seventeen paces to his right then retraced his steps to his position, seventeen paces to his left then back again to his central place where he stood on an area where there was a particularly hard bit of clay. His feet were two plates of frozen meat held together with iron hard laces. His toes were a tired set of pain and misery that echoed the cold of his calloused heels. Even the full moon sailing over the scene in its grandeur provoked a shiver that seemed to start at his back and travel down to his feet.

The moon's brightness did not affect the occasional shell that seemed to burst on a trench a bit farther on up the British lines. In the moonlight other muffled shapes could be detected, wrapped in an assortment of greatcoats and blankets to keep out the cold of the night.

Smithers had a small section of the trench to guard, where he met his opposite number, Private Waites, who did the next part of the patrol. They often met on the nightly march and always in the same rig-out, carrying the same arms; a rifle with the bayonet fixed. He saw the gleam of the bayonet when his opposite number turned to repeat his march and caught the glitter of the bayonet as it shone in the blaze of the full moon.

Bit by bit the moon edged over the trench, accompanied by a bevy of clouds that had appeared from out of nowhere. It slowly started to descend as Smithers' guard duties came to an end. His relief was obvious when another soldier, wrapped in the usual greatcoat and steel helmet, nodded to him and took up the same position he had vacated less than a minute before.

"All quiet!" whispered Gunn, who had arrived quietly as the two had exchanged guards.

"All right, Corp," replied the man as he looked at Gunn in the half-light.

"You're Private Street, ain't you?"

"Private William Street," replied the soldier, rubbing his hands together.

"I thought you were. Keep a sharp lookout, Street, the moonlight has gone."

"You think they will mount an offensive now the moonlight has gone?"

Gunn tipped his steel helmet with a gloved hand.

"You never know your luck," he said, pulling at his chinstraps. "One minute they are there, the next they will strike at you with everything they've got. You can never trust a Hun to do the ordinary. Keep a sharp lookout, Street, it could come at any time."

The shadow of the corporal moved away down the trench.

5

THE AREA WHERE THE fighting was taking place was the River Somme. The river started in Northern France in the Aisne department, flowing west through Amiens and Abbeville to the English Channel beyond.

A number of pretty villages lined the banks of the Somme and outlying districts, but the area where the struggle for supremacy reigned between the two opposing armies was pockmarked with shell holes and other evidence of destruction. It was endangering your life to venture across this wide gulf of frenzy. Every day figures of grey and khaki risked life or limb to gather the many corpses that lay fallen. They were mostly the ones who had made the dangerous crossing from the enemy lines and had been killed in the process of trying to do the same thing to the opposing army.

The men who risked drawing the opposing side's fire were those who wore red crosses on their arm. They cleared up the results of war that lay silent on the blood-soaked soil of the Somme battleground. They were seen pulling the many bodies from the barbed wire entanglement planted by each army.

The rifles were silent at these interjections as was the vicious sweep of the machine guns. These modes of death and destruction were stilled when the few stretcher bearers of each side were in evidence at the scene of great carnage. Even the toll of the crack shot, rifle-shooting snipers was temporarily suspended while this operation was being carried out. The momentary lull saw the medical arm of the each side launch a stretcher-carrying couple of men after a particularly horrific battle had been perpetrated. They seemed to ignore the danger of one or more soldiers deliberately or accidentally pressing a trigger. They just took it as natural that the men on each side would exercise convention and hold fire. The battlefield seemed to hold its breath when the downed men were collected and transported away to their graves elsewhere.

The rest of the war-torn area of hideous death and destruction also held the bodies or parts of bodies of those who had been killed in the many ways of dealing out death to them. The men sporting red crosses unhurriedly cleared the field of dead or dying men, who called for water or cried out in great pain for relief from the torture. The men of mercy carried the last of the fallen and transported the dead or dying, no matter for which side they were fighting. Although they realised what was happening out in the battlefield, they ignored the daily occurrence that was being enacted before their eyes. It was merely being brushed aside as the ordinary cares of men who vied with men for supremacy.

Smithers, well in the safety of the trench, eyed his mug of tea and took a sip of the tepid liquid. He was used to drinking cold tea and was fed up with complaining about it to the corporal.

"At least it is sweet," said Hartley, licking his finger after trying to stir the sugar into his tea.

"There is that," scowled Smithers, "but it would be nice if it was just that wee bit warmer."

They were sitting around a fire in a circular tin can, and toasted their knees at the flames coming from the fire. The group also included Willcox, who was frying a big chunk of bully beef in a black-looking frying pan. The other two watched as he added two large potatoes to the spitting bully. The delicious smell of the cooking food wafted on the wind and made the other two hungry.

Willcox stood up and grabbed the hot handle of the frying pan with much pain, as it was too hot to hold. He wrung his hand to ease the pain and wrapped it in a sheet of a daily newspaper someone had given him.

"*Fuck it!*" he swore, waving his hand around. He blew on the burned hand and tucked it under an arm. "That was bloody hot."

He brought the hand to light and showed them a blister that was beginning to show on the palm. He shook it a couple of times and again gripped the pan, this time with the cushion of the newspaper sheet to protect him from the heat of the blazing fire. The pain from the blister taught him to steer well clear of the hot fire as he stirred the bully beef and potatoes with the point of his bayonet. The heat from the fire was beginning to burn the mixture, so he turned it over with the flat of his blade. He skewered the two slices of bully beef and, using the tip of his bayonet, punched a slight hole in the top of the tin. Avoiding the flames of the fire, he tipped the contents into the frying pan and held it over the fire.

He regarded the other two with a wide smile and remarked as he stirred up the mixture:

"Dinner is almost served. I'll have to ask you to get the three plates, so I can divide the dinner equally. You've had your tea just now, so there's no need to make any more before teatime."

Hartley went for the plates and washed the tin surface in a nearby bucket of cold water. He shook the drips from the plates and handed them to Willcox.

The machine guns then decided to open up from the German side of the battlefield and the resultant fire slammed into the head of the trench and dislodged a chunk of mud that fell onto the frying pan and the fire. The mud hissed in the flames and almost shook the frying pan from its place on top of the can.

Willcox just saved the pan from the clay, to the cost of his hand, which he burned in a different place. He yelled with pain again and hung his hand under his arm to ease it.

"Not that hand *again?*" said Smithers, with a ghost of a smile edging across his face.

Willcox was unable to answer as the pain knifed through his hand. Hartley saved the dinner from disaster as he grabbed the newspaper sheet and wrapped it around the handle of the frying pan. Willcox was still doing a war dance with the pain of the two blisters.

Hartley swept the food onto the plates with a sideways motion of his hand, emptying the gravy until it was lying there alongside the cooked food.

Later on, through the grapevine, they learned that they were expected to form another foray into enemy-held country.

"That means we are in-line to do the thing we are paid for - to fight," moaned Smithers, through the hail of machine gun bullets that periodically opened up. "Maybe they will increase my pay in-line with the danger to my life."

"Don't break a leg in sweating on them to increase your pay," said Hartley with a look of contempt on his face. "We are the world's worst paid and the world's most hard done by army."

"You can say that again," echoed Smithers. "You're right on both counts, mate, especially the pay one."

"You can't spend it out here in the trenches," said Hartley, drawing on his cigarette.

"Yeah, but I can die happy knowing I have a few shillings to rattle together in my pocket."

"I know the feeling. I have been hard up when you have been hard up," said Hartley, pinching out the fag and putting it behind his ear for later.

The next morning as it was growing light the entire company of the Ninety-ninth crowded the space of the trench and lined up, gripping their weapons near the bottom rungs of the ladder.

The tension of the coming battle brought out fresh beads of sweat on the faces of the waiting troops. In the half-light the waiting men coughed, groaned, hitched up their heavy packs and waited to hear the whistle.

The machine guns had lulled for a few minutes as the enemy gunner decided to change magazines. The wind was blowing along the packed ranks of soldiers, drying the drips of sweat staining the features of the waiting men.

A thin officer with a lanyard around his neck, pushed past the tightly packed men, the faint light of the morning reflecting on his steel helmet. He was waving his revolver in one hand and gripping the glinting whistle in the other hand. He was waiting for the okay from another officer, who as standing several feet away from him.

The officer with the whistle now held it with his lips, which were trembling with the pressure. The other officer put a hand on the shoulder of the nearest trooper and felt him tremble with nerves. The man in charge nodded in the half-light and as he did so the shrill blast of the whistle echoed above the crowds of packed men. In answer to the whistle, the steel helmets began to crowd together and mount the ladders.

The machine guns began their song of death as the soldiers piled up the wooden ladders, catching the first as they slithered over the sandbagged tips of the trenches. Most were able to slip into the welcoming shelter of a nearby shell hole. The first of the men were cut down by the unwavering toll of the machine guns that left them draped over the coils of barbed wire that stood in their way.

Slowly the men surged over the lip of the trench head. They trod the ladders into the unknown, armed with hope and blind luck. Of course, they had their Lee Enfields to back up their luck, and their bayonets as a second reminder of the power necessary to force the adversary to heed their warning. As yet they were on the bridge of death and destruction, on the verge of their foray into danger.

The two soldiers, Smithers and Hartley, were in the centre of the force, trying to present as little a target as possible to the opposition. They squirmed over the fallen bodies of their mates and in several cases helped a man to return to the friendly trenches while they crouched down on the mud of the battlefield. This time they managed to make the first line of the masses of barbed wire blocking their way. They slithered to the left where there was a gap in the wire. Others on the same course passed them as they hesitated at the parting of the barbed wire hindrance.

The machine-gunners changed canisters of bullets, and the constant barrage ceased while they did so. This gave them the chance to slither through the coils of wire and lie down behind the foggy shape of a ditched lorry. They heard the ping and ricochet of the deadly spray of bullets as the machine gun resumed its lethal fire. They poked their heads around the sides of the lorry and waited as the episode of death came to an end. The few seconds that it lasted gave them a chance to change their positions for another.

All the time they came nearer to the enemy trenches, noting with a realisation that the nearer they got to the enemy the greater was their danger of being killed or wounded. Of course, this was in the back of their mind, but they chose to ignore it in their ineptitude.

As the other men joined them on the mud about twenty or thirty yards way from the likelihood of meeting the opposition face to face, the meeting didn't seem so attractive as it had been a few moments ago. They ducked back to the shelter of the abandoned lorry and took a breather.

"Well, old sport, we've done our bit, now it is the time to make a hurried withdrawal," grated Hartley as he slid backwards down a muddy slope.

He was just about to put another foot backwards when his left boot encountered a hard round object. His heart skipped a beat as he realised the object he was touching was an unexploded shell casing. Carefully he lifted his leg, put it back to where it had been and whispered to Smithers.

"I think we're lying on a unexploded shell. We can't go backwards, but we can go forwards to our original position, you game to try?"

Smithers nodded numbly.

"We must go forwards then, but if we do we will be exposed to the fire of the machine-gunners and others," he replied.

"Yeah," agreed Hartley, "but even that is preferable to being blown up by a shell."

With their heads so low their chins were scraping the muddy ground, they edged forwards, nearer to the enemy trenches.

"I just can't be doing this," muttered Smithers to himself, walking on his elbows and sliding his lean body across the mud. "I must be wrong in the head to be doing this." He slid over to Hartley and moaned, "Can't we go back to the wire? This is downright dangerous if we stay here."

Hartley ignored him and slid away from the shell.

"I'm getting as far away from this shell as I can go; it might just decide to explode under me."

"You're wanting to go one way and me another," Smithers said. "I wish I had a coin to toss up where we go."

"You *are* joking! "Hartley exclaimed, fuming and sliding forwards. "Out here? You must be a little mad, and where are we going to get a coin out here?"

"I was just trying to find out what we should do to get us out of this shit hole of a place to safety."

"I know what you were doing. I'm doing a good job of getting away from this shell, and that is my main aim."

Little by little they inched themselves forwards, around the silent form of a khaki-clad man lying face down in the mud, bleeding from his head and nose. The day was going fast while all about them others were trying to prevent the bullets and the exploding grenades from reaching out for them.

Suddenly, as an accident of intent, Hartley put out his hand to grip something and dislodged a fat stuffed sandbag, which fell into the German trench. I've made it, he thought, sliding his rifle to the tip of his steel helmet and waiting for the reaction of the Huns.

Smithers edged up beside him, ears strained for any sound. From below the sandbag came the faint sound of voices. There was the smell of strong tobacco smoke rising up from the well of the trench and they could hear someone coughing.

"I can hear three voices," hissed Hartley into Smithers' ear.

"I can hear three voices as well," said Smithers, almost touching Hartley's ear with his lips.

They waited, waiting for the opportunity, squaring up for the fight of their life.

"I'm going back," said Smithers, ducking his head as the voices got louder.

"Come back, you fool, you could get killed crossing the field again. Anyway, it's just the same as the other time. We've got to the Huns' trenches this time, so we might as well go the whole hog and fight. There's no other way. We have to fight or give ourselves up to them."

They were whispering above the relentless gunfire and echoing shell explosives.

6

They inched their way along the sandbags until they found a gap in them. The sand and earth were spilling from the ruptured sacks. The gap was three feet wide and slowly getting wider as the contents of the sandbags was poring out through the rips.

They could not believe their good fortune as they slipped down the lines of sandbags to the floor of the German trench - but things were about to change...

A fat German carrying a tray of tin mugs turned the corner of the trench. His eyes goggled with surprise as he dropped the tray, lifted a rifle to his fat jowls and scurried back around the corner.

The element of surprise was over and they knew it. They were just about to beat a hasty retreat up the sandbags again when a slug from a German rifle clipped a shower of earth from the area just above Smithers' head.

Another German soldier advanced and Hartley shot him. Another grey-clad figure hove into sight just as Smithers pressed the trigger. The gun jammed and he was left with his bayonet and silent rifle. He feinted with the blade of the bayonet and knocked his enemy's rifle aside with the butt. He pushed the wooden haft of the rifle into the face of the German. The soldier was knocked off balance by the butt, leaving Smithers an opening to plunge his bayonet into the big midriff of his opponent.

Hartley was being besieged by two big German troopers and was getting the worst of the exchange. Smithers picked up his adversary's gun and shot one of the Germans in the belly. Immediately, Hartley rammed his bayonet into the chest of the remaining soldier, twisting the blade to stop it from wrapping itself in the entrails of the downed man.

Hartley, breathing hard with the effort of the fight, leaned against the side of the trench holding his rifle at the trail, waiting for the next assailant to appear. He looked down at the groaning man and kicked his rifle away. He bent down to the dying man and saw the blood issuing from the wound in his stomach. He had the look of the dying and very soon he did die. Hartley laid the corpse against the side of the trench and placed his German helmet on his chest. That was all he could do, and straightened up from the cadaver.

Smithers was wiping his bayonet on the uniform of the German soldier he had killed.

"We'd best make ourselves scarce," he grated, looking down on the result of their brief battle. "There don't seem to be any more of them," he said as he quietly made for the intersection from where the men had come, and peered around the angle of the trench.

In the distance there was a gramophone playing a cracked record of a man singing in German. He heard the record jump the crack, then begin to sing the words of the aria again. Smithers heard the same words a couple of times before he made a move towards his waiting companion.

Hartley produced a small ladder he had found and leaned it on the sandbags once more. He waited, his heart beating loudly in his chest, then climbed up the first few rungs of the ladder. He felt Smithers' hot breath on his neck, feeling his rifle touch the back of his helmet.

Above the noise of the machine guns hammering out their message of death, they waited on the topmost rung of the ladder, ears peeled for any foreign sound. Their luck held and they slid over the topmost sandbag, still holding on to their rifles, the bayonet still attached in both cases. They had enjoyed phenomenal luck up until now and they did not want to spoil it by following the same route as before.

Hartley pointed to the hump of the unexploded shell and whispered to Smithers.

"Watch the shell where I touched its casing. We'll go around it and give it a wide berth."

This they did, sliding their rifles along beside them. The lull of fighting was beginning to tail off to a murmur of single shooting as the snipers took over. They felt the rain pitter-pattering on their steel helmets and starting to drip down their faces.

"That's all we need," muttered Hartley, wiping the fringe of drops from his helmet with a finger.

They skirted two dead bodies caught by the machine guns, lying in the position where the slugs had caught them in death. The two men slewed into the enfolding arms of a deep well of rainwater. Smithers slid down the muddy sides of the shell hole, dislodging a dead man who had been caught by the shell. He eased the dead soldier aside and rolled him over to the bottom of the hole.

The shelling of the German trenches had tailed off to nothing. Testament to the accuracy of the British gunners was the amount of shells that had missed the trenches when they were in them not an hour before. Still Smithers reflected it could be worse; they might have scored a hit and wiped out one of their own side. Now they were stuck in this godforsaken hole in the ground.

"Let's hope another shell does not land here in the same spot," said Hartley, looking over the rim of the shell hole and gazing at the depressing sight of the hellhole of bursting shells and raking machine gun fire.

The firing seemed to be coming from the place where they had been recently.

"Humph, they seem to be awake at last," enjoined Hartley, after noting the fire from the trench. "Our effort seems to have stirred them into activity."

Smithers had his own problems. He was forever slipping on the muddy surface of the shell hole and sliding back down into a pool of freezing cold rainwater that always seemed to be at the bottom of each hole. As always, he put his foot into it and had a cold pair of rain-sodden boots. He hitched up his heavy pack, pushed up the Lee Enfield ahead of him and, with an effort, made it to the lip of the crater where he joined Hartley.

"How're we going to get back to our lines?" he shouted, trying to make himself heard above the terrific din of the explosions. "We've got to start crawling in the mud once more."

"You're telling me," grated Hartley, ducking low behind the safety of the dirt rim blown by the shell explosives.

He lifted his head above the blasted earth, turning his helmet towards another shell that burst in smithereens less than twenty yards away. Their own friendly trench seemed to be miles away, but in realty was just fifty yards ahead of them. The enormous distance was heightened by the prospect of sliding the rest of the way on their bellies.

There was a brief spell of inactivity as the machine-gunners and the shells decided to end the onslaught together.

Far away the rest of the company was crawling through the same mud and rainwater, doing the same thing; trying to crawl the distance to the relative safety of the British trench.

A few made it, others making a quick dash risked life and limb as they made a wild dive for the safety and security of their own lines.

In some cases they paid the ultimate price by receiving a bullet. The fortunate remainder gratefully gained a few extra yards nearer their goal.

In many cases they scrambled into the welcoming hands of other troopers who were sheltering from the return fire of the German hordes. Altogether they welcomed the chance of escaping the terrible bombardment that was being waged on the battlefield behind them.

Hartley and Smithers were still stuck in the shell hole and likely to remain there until the terrific part of the bombardment was at an end.

They endured the German answer to the incursion and turned their faces to the explosive force of the shellfire, then came a brief respite as the guns suddenly stopped their rain of shells. They lifted up their heads and for a few seconds were unable to believe it. For an instant they listened and looked for the reintroduction of the shells. The lull lengthened into a minute and their joy started to emerge.

With desperate movements they squirmed up the sides of the hole and slid into the soft and squishy mud that had collected on the rim. With their faces and chins scraping the dirt, they slid a few yards nearer to the trench and salvation, but they could see they still had another fifty yards to go to reach safety.

The day was still advancing into the rainy afternoon and they had the dubious pleasure of sliding in the mud and slime of the pock-marked earth. They avoided the still forms of the other troopers, in some cases sheltering behind a cadaver, but they still had to make the final distance between the dead body and the wall of the trench. They had to continue and they knew it.

If they were to make the safety of the trench and the welcoming arms of the other soldiers they had to cross the rest of the ground between where they lay in the mud and the haven of the trench. The sliding went on, every inch nearer was a small distance away. It seemed as though the gulf between them and the remainder of the blood-soaked ground was an enormous gap, raked by incessant machine gun fire that pinged off every object in the direct line of fire.

Smithers noted a rock in the ensuing distance of the remaining ground between the lip of the trench and his position. He slid this stretch of ground and counted the inches between himself and the rock. He passed it and tried to engage another object on which to concentrate. He slid this distance then did the same with a piece of wood a further three feet away. This way he covered a few feet nearer the haven of the British trench.

Hartley was very near him, sliding beside him uttering hoarse breaths from the slack-jawed opening of his mouth. They were coming within fifteen yards of the lip of the trench when the machine-gunner stopped to reload his magazine.

The next time he reloads, Smithers mused, the very next time he changes the belt of bullets before firing, I will try my luck and make a dash for safety. The bullets continued to fly within seconds, so Smithers gauged to the second how much time he had to leap the last few yards to safety. In his mind's eye he saw the two men go through the motions of reloading the machine gun, and counted the seconds they took until the next fusillade.

He had just seven seconds to jump the remaining few yards to the safety of the trench. Could he do it? Did he have the necessary speed to jump up and throw himself over the sandbags lining the edge of the trench? He reckoned he did, and was willing to risk everything in the final leap for the sanctuary of the trench.

Keeping his head down low he waited for the moment to come. He keyed himself to a high pitch, steeling himself for the plunge forwards. As the rain of bullets came to the end of the bullet belt he leaped up and, not heeding the warning shout from Hartley, made a wild dash for the sandbags. He just made it as the first of the slugs hit the wall of earthen bags. He heard them slam into the protection of the trench, and fell into the welcoming hands of the other troopers pressed against the trench sides.

Now it was Hartley's turn to try his luck.

Smithers called to his partner to keep his pecker up. He tried to bolster his confidence by shouting some advice at him.

"I have worked it out. I noticed the two gunners using the machine gun when changing the ammunition belts take several seconds to do it. You've got to count to seven as they do so, that is all they take to change the ammunition belts. After that it is dangerous to attempt the run in from your position. You got it? Wait until they run out of ammo then count seven seconds - all right?"

Back came the reply.

"Supposing they saw you try it and are daring me to try the same method? They might be waiting for me to do it."

"Then you'd better start praying if they are."

The bullets were still coming, and Smithers waited till they tailed off. He started to count and just as he got to seven the flying form of Hartley scrambled over the rim of the trench and slid down the slimy walls into his outstretched arms.

Machine-gunners' mate, Glenn Ehoe, had a twofold job to perform every day. He had to clean the Vickers Supermarine Machine Gun, of which he was the loader and sometimes firer.

In his first job he had to keep the machine gun in tip-top condition. This he did every day, rain or shine, snow or brilliant sunshine, winter or summer. He could be seen polishing the brass or the ironwork and whitening the pull string of the canvas cover. That was when the gun was not operational, but when it was used he could be seen loading the ammunition belt of the gun as it sprayed its deadly fire of .303 bullets.

The gun was housed in a tin hut just beside the trench head. The corrugated roundels of the tin hut were camouflaged with tin cans, paper and a general selection of other bric-a-brac collected from inside and outside the trench; anything to disguise the appearance of the hut, so it would not draw attention to its lethal side.

Only this morning, in support of the troops sallying forth into the enemy side of the Somme Valley, it had spewed out its message of death and destruction, and cut down any opposing enemy forces seeking to stop the British push.

Now Ehoe was taking it easy by cooking his breakfast, and his mate, the corporal gunner, his superior, Corporal Doust, was enjoying his rest, which had been curtailed that morning after a night of intermittent shelling.

Let him rest, thought Ehoe, frying the bully beef and breaking an egg into the mess. Most of their cooking was by way of the frying pan. It was simple to clean up the pan by wiping it with a piece of rag or an old letter from home. The range could be used again, and the greasy paper could be saved to start the fire in the morning.

The heat from the fire was burning his midriff, so he stepped back apace. His boots were covered in slimy mud that never seemed to dry. Even in the morning they still had the same blanket of grey mud attached to the soles from the night before. To save on effort and hot water, he ate straight from the steaming frying pan, burning the inside of his mouth in the process.

Other people went by; messengers on their way to deliver the latest report from the top brass, other NCOs on their way to meetings or from meetings, probably with the date and time of the next general push against the enemy. Other privates were going somewhere or coming from somewhere. They all acknowledged the machine-gunners' assistant's grin with one of their own.

They all had to eat, so they inhaled the smell of the cooking breakfast with hungry glances at the frying pan, his plate and the food, which was vanishing fast under Ehoe's ferocious assault.

7

THE PERSISTENT RAIN HAD eased off and Doust made an appearance at the entrance of the tin hut.

"Morning, Corp," said Ehoe cheerfully.

He produced a plate with a share of the recent repast. Doust acknowledged the greeting and sat down on a rickety wooden box. He gave a great yawn and picked up the fork Ehoe had been using.

"Morning, Glenn," he said, yawning through a mouthful of breakfast, "how's tricks?"

"Not so bad. Been quiet for the past couple of hours, how did you sleep?"

"In snatches; I kept waking up then dropping off again. I dreamed I was at home with the old woman."

"You did, did you?" gushed Ehoe. "I bet you gave her one."

"Didn't I just. I was back in my old bed and just after - then I had to open my eyes to see the same old faces. It was not a welcome sight, I can tell you."

"I bet it wasn't, Corp. You've got my sympathy."

Doust nodded with a mouth full of bully beef and fried egg. He watched Ehoe start on the gun. He was oiling the mechanism and the breech then he cleaned off a tiny bit of rust that was beginning to form on the trigger guard. He polished this off with a bit of rag dipped in oil dregs. He was sparing with the oil can and replaced it in the cubbyhole with another full can. Very soon the gun was gleaming and back to its original position.

He picked up the belt of rounds and counted the remaining bullets. Just twenty-three, we used thirty-seven on the last burst of fire, plenty more in the ammunition box though, he mused. That'll be over five hundred used since yesterday.

Doust watched him cleaning the gun and counting the rounds expelled. He seemed to be proud of his job as a machine-gunner's mate. He could operate the machine gun as well as he could, the only difference being that of rank. He had a few years seniority over Ehoe, and the fact that he had two stripes on his arms while Ehoe had none.

Ehoe studiously worked on the machine gun. He had the right, he figured, by virtue of his work ratio and his ability to fire the gun when they exchanged places. He could work the gun over the square allotted by the other machine guns and always managed to keep the arc of fire within his range, the reason being because the powers that be had decided to allot the machine gun its arc of fire. It had its only range of dealing out its deadly fire in one area, so that it would not impose on the other machine-gunners' arc of fire. This way they covered all tracts of the field and no other. Of course, when the other gunners allowed it, they impinged on other's territory, or when ordered to do it by the higher authority.

Ehoe loved the Vickers machine gun. He cared for it, cleaned it and even dreamed about it. He was happiest pressing the trigger and spraying lead, but he was always a happy man. He hated the enemy and set out to destroy him, but he had a streak of conscience inside him that was always evident, and that is where his evidence of cruelty always let him down. He had a big conscience and he knew it.

Of course, he was a cruel man to the enemy and set out to kill him in any way possible, at every opportunity. When he pressed that trigger he was fighting for his country against an aggressor. It was kill or be killed with him. Either he or the enemy was finished - there was no other path. They had to be eradicated or finished off, no messing. He was ruthless to the enemy, but not to anything else.

He thought even the rats that frequented the trench by night had a right to life and liberty. Perhaps they had a filthy way of surviving, but it was their way and they bore the fruit of prosperity and life with every baby they produced, which they did with impunity every so often, four or five of the dreadful little beasts.

Apart from the reputation of eating dead bodies and other disgusting things, they were a constant pest in raiding the men's rations. They chewed a variety of things like clothing or paper, bits of waste food left around, even explosives and other indigestible things, which when left for a while, showed traces of rat gnawing. They ate other things with gusto. Until rat droppings were seen in the vicinity as evidence, the humble moth was blamed for the holes in cotton and khaki uniforms. They were never eradicated. As fast as one rat was killed, another popped up his features and carried on where the other had left off. It was a case of keeping the rat population to manageable proportions.

Private Ehoe diligently polished the bright work of the machine gun until his face was reflected in the brass. He stripped the barrel off the 'V' of the two legs and laid it aside. He saw the previous day's oil receptor and dripped a spill from its tip. He worked the spill into the gunmetal and brought the ready shine back to a gleaming lustre. He wiped the barrel clean of the oil and reseated the rest of the gun on the two legs.

Doust watched him working on the machine gun and held the gun in his lap as he replaced the two handles.

Ehoe worked the firing mechanism of the gun with several jerks of the loading cartridge bolt. He was just going to inspect the ammo box when a huge brown rat jumped out and scrambled away. They tried to catch and kill it, but it was too fast for them and escaped out through the tin hut porthole.

The rain came again. The clouds shifted overhead and a great big grey one that stretched from horizon to horizon dripped constantly for hours and made it uncomfortable for the men. It ran down the necks of the soldiers and made everything damp and miserable. It was cold as well. Without hindrance it soaked the already soft clay and washed the dirt to the trench underfoot, producing a soft and clinging mud that covered the boots of the soldiers in a film of watery earth.

Every man wore his groundsheet over his head, around his shoulders, even around his middle to ward off the trickle of water that persisted in wetting his khaki trousers and dripping down to his puttees. To prevent rust they nursed their Lee Enfield rifles beneath the shelter of the groundsheet.

This was the favourite time of the opposition to launch a counterattack, and the British soldiers waited in expectancy. It was not to be so. The Germans were suffering as well. It was the same rain falling on them as well as the British side.

The bad weather increased in severity. It started to hail. Very soon the hailstones got bigger until they were the size of marbles, which pattered on the steel helmets of the troops in a fast crescendo. The hailstones hit the sides of the trenches and other hard surfaces in a rapid tattoo. They rattled on the tin roof and sides of the machine gun emplacement, managing to find anything that was hard and unyielding.

Officers and men suffered in the downpour, which streamed down the sides of the trench to the soft mud underneath the footwear of the soldiers.

One of the lookouts lifted his field glasses and watched a pair of planes zooming in the grey of the sky. They were ducking and diving to escape the attention of each other.

First one came in fast to dodge the other aircraft then zoomed up to twist out of a roll, then this one, a triplane, twisted away to avoid the other's unwelcome attention. The hesitant stutter of a machine gun was heard as the triplane tried to get away. The following aircraft, one with the roundels of a British plane, was trying to shoot the first one down. They twisted and squirmed together in tight rolls, and sailed away to fight each other.

The triplane with the black marking of the German cross, tried to get away once more. The second one fired a quick burst at it, the German managing to roll away from the hail of bullets. The British plane followed the spinning German and opened up with an equally quick burst. The two planes roared away into the distance, out of sight of the observer.

Smithers and Hartley had copped again. They had regained the job of getting the tea and doling it out to the various sections of the company. They were waiting outside the cookhouse trench, waiting to collect the tin drums of foaming tea. Of course, they were experienced in the procedure of carrying the heavy brown liquid and knew what to expect. They waited as the cook sergeant tipped the sack of sugar into the two tin cans and stirred it up.

"All right, you two," he growled, wiping the ladle under his arm then trailing it. "Orf you go, and this time try not to spill it too much. I have only my tea allowance to make it, so when you do, I have to make more out of my allowance to cover it."

He stood back while they tucked their rifles into the carrying ropes. When they looked back to see if he was watching them, he had gone.

As usual they spilled the tea, which was expected, for it lapped the sides of the two tins and ran down the battered sides. Corporal Gunn was first in line this time, holding out a dilapidated tin mug and eyeing the two troopers with mistrust.

"So, now you pair of misfits have the tea boat again? What goes around comes around. You do it right and you will be doing it for a month this time." He held his mug to wait for them to fill it up to the brim. He sipped the tea and retorted, "Of course, it's just warm, why don't you bring it a little faster?"

He went away shaking his head. Gunn looked back at the two privates and in so doing, barged into Sergeant Cox.

"Sorry, Sarge," he apologised, "but I was watching those pair of troopers carrying the tea boat. I don't trust them any more than I can see them. They're after something, probably trying to sell the milk or sugar, or *both*. I wouldn't put it past them to steal them both."

"Probably, but I wouldn't trust them either," said Cox, smiling. "They're all tarred with the same brush when a fiddle is in the offing, but it is just their way of living, like all my boys. It's just the way they were brought up. They were born with nothing and will probably die with nothing, most likely here in the Somme. Don't let it worry you, Corporal, it doesn't me in the slightest way."

Gunn gave a hesitant smile at his superior.

"I'll try to remember those wise words, Sarge, but I still say they will bear watching."

Smithers and Hartley eyed the two NCOs talking together.

"Look at that Gunn tearing us apart," grated Hartley. "He suspects us 'cause we got the tea boat back. I have a suspicion he don't like us doling out the tea, prob'ly thinks we should be digging the latrines or something just as nasty."

"Maybe he will have us carrying the wounded or the dead back to the hospital station," moaned Smithers.

"Don't put that idea into his head or he might just give us the job of getting them back to our lines."

Smithers groaned in misery.

"I can't face going out there again; we might get killed this time."

"They stop firing to allow for the collection of the casualties," said Hartley, in a dry voice.

"Yes, but it only takes a slight twitch on the trigger finger to kill you," added Smithers in a low voice.

"We are expecting another big push in the near future," Cox was saying. "As you know, no man is allowed to say when, but *soon*."

"As usual, we are the last to know, but the ones to suffer," said Gunn in a quiet voice.

"It will always be that way," replied Cox with a smile. "It is the same in all our wars - *them* planning the different campaigns and *us* doing the actual fighting. As I just said, it will always be this way and I can't ever see it altering."

"More's the pity," echoed Gunn.

"If it was the other way around we'd be out of a job, you ever think of it that way?"

Gunn held his council and bit his lip to bite back a retort to answer the jibe. Instead, he changed the subject.

"We are due a bit of leave in the near future. Is there anything around here where we can get a pint of beer?"

Cox shook his head.

"Around here, no, mind you, there are a number of villages that have not been touched by the war. They might have a pub or beer parlour in one of the cafés. They used to sell wine or beer at the café. They will most probably have beer, not all the locals like wine."

"Have you been in one of the cafés yourself, Sarge?"

"One or two. They are all rationed, so I think it will be difficult to get something to eat."

Corporal Doust tried the mechanism of the Vickers and held the firing pin of the gun to the light to see if he could see any dust on the breech. It was testament to the work of Ehoe that he could not see any in the light of the weak sun that was shining through the door of the tin hut. As he inspected the breech further he noticed where Ehoe had been working on a patch of rust on the firing chamber of the machine gun.

The patch of sunlight clouded over as an explosion occurred in a far away part of the trench, and the dust motes danced in the weak bar of sunlight. He watched the dust whirl into a miniature storm as it waved on the wings of the slanting sun. It seemed to fascinate him as he gazed at the whirling specks.

As Ehoe entered the gun emplacement, Doust tore his eyes away from the weak sunshine. He nodded towards the gun.

"Good job on the gun, that rust mark has gone," he remarked.

"I worked on it for an hour or more," retorted Ehoe, dropping a boot onto the dirt floor. "I also greased the mechanism and wiped the barrel clean with a greasy rag. It should be clean now."

"I've seen it just now," enjoined Doust. "Keep up the good work."

"I will," said Ehoe, picking up the boot, sitting on the wooden box and polishing the boots with a scuffed rag.

"Are those my boots?" Doust asked, watching the man buffing them.

"They certainly are, Corporal, I'm just giving them the once over to bring the shine back to the leather."

"Good man. You're a good soldier, no messing."

8

SMITHERS WAS BORN ON a farm in Essex, located just on the edge of the seaside resort of Southend-on-Sea. It was a smallholding really. The farmer, Smithers' father, had a couple of cows, four pigs, several chickens, a couple of ducks swimming on a small pond in the front garden and one solitary sheep cropping the grass and the surrounding garden.

As a small boy Smithers used to ride on a swing in the front garden. He used to swing it high, getting higher with each pull at the ropes. He purposely used to miss the sheep with his wide sweeps, trying to just miss it - just - by two or three inches at the most. It was just boyishness really, and there was never any intent to do the animal any harm.

He had no brothers or sisters; no one to romp with and no one to play those pretend games that boys are apt to indulge in. It was a lonely life for him; no one to listen to his pretence of acting as a pirate or a smuggler, or one about to experience the life of a great explorer. He had a tent in the front garden, an old sheet that his mother had discarded and was about to throw away. He rescued it from a pile of old material his mother had saved for cleaning rags. In that tent he rescued young maids in distress and fought off the opposing armies of Napoleon and other despots, while holding back countless antagonists bent on causing havoc and unrest.

In his dreams he used the sheep to serve as a horse, while lancing other knights with the branch of a tree. The sheep objected to him trying to ride it and frequently threw him off with a shake of its head. That never seemed to deter him. He just remounted the animal whenever it shook him off.

His school was about two miles distant. His mother used to pack him a lunch to eat for his midday break. It was always the same lunch - two slices of bread and jam, and an apple picked from the small tree in the back garden.

He had a schoolmate, a ginger haired boy named Denis Thrower. From the time they met he called him 'Ginger' and the name stuck. The other boy had a bicycle as well, and together they used ride over to the girls' school and call to the girls from between the iron bars of the school fence. Like all children they used to call out to each other and playfully deride their different appearances with whispers of, 'Look at those red lips, she must be using lipstick. I bet she has been using her sister's powder'. On their way back from the girls' school they always ate their sandwiches on the same stretch of grassland.

One day a motor car passed by the boys and they goggled at the sight of the great belch of smoke pouring from beneath the vehicle in great waves. It passed them by with a couple of bangs of the engine and disappeared from sight, over the crest of the hill in a blinding cloud of greasy grey smoke that enveloped the car and the driver.

Apart from that isolated incident, the road was entirely free of any other vehicle. The fields were frequented by chewing cows and sheep that cropped the grass. The boys collected firewood from the trees and tied it on the crossbars of their bikes.

When the fork of the road was reached, Ginger waved goodbye to his schoolmate, who continued on along the road to his father's farm. As usual, Smithers' father was waiting at the garden gate for him to come along. He took the bundle of sticks from his young son and dropped it at the corner of the farmhouse.

The elder Smithers was a bearded man of some thirty-five years of age. He was big, and his barrel-chest was covered with a dirty singlet that had a grey patch on the front. He was balding with a wrap-over of hair that covered the naked patch in the centre of his head. He spoke in a deep voice.

"Wash your hands, young 'un, Mum is just getting your tea ready. Where's your school cap? I told you to wear it today."

"It's too flashy. All the other boys keep 'em off. I will be the odd one out if I wear it."

"Ahem," muttered his father, "that cap cost three and six. That's what it is worth in animal meat for the three of us."

"I will catch a rabbit to make up for it," young Smithers said, dropping his bicycle onto the grass.

He skirted the sheep and made for the tent. He parted the two sides of the sheet and dropped onto the two bits of rag that served as a bed. He pulled the two halves together and pinned them with a large safety pin. Inside the tent he sat on the old rag and felt really at home there.

His father called out to him as he passed the tent.

"Your mum says your tea will be ready in ten minutes. It's stew this evening, young 'un, so don't be late in getting it."

———

The younger Smithers hungrily ate the dinner placed before him. He forked the stew into his mouth and looked all around the table.

His mother, a mousey woman with a straight head of hair, looked at him.

"How was school today? You up to your mate's standard? He seems to be getting on with his sums more than you."

The younger Smithers eyed his mother across the table.

"He likes school more than me. I think he likes sums and I like writing an' drawing. We're not the same - he gets on with his homework, I like drawing patterns. We both like riding our bikes, though."

"I suppose you do," his father interjected, "but you've got to go out and earn your living soon, just think of that, my fellow me lad."

"I'm doing it all the time. I want a job as an artist or something."

"There's no money in artistry," said his father. "They are all starving because they can't sell their paintings."

"Why can't you go into something like carpentry or bricklaying, even farming, like your dad?" asked his mother, gathering up the dirty crockery into a pile. "There's the farm, you could help your dad."

The boy pretended not to hear and stooped down to stroke the tabby cat that was eating the remains of the stew left by his mother.

"Hello, Whiskers," he said, petting the cat and stroking his lush fur.

The cat ignored him and went on wolfing the stew.

After eating his dinner his father went out to collect the eggs left by the chickens, while his mother washed up the dirty crockery. Smithers was left to his own devices and soon made his way to the tent. Very soon he was riding the sheep and pretending to be a knight on horseback.

The animal soon shook him off and moved to a fresher patch of grass farther away. The pretence of being a knight very soon paled and he looked around to see what he could do to while away the time. It was then he made up his mind and decided to give his father a hand on the farm.

His father was pleasantly surprised to see him take up a rake and pull out the straw of the rabbit hutch. The surprise went further as his father saw him take out the big buck rabbit, place him on the ground beside him then replace the straw with a fresh batch. The elder Smithers pretended not to see him, but he was pleased the boy had begun to show an interest. His breast swelled within him as his son shot a look at him and saw the quick wink he gave him. The boy reciprocated and smiled at his father, who watched as he walked over to the small chicken run and threw a few crumbs through the wire.

He worked for a full hour before he sat down on an old chair. He shucked a few peas and tossed the pods to the chickens. Suddenly he stood up and smiled at his father, before returning to the tent in the front garden.

So, he has had enough, his father thought, but it was a small start and a valid one. He had not been ordered to help his father. He had done it out of the goodness of his heart, and the elder Smithers was thankful for that.

His mother, Edna Smithers, noticed the change in the lad and was glad he was beginning to grow up, but she was in for another surprise when her son picked up a tea towel and started to dry the crockery. She was so surprised she had to sit down and watch him dry the things and lay them in a row on the wooden draining board. Of course she thanked him in a motherly way and the boy liked the cuddle that followed.

Wonder of wonders, Smithers ended the day working on the problem his teacher had prepared for him. That evening as his mother and father watched him work on the page of simple arithmetic, they wondered whether it was a five-minute wonder and he would return to his tent and his pretending.

The younger Smithers bent down and stroked the cat, which responded by arching his back and stretching his back and legs. The cat accepted the morsel of bread and watery milk offered.

The surprise continued the next day because instead of daydreaming in the tent as he usually did, Smithers changed the rabbit hutch straw and made the animal comfortable by giving it a carrot bottom to gnaw. His mother, to save on vegetables, always kept the carrot skins and, after washing them, she cooked them on the kitchen stove, but she sliced off the carrot bottom and saved it for the animals outside. She never wasted a piece of vegetable, no matter what.

That evening, as a treat, she had bartered a marrow for a jelly and was setting the delicacy on the table, just after the meat pie. Smithers looked goggle-eyed at the red jelly resting at the centre of the table and wondered whether it tasted as good as it looked. They seldom had any afters, except once a month when they had a big lump of pudding. The pudding always seemed to be accompanied by a small blob of homemade jam. The family liked the special treat and they thrived on the extra part of their Sunday meal. Smithers elder always grew his own vegetables and with the occasional meat of a chicken or rabbit it was not much, but adequate.

Smithers' father was born in the same cottage where his father before him had come into the world. He married his childhood sweetheart, Edna, and they made a home at the farmhouse, carrying on in the same tradition of farming. Of course, along came Smithers junior and he was the spitting image of his father, so his wife maintained, but junior doubted that because he said he didn't have the bald patch that his father had and he parted his hair on a different side.

Of course the boy was happy at the farm, but he did not like the bicycle ride to school in the morning, especially if he was late. It was two miles or more if he was behind time, and he had to pedal hard to make it to the school before the bell was rung to indicate the start of school hours. He had to sneak in through the front door after tying the bike to the handrail.

Many a time he was called up before the headmaster when his bike was missing. He was a shrewd boy and worked it out that this was the only time he was reported to the headmaster. He racked his brains to see if this situation could be changed, then the realisation hit him that the only way of not receiving any punishment was to get to school on time.

Smithers feared the stick mainly because the headmaster was a big man, who hit the hands of the offender with a big wallop. He made certain you remembered the beating because he had a way of hitting you on the ball of the thumb where it hurt the most. Smithers hated the headmaster the most and tried to get to school at the right time, but he maintained he couldn't help oversleeping a couple of times.

Times were changing and he was growing up. He still managed to get to school, but he was approaching his fourteenth birthday and it was time to think about getting a job. Work was almost unavailable locally, so he decided to earn his keep by working on the farm with his father.

He dug a patch of earth and sowed a selection of seeds, marking each row with a symbol of what he was growing. He was a good artist and made a drawing of the vegetables growing in the patch. He had no money, so when his bicycle tyres wore out, he bartered a few potatoes for a worn tyre that fitted the wheel of his bike.

One day he got a brand new pump. How he managed it was this way. He exchanged a small marrow with a man for a wooden wheelbarrow and the wheelbarrow for a few hours' work on a neighbour's front gate. The money he got - one shilling and ten pence – was for a brand new bicycle pump. He now had to use his pump to blow up his tyres instead of borrowing his mate's pump every time the tyres deflated. The inner tube was a mess of patches on the rear, and the front was already showing more patches.

He then had an idea; he would fix a wooden platform to his bike and make it a sidecar. That way he could carry more on the combination. He borrowed his father's saw and hammer, and using a little common sense, attached the wooden platform to the side of his bicycle. It made the combination a bit lopsided, but he could right that with a jerk of the handlebars.

His father watched the work on the platform as it grew to fruition.

"What are you going to carry on it?" he questioned, after rescuing his precious box of screws.

"Small things like vegetables and Mum's homemade jam. I'll give her a bit of money to pay for her time and the fruit she collects from blackberry picking. It will come in handy in paying a few bills like oil for the lamps at night."

Secretly he was proud of his son's achievements, but he never said so. Instead, he made an arrangement to give the boy a few potatoes to sell to the villagers. Thus, with his own ingenuity, Smithers was able to make a few pennies a day selling his wares to local customers.

On his sixteeth birthday he bought a horse and cart, and expanded his business to include the next village. For a few months the business prospered, then rivals appeared. Others, jealous of his success, copied his enterprise. A local farmer included a horse-drawn milk cart, with a selection of fruit displayed in cardboard boxes.

9

ONE DAY DISASTER STRUCK in the shape of Smithers' horse getting a form of ague. His fever worsened and as he watched him in the stable, after a series of violent shudders, he died. He received several pounds for the corpse and as he saw the body being carted away, realised he was now unemployed.

He thought about going back to the bicycle, but that was going backwards. He needed a horse and the only one available was too dear. The horse seller wouldn't reduce his price and Smithers had no more than twelve pounds. The seller was adamant he wanted fifteen pounds for the horse, which included the reins.

Thus, the future of the young man was shaped and designed.

Things were happening in Europe after a dignity was murdered in Bosnia by a Serbian nationalist. Germany and Austria declared war on France and the UK, and we were at war again.

Young Smithers looked at the shape of the news from Europe and decided to join the army. He journeyed to the nearest recruitment centre at Southend-on-Sea and queued up with a bunch of hopefuls waiting at the building.

It was there he first met Hartley. It was there he also found out that Hartley lived a few miles away from his village in Essex. Hartley mentioned the name of his village and Smithers exclaimed:

"Well, be Gawd, I know it well, I was there only just a week ago!"

"I've never seen you before," said Hartley, cuffing his nose with the edge of his coat.

"I was there selling groceries. I had a vegetable round around there."

"Why're you trying to join the army if you were in work?"

"My horse died. I was left without something to pull the cart."

"Shame," retorted Hartley, "so now you want to join the army?"

"Better 'n being unemployed, how about you?"

"The same. I was working as a general labourer in a forge. It was hard work, but I stuck it until I was sacked because of no work. There was another forge that done the work cheaper."

The queue lessened and soon they were let into a building that was equipped with drawn blankets that sectioned the room into spaces, each one occupied by a man in uniform. The soldier asked if they could read and write, and when told they could, he gave them each a form to fill up and sign.

Another man wearing a white coat told Smithers to strip to the waist, and pressed a pair of instruments to his chest and listened. This was followed by the partial removing of his trousers where he was asked to cough. The doctor signed the form to say the patient was in good health and ready to sign his signature to the paper - and that was it. He was now a member of the armoured force, and waited for the sergeant at the end of the line to tell him what to do.

He then received his first order. "Smarten yourself up," the sergeant roared.

This was Smithers' first introduction to an order and it surprised him almost out

of his socks. He jumped, having forgotten to lace up his boots. He treated the sergeant to a look of astonishment and looked from Hartley to the sergeant then back again. Before he had a chance to reply to the NCO, the sergeant shouted.

"Yes, *you*, I'm talking to you, Private Smithers. You smarten up and stand to attention when told by a senior NCO, is that clear?"

The young man reddened and was just about to say something when Hartley shook his head. Smithers stood to attention and looked at the ceiling. The sergeant relented and turned to other things, mainly doing the same thing to a skinny youth who was smoking a cigarette. The roll was hanging from his lip while he issued a small cloud of smoke from his thin nose. He casually turned to the sergeant who was upbraiding him in no uncertain manner. The youth shot a quick look at the NCO before snatching the cigarette from his lips.

"Sorry, Sarge," he said as he ground the remains under his booted foot.

"*Sergeant, sergeant*," bellowed the NCO, his face barely an inch from the other's cheek.

The man copied Smithers' example and looked at the ceiling.

A bus came and transported them to the local depot of the army barracks. The sergeant accompanied them all the way to the regiment's army barracks and they stepped down from the bus at the gates of the regimental parade. The iron gates had a crest emblazoned on the bars; a picture said to represent Zeus in flight. They eyed the flying crest and were interrupted by the sergeant bellowing an order.

"All right, you men, stand to attention, that means to stand up straight and face ahead. You will walk past the guardroom, that house-like building on the right. You will then be led into another building that houses the place where you will draw your blankets and straw biscuits. These are government property, as is everything that is issued to you. In the next room there are orderlies to issue you with your uniforms, boots and puttees. They will also issue you with a great pack, a side pack, a rifle and bayonet. They will also issue you with a set of utensils, a mess tin and a tin mug. That is all you need to know for now, so march to attention and follow me to the first of your issues." He puffed out his chest and shouted, "*Squad, squad, attention, move to the right in threes, quick march!*"

The civilians tried to keep in step, but their pace was woefully inadequate. They see-sawed a way across the parade ground and came to a ragged stop when he called a halt.

"*Queue up,*" the sergeant bellowed, poking the men with his staff. "Form an orderly queue."

The men dutifully did as they were ordered and filed into the room. They lost the sergeant then as he returned to his station at the recruitment centre. One by one they moved forwards, collecting each item as it was issued, until they were each laden with the accoutrements.

Another NCO appeared at their side and shouted.

"I'm Corporal Gunn. I will be with you all through your training. You will follow me and I will show you where your bed space will be. There you will find a bunk where you can deposit your blankets, and a locker where you keep your things. You will start to look like soldiers by folding your blankets and pillow the right way, the other men will show you how. Remember these things were issued for you to use, but they are still government property and will always remain so.

Your webbing equipment and your personal things are issued to you on the understanding that you will keep them clean and tidy, especially the boots, the rest is up to you. The boot blacking can be bought at the regimental shop, as can the Brasso to shine the bits of brass on your packs. Supper will be at five o'clock, this and all other mealtimes are on the company board. Welcome to the Ninety-ninth Company of Foot."

The next thing they were led to a barracks room where they found a wooden bedstead for each person. Gunn disappeared from sight and the men sat down and contemplated their induction into the army.

The two men looked forlornly at the bare room and wondered what on earth they were doing joining the army. Hartley echoed Smithers' feelings.

"You think we did right in joining the army? Why not the navy or the marines?"

"I can't, I get seasick on the Woolwich free ferry. I tried it once, but no more," replied Smithers, pulling a face at the memory.

"I suppose we did the right thing in joining the army. I'm not much of a sailor either. I can't see myself in that sailor suit and, as for the hat, I can't see the sense in wearing that thing."

They wandered the alleyways of the barracks and found the essential things. They found the toilet after bursting for a pee, they even found the mess hall and, after getting their tin mugs, queued up behind a knot of other civilians and partially-changed soldiers.

That evening just before lights out, they wrote home and posted the letters in the postbox beside the barracks.

Smithers wrote he hoped both his parents were keeping all right and his cart was safe. Hartley's letter was almost a replica of Smithers'. He had no knowledge of a cart though, and wondered how his mongrel dog, Shep, was doing. Both letters ended with the same theme - look after yourselves.

The next day, just after five a.m. the light flicked on and the dulcet tones of the corporal echoed through the barracks room. He demanded they each, ninety or so persons, get up and get outside in full kit and rifle, ready for inspection within half an hour.

The mad rush for compliance to the order was accompanied by the noise of ninety men scrambling to get out to the parade ground before Corporal Gunn's appearance. The entire company of the Ninety-ninth was on parade for the first time and stood there stiff and upright, clad in full equipment with the rifle at the trail.

The corporal duly arrived on the scene and proceeded to start by commanding the company to come to order and slope arms. During the next two hours he put them through a course of physical exercise that had them groaning with the force of the act. They found pain in the condition then found more pain as the exercise carried on. They used muscles they never knew existed and they ached and throbbed with the effort.

After about the first hour they fell to the ground exhausted, panting hard with the unusual exertion. The corporal let them recover before he commanded them and led them over a run of several times around the parade ground until they again collapsed in agony.

"Look at the state of you," Gunn said, laughing. "All flab and fat, you should be ashamed of letting yourselves get in such condition. In days you will notice the change in yourselves; these exercises will seem like child's play. You will sleep better and feel better, every day the change will happen. You'll eat more and you will work harder, but to be honest, there will be others who will let you down by slacking. These you must root out, encourage them initially, but don't let them get away with it. This you must do if you are to be a soldier. Remember these words if you want to be a member of the Ninety-ninth."

It was midday, time for the midday meal. They scrambled for their eating irons and mess tins, and made a wild dash for the mess hall. The troops talked wildly about the coming meal, the prospects of getting a drink of tea and the corporal who had taken them through the first day of sheer hell. Although it was their first day and the corporal had worked them extra hard, they secretly did feel better for the few hours of physical exercise they had received. They had the afternoon to look forward to, but it was with laughter and relief that the hard day was beginning to wane.

Smithers and Hartley were resting their tired bodies and tucking into a meal of corned beef and potatoes, the army's staple diet.

"These potatoes are not cooked," complained Smithers, digging into a particularly big potato, "and this gravy has bits in it, it ain't been done right."

"Get on with it and eat it," growled Hartley, treating him to a look of hatred. "You always like this, complaining?"

Smithers gave him a sly look and cut up the potato, ignoring his remark.

That afternoon they went on the rifle range. Hartley scored two bulls and an outer. Smithers also scored two bulls, but missed the other shots entirely. He was gnashing his teeth together in rage at the missed shots.

"Something's wrong with the sights," he complained, dismissing his losses as the result of poor equipment.

They had to ring the holes of the bullets with a pencil. He just pushed the pencil through the paper target.

"Let them figure it out, it just looks like a bullet hole."

The corporal looked at the target.

"The holes mean nothing, we can easily make one with a pencil," he remarked.

Smithers tried to avoid his accusing eye and looked the other way.

On the range, where they were told how to use the bayonet, they lined up before a row of straw-stuffed dummies. Gunn told them how to use the bayonet in no uncertain manner.

"Remember my words as you thrust it in, on guard, thrust in the bayonet, twist to release the entrails from wrapping around the blade then pull out. If it is hard then put your foot on the body, pull it out, easy, if it is still catching, fire a round to release, but keep one up the spout to do it."

Smithers found it easy to push the bayonet through the straw dummy. He found himself repeating the corporal's words.

"On guard," he whispered. "In, out and on guard," he muttered, twisting the bayonet from the dummy.

He lips moved as he repeated the words of the corporal. He was still muttering as he sheathed his bayonet. Hartley was doing the same thing just behind him.

"What do we do before starting the action of fighting the other soldier? He might get the better of the other man and beat your weapon away."

"Then it's goodnight to you, soldier," said Gunn. "We always speak in the positive sense in this company - we always win. Remember that, trooper, no negative thoughts allowed."

"I'll try to remember that, Corporal," said Hartley, dropping his rifle to the ground by his boot tips.

"See that you do. We never allow the enemy to get the upper hand, which means you are a write-off, we can't afford such losses."

The corporal walked away then and shouted to the other men to hurry it up and line up for inspection. It was the end of the first day of learning to be a soldier. The corporal dismissed the men with a final warning.

"You will spend the evening learning how to clean your rifle. This you must do until you know how to do it blindfolded. Your personable dress will be inspected every morning just before physical training. You will be expected to be well shaven and ready to face the day training to be a soldier - *dismiss!*"

The men turned right at his command and broke away.

"I'm hungry," complained Smithers, shouldering his rifle. "I wonder what's for supper."

"Probably hard tack and watery soup, spuds and greens if we're lucky, what lovely grub we get, don't we?"

Hartley sat on his bunk and unlaced his boots. He sat on the bed springs and rested his head against the wooden bed top.

The next two days were replicas of the first.

It was Friday, and as the corporal dismissed the section he announced they would all get a pass until midnight. The ruling was received with glances of delight by the troops; it was the first free night since their induction into the army and they looked forward to a free evening without bullshit.

After the evening meal they washed, dressed and donned their best uniform. They shined their boots until their faces were reflected in the leather, then they collected outside the corporal's office where their passes were issued. The corporal was there to warn them about their behaviour in the local town.

"The redcaps will be there to ensure that you don't get drunk or do any fighting. If you do, you will be hauled up before the old man. He will be a lot harder than the redcaps, I assure you."

At six o'clock they were let out of the gate to the barracks and let loose in the town of Gildersthorp. Although the locals avoided the soldiers, the licensees welcomed the addition to their coffers with arms outstretched. The local whores also celebrated their temporary business, but in a different direction.

The pals made straight for the pubs and fought to get in to order a pint. The smoky atmosphere attracted the troops and they found it hard to get to the counter. After about ten minutes of trying to wade through the crowd, Hartley and Smithers gave it up and decided to find another pub. They found a quieter pub and sat in upholstered seats at polished wooden tables. As usual they had very little money to spend and pooled their resources to order a couple of beers.

The man behind the counter was wiping the beer rings off the bar top. He gave them a cheery grin and asked them what they wanted to drink. He had an enormous moustache that curled from his upper lip and spread over his cheeks in a twisted spiral. He was forever twisting it with his finger and thumb, even when talking. He guessed their drinks and was already pouring out the two pints as they waited.

"There you are, lads, two pints."

They plonked the coins onto the counter and counted them out before him.

"There you are, lads," he continued, "tuppence exactly, thank you."

"How did you know what we wanted? We might have wanted bitter," grated Hartley.

The moustache was twiddled as he replied.

"I was in the same mob as you, so I know what you are paid. I got starvation pay the same as you. I could only afford the cheapest drinks. The government doesn't pay its soldiers well. I was a sergeant and the lads told me what they got weekly."

The two pals sat on the chairs in the tiny barroom and contemplated the situation. They were short of money, which was obvious as they pooled their few coins together and mentally gauged whether they had enough to pay for another two pints. Hartley produced three pennies and a button, Smithers added another three pennies, and the smiles came back to their faces as they realised they had enough to get merry.

Smithers rolled a fag and struck a match. The light reflected in his eyes as he breathed in. He coughed a slight wheeze and, as the tears came to his eyes, coughed again. He drank the top off his beer to ease the tickling in his throat.

"I've got to stop this habit, the tobacco is killing me," he said, breathing with a whistle.

Hartley had often heard him complain about the smoking habit, but learned to ignore his promises.

"I wonder where the local talent is?"

Smithers seemed to know what he was talking about and laughed.

"Women? We ain't got enough money to pay for booze *and* Judies. I prefer the beer."

"I want *both*!"

Hartley was saying it in a smoke cloud that seemed to wreath up as Smithers smoked.

"Don't we all, but we can't afford it," repeated Smithers with another cough. "The only way we're going to afford it is to get a stripe, which means another one and six for a lance corporal's pay, that's six and six per week. We might be able to afford it then."

"Where are we going to get a stripe from, I ask you?" Smithers scoffed.

"We might get one stripe in a year or two," his mate replied.

"We might be dead and buried by then," said Smithers, coughing.

"There is that," rasped Hartley, sipping his beer.

10

THAT EVENING THEY WERE using the rifle pull-through and greasing the mechanism. Hartley was tipping the rifle upwards and eyeing the gleam of the barrel.

"Clean as a baby's bum," he reflected. "Not a speck of rust or dirt - the corporal will be proud of me."

"I bet he won't," said Smithers testily. "He wouldn't be proud of you if you bled all over the gun."

One of the lads, a tall individual called Tom Holt, tried to borrow sixpence from Hartley.

"I only want it to buy my mother a birthday card," he explained. "She is sixty this Saturday and I ain't got any money to get it. I'll give it back to you on payday."

"Sorry, I ain't got any money. I spent the last in the pub this evening," explained Hartley, treating the recruit to a look of sympathy. "Try someone else."

Holt shrugged his shoulders in resignation.

"I have tried the others, but they said the same thing."

When he turned to Smithers he received the same reply.

Smithers ran the words of the corporal through his mind.

"Ready, on guard, thrust the bayonet through the man, twist to avoid the entrails then pull out," he whispered as he pushed the bayonet through the dummy.

Gunn was there, gazing at him as he did the job. He tried to encourage him by bellowing:

"In, out and twist, Private Smithers, remember to twist the blade."

Smithers tried to imagine the dummy as an enemy and drove the bayonet in up to the hilt. Gunn saw him get mixed in sacking and straw, and shook his head in wonderment. The soldier finished by picking the straw and sacking off the gun by hand.

The next stage of the training was the rifle range again, but Gunn was there to watch over the proceedings as the recruits emptied their rifles at the targets. Smithers still managed to score a couple of bulls, and the corporal was pleased with the target practice.

"Good shooting, Smithers, you're learning," he said, kicking his legs apart to balance his body, "but keep those legs apart to shoot straight. I'll make a soldier of you yet."

They were in the mess hall that evening.

"He has a special interest in your shooting," Hartley remarked. "He don't do that for everybody, Smithers, only the ones who show promise, either that or he is a bum boy and I don't think he is, so keep up the good work, lad."

Smithers liked the feel of the gun. He knew he had a natural aptitude with the rifle and was glad it was with firing at the targets, something he was at home with. Hartley hoped it was not a five-minute wonder as other things were with Smithers.

The pair ate heartily and enjoyed the dinner, not because they had to, but the hunger in them was an urge transcribed by the daily prescription of physical labour they were subjected to by the enthusiastic corporal.

The main daylight and also the evening hours were devoted to bullshit. As fast as one item of their kit was dirtied so another was waiting to be done. If it was not the brass work on the packs then it was their boots that had to polished. Their kit and the presentation of it happened every day. It was just one long round of cleaning, polishing and buffing their kit with an added assemblage of bed making and stripping after each night, plus a daily show of the items used.

Their eating irons had to be cleaned and displayed on a daily basis, including their mess tins, tin mug and shaving and washing materials, and implements used. Their bedding had to be stripped and folded up to display the three blankets rolled to show the pillow and the slips held by one blanket, rolled to contain the three items in the centre. This had to be done every day, especially on inspection days. It was done every day without fail, as well as rifle maintenance and cleaning.

Gunn was always around to see that these tasks were executed. He poked into every nook and cranny, weeding out the wayward things and pointing them out to the soldier with an accusing finger. He made each person aware they could be on a charge and marched up before the senior officer, charged with neglect and unsoldierly conduct. Every man of the entire barracks would be on a charge as well. This was to ensure that no lazy slackers were to be tolerated by the rest of the barracks room. Gunn made this very clear to everyone - if one let the rest down, the entire room would suffer by withdrawal of all privileges like evening passes and evenings out in the town with the ladies of the night.

This proposed turn of events was viewed by the troops as drastic and to be avoided. They worked with a will and made the barracks room spick and span. Woe betide the person who fell down on his daily schedule of work. He would be ostracised and made to complete his share of the responsibility. After a time of this treatment they all fell into line and complied.

Even Smithers helped to shine the oilcloth with a sack attached to the broom and tied around the handle, but he was growing muscles he never knew he had and easily managed to swing the polishing sack around the entire length of the floor. He and Hartley were shining the floor and putting down bits of paper for the others to step onto. The rest of the men either used the paper or went out through the other doorway - except Corporal Gunn. He thought he was privileged and left marks behind him with his boots.

Smithers polished his boot marks with his teeth gritted, for the fourth time. After a time he got fed up with redoing the oilcloth.

"Please, Corporal Gunn, that's the fourth time I have polished your boot marks, I'm running out of polish," he rasped.

He was just going to say he was running out of patience as well, but he did not have the nerve to say it anyway because Hartley was shaking his head slightly and warning him. Gunn stepped across the bits of paper and ignored Smithers, then with a withering look clumped out of the barracks room.

Hartley wiped a sheen of sweat from his brow.

"He must be in a good mood or he would've picked you up on that last remark."

"I only said what was the truth. He *did* make boot marks on my polished floor," protested Smithers, leaning on the mop.

Hartley blew a hot breath.

"But you didn't have say nothing, you could have ignored his remark."

"Well, I didn't," Smithers said, running the mop around his own footprints. "Anyway, it's said now and the floor is polished, I only hope it stays this way."

"I only hope he don't hold it against us," Hartley grated.

Gunn didn't; he must have forgotten it or thought it too trivial to bother.

Corporal Gunn ran into Sergeant Cox on the parade ground square and the matter of the boot marks had been put on the back burner.

"Ah, Corporal Gunn, just the person I have been hoping to meet. I have some news for you."

"Sergeant Cox," said Gunn respectfully.

A passing platoon of soldiers was counting as the corporal in charge was shouting in time to the men's marching feet. Cox pulled the corporal to one side as they passed out of earshot, and waited as the noise faded away.

"We are pulling out, Corporal, we are moving to a place called Berryfields. That's a place in Wiltshire, we are taking the whole regiment and a few things with us. The men have got to get ready on the fifteenth, that's just a month away, so they need to be warned about the move a week from now." Cox had beads of sweat under his nose and he wiped them away with his hand. "The lads must be told, so they can let their family know where to write to. We need a lot more room to accommodate new recruits we are expecting to come, we also need room for expansion to build more huts to house this explosion of manpower, that's the main reason we are moving. The big brass as well, they are all coming. They are thinking of making it the area headquarters, which means we will have a general to command us, will you see to it, Gunn?"

The corporal nodded.

"One month away you say, Sergeant Cox? That will be tight. There are a multitude of things left to do before then. The men will not like shifting their kit and everything. It will take all of a month and more to pull it off."

"Just one month, Corporal, lock, stock and barrel, the lot," insisted Cox. "The colonel is insisting on the move. He says we must be out of here by the said date. That's a must, Corporal, see to it."

Cox gave a curt nod to Gunn and walked away, tucking his regimental staff under one arm.

Gunn bit his lip. A month away, it seemed to be impossible to undertake. Even his own kit would be a lot to organise, especially his living quarters at the end of the men's barracks room. It had taken him several years to move into the room and more to find out where he was. Now they are asking, nay, *ordering* him to tear it all down and start afresh somewhere new. There ought to be a law against it.

This new command drove all thought of repercussions from his mind with regard to Smithers' remark, so Smithers could thank his lucky stars that this state of affairs had come up.

11

A FLEET OF BUSES WAITED on the lines of standing men.

They were dressed in best khaki and material puttees, with feet encased in highly buffed boots that reflected the light. Every man carried a pack, even Corporal Gunn. He also had a rifle, but that was consigned to a private who also carried his own weapon and bayonet.

"Officer on parade!" called Sergeant Cox as the commanding officer appeared on the rostrum.

He saluted the colonel and waited for him to start the talk. The colonel addressed the men and was well into the speech as the men waited in the light rain.

"You men of the Ninety-ninth have a proud heritage to maintain," he was saying, eyeing them through his eyeglasses, "and we mean to carry it on no matter what. We are moving to be nearer to the port of embarkation. This is deliberate, so you can imagine why we are doing it - so it is cheaper to move a quarter of a million men to France and beyond. In your next move you will be engaged in the various forms of actual combat. You will learn how to engage and fight the enemy in the tradition of the British Army. We all know what that is. Well, the Huns will find out when we get over there. When we do, they will find out what the British Army is all about. Good luck to you all, and God bless you and keep you every one."

The small military band struck up a march and the troops marched away to the waiting buses. The colonel took the salute as the ranks dwindled and ended.

The ride took three hours and the men looked through the stained windows for the umpteenth time. The bus Smithers and Hartley was riding in bumped and clanged over ridge-riven roads, narrowly missing farm animals as it passed. The landscape was changing all the time. They crossed several rivers by way of bridges and swept by one river alongside the outskirts of a big town. They had no idea where they were or where they were heading. The only thing they were certain of was the end of the journey would be at Berryfields in Wiltshire.

The bus was wreathed in cigarette smoke. Smithers coughed in the thick atmosphere and lit up another cigarette.

"Gawd, the air in this bus is as thick as a bill sticker's bucket, can't they open a window or something?"

Smithers puffed on the rolled fag and happily coughed into the smoke.

"It might be smoky, but it's warmer without the windows open."

The raindrops were hanging on the window frames of the bus and running down the dirty panes. The driver was framed in the front section of the bus, wrestling the huge steering wheel. He ground the gears together and trod on the foot brake. He did it as they watched, then, to avoid another animal on the road, brought the bus to a squealing halt. The engine opened up to a squeal and the bus lurched forwards again.

Smithers was almost dropping off to sleep as the bus stopped amid woods and smoke-filled trees. The clearing was filled with wooden huts, and a selection of furniture and wooden beds. A few people were passing the bus windows and treating the passengers to stares of mild curiosity. A corporal with a list of the passengers ticked off each man as they all spilled from the interior of the omnibus.

The rain had stopped and a watery sun was filtering through the trees.

"So this is Berryfields?" sniffed Smithers, hitching up his pack. "It don't look like much."

As they were standing there, the corporal was shouting out their names and assigning them to a hut. When Smithers and Hartley heard their names they trooped into the empty hut and plonked their packs onto the bare wooden boards.

After finding a couple of beds, they carried them into the hut and, amid the bedlam from the other soldiers, they managed to find out about their bedclothes. The bedclothes section was nearby, and finding and signing for the blankets took all of half an hour. They eventually got the blankets and a pillow each, and carried them over to the hut.

The hut included a pot-bellied coal stove, a coal skuttle and a half-burned away poker. They positioned their beds so they would feel the warmth from it.

In keeping with the other troopers they went to hunt for the mess hall and a mug full of hot tea.

"Guess what's for tea," trooper Holt said, coming back from his fact-finding mission. "Stew and potatoes; same old food cooked in the same old way, does nothing ever change?"

"Well, it's *food* after all," commented Hartley. "It could be worse, there could be nothing."

"I suppose so," said Smithers, "but highly unlikely as they're all getting paid for cooking it."

The pals exited through the doorway and with their irons rattling in the mess tins, went to the mess hall.

Slowly the new camp came into being.

The first thing to get was a fire going in the stove. They found the

coal heap and, with the skuttle at the ready, filled it to the brim. Others
were splitting sticks for kindling and soon a blaze was started in the
stove. Smithers emptied the coal onto the flame and with a little help
from a bit of waste paper, encouraged the wind to catch the wood
sticks. Others of the hut gathered around the stove, waiting for it to
warm up. Of course, Smithers had the best position with Hartley on
the bunk next to him.

True to form, Corporal Gunn made an entrance at this time. He
was carrying his swagger stick under his arm and he lifted it to pull
off Smithers' top blanket.

"Well, all comfy and cosy, Private Smithers," he sneered, "trust you
to get the warmest place in the hut."

Smithers jumped to attention.

"All ready and correct, Corporal."

"I hope so, 'cause we are doing a big course of exercise in the morning, so to get you all in the mood we will start on rifle cleaning right
away. You..." He swung around to include the rest of the men. "All of
you are confined to barracks until this hut is just right, that is until
it is cleaned to my satisfaction." His eyes took in the rest of the recruits as he continued. "Outside you will find several pieces of oilcloth
and half a dozen brooms as well. We have all seen what we do with
them, haven't we? We use them to sweep the floor and when we have
finished we lay the oilcloth, then polish the floor cover with polish
then buff it like you did at headquarters. It's so simple a child could
do it, so it should be easy for you to carry out my orders, so see to it,
that's all."

The men watched his husky form go through the doorway to his
room at the barracks entrance and slam the door.

The next morning it was raining as usual. The raindrops hung on
the branches of the trees and dripped on the heads of men as they
brushed through them.

Everything felt damp; their packs were damp and their uniforms were damp, their side packs were damp as were their rifles. The rubber groundsheets were running with raindrops, their puttees soaked with the continual passage through the wet grass.

Gunn never seemed to notice the raindrops, seeming to ignore the dripping and the cold of the rainfall. He was the same as he usually was, and tried to show it at every opportunity.

"Left right, left right," he chanted when he suspected them of faltering. "Left right, keep in line, Private Holt, stop talking, Private Smithers, left right, left right."

Sergeant Cox watched them marching to the gun drill and the practice ground where they used the bayonet once more. Other troops had been using the same equipment and the straw-filled dummies were hanging in tatters. The chill wind caused the dummies to move and the ends of the sacking were waving in the wind.

The corporal commanded them to halt, and obediently they slid to a stop in the mud of the practice ground.

"Left turn," he ordered, and watched them follow his orders. "You all know what to expect now," he shouted, walking up and down and eyeing the packed ranks. "For the benefit of those who were absent from bayonet drill the last session, I will repeat my orders. When you push your bayonet through the sack, twist it sideways to see that the entrails of the supposed enemy don't wrap themselves around your blade. This is important 'cause it sometimes does. If you find this is so, place your foot on the body and yank it out with force. If it still doesn't want to come out, use the remaining round to jerk it out."

The next hour was filled with charging men howling like devils and plunging the bayonets into the hanging dummies. In Smithers' case, he repeated the corporal's words ad verbatum as he plunged his bayonet into the hanging sack of straw.

At the firing range he again scored two bulls, this time with an outer to go with it. Gunn was there to see him score, and watched the target as he shot at it. He said nothing this time though, then turned away to oversee the rest of the section.

The rain stopped just as the lunchtime whistle sounded.

Hartley rattled his eating irons on his dixie in exasperation and moved up the queue to the tea urn. He was thirsty as well as hungry, and wanted to have a drink.

"Thirsty work, all that screaming and hollering," he observed to his mate, who was standing beside him. "I'm as dry as a desert. I could drink the tea urn dry and still come back for more."

"Me too," said Smithers, looking at his tin mug.

"I wonder what's for dinner," Hartley said, dangling his mug on the end of his finger.

"Something not cooked very well," was Smithers' instant reply.

The pals were due some leave, so they put in for a forty-eight hour pass.

"A fat lot of good that will be to me," Smithers bleated. "It will take me all of a couple of days to get home on the railway, plus two more to get back. I won't have no time to wave hello to my parents."

Hartley had to agree with him, as he had the same journey back to his home in Essex.

"You could save up all your entitlement until your leave is due and then take it," Gunn said when they complained about the distance they had to travel.

"Can you do it under this rule?" Hartley enquired.

"If you are entitled to leave, the old man will see you get it. He's a reasonable man," Gunn replied with a smile. "Everything will be all right if you toe the line and return on time."

"Oh, we will," they both chimed in unison.

"Well, a forty-eight hour pass won't suit you, but it's the best I can do at the moment," said Gunn, once more beaming a large smile at the pair. "You can use it to go local, that is go no farther than Trowbridge or Devizes."

"I was just about to suggest the same thing," said Hartley, looking at Smithers.

"If you have the money you can go to Salisbury Plain and see the ancient monument of Stonehenge. I sometimes go there myself," observed Gunn, staring at the two men.

Smithers laughed nervously.

"I was thinking of going to town to sample the favours of local whores. The last time I had sex was with a lady in my hometown."

"It's not our scene," ventured Hartley, eyeing the corporal. "We are not into highbrow stuff like old things, we like to use the taverns and get pissed, Corporal, if you excuse my old English. We ain't got no more than enough to get tiddly. We pool our coppers and buy pints of mild, the cheapest beer we can afford."

He looked at Smithers, willing him to back up his story.

"I'd say the same," commented Smithers. "We both like the same things, we only want the things others do."

The corporal looked from one man to the other.

"There's no interest in going to these places if you don't like them. I like 'em and I'm not going to force you to do things you don't want to do, that would be wrong. Anyway, you are due a thirty-six hour pass. You will collect it before you go - dismiss."

He turned away from them and seemingly erased them from his mind.

The other men questioned the pair, asking them what the corporal had said and whether they had got the passes. Private Smithers was adamant they were entitled to the leave. He argued they were entitled to have leave even if it was only a twenty-four hour pass.

"You go and tell *him* that," flared Hartley. "We almost didn't get nothing."

12

THE DAYS FLEW BY and the weeks with it.

During this time Smithers and Hartley both got leave, and travelled together to Essex on the train and decided to visit each other in their homes. Hartley met Smithers' parents while Smithers travelled over to Hartley's home and introduced himself to his mate's mum and dad.

The days of their leave seemed to flash by and soon it was time to say goodbye to them. The two soldiers travelled back to their unit, and everything was as before.

The end of their initial training was almost over and they looked forward to their passing out ceremony.

The men were tired but happy as they marched onto the parade ground, secure in the knowledge that the bullshit was finally over and they were free of training and ready to be dubbed soldiers. The regiment was lined up on the parade ground, all in suitably pressed khaki, with buffed boots. Their packs were square, and sparkled in the weak sunlight. The NCOs were in attendance as were the officers, junior and senior.

They had been up half the night bulling the equipment and shining the brass work. The carpenters were up half the night as well, building the rostrum since dawn and making a row that kept the rest of the men from sleeping. This all added to the noise from the band practising the different marches.

The entire regiment was present as was the company known as the Ninety-ninth. Sergeant Cox was there as was Corporal Gunn. They were there as the permanent NCOs and would soon be travelling to France with the men of the company.

As the men stood in lines on the prarade ground in their best khaki uniforms and highly polished brass, they little knew of the horrors they were going to be subjected to in the near future. They laughed and joked among themselves behind the backs of the NCOs and officers.

A little while later the commanding officer with his retinue of junior officers, mounted the rostrum at the front, only this time he was accompanied by his wife and several ladies of senior ranking officers. They all stood or sat on chairs the orderlies had presented for them. For a while the military band struck up a couple of marches and as they were playing, the figures on the stage were talking among themselves. The drum thumped and the bugles blared, the trombones whomped and every other instrument joined in the fanfare. This continued for half an hour, playing all the well known marches and even a few tunes to mark the occasion.

As the music died away the commanding officer stood up to deliver his speech. He only had a soft voice, so the men at the back could hardly hear. This prompted one of them to speak in a low whisper.

"Speak up, Sir, we can't hear at the back."

Gunn heard the remark and half-turned to reprove the offender. He thought better of it and agreed with the man, although not saying it out loud.

"I know you, all of you will do your duty to king and country, and fight," the high-ranking officer was saying. "You have received tremendous support from your leaders, officers and NCOs, and I cannot speak too highly about their wonderful teaching, on and off the parade ground. You have got the finest NCOs and officers in the world to show you how to conduct yourselves and fight for your leaders. This will aid you in your fight against the Hun oppressors." He paused to gain his breath. "The Germans have declared war on France and in return we have declared war to help our allies. We will help them to drive back the warlike motions of the Huns. This we are determined to do, and with God's help and your service we can pursue and gain these initiatives. May God protect and deliver you in your hour of great need. I know that the Lord God, in his mercy, will protect you, but until that time you must fight to save the world from those who seek to oppress us. This we must do, nay, *will* do, to save the world from the German yolk."

As the band struck up the 'National Anthem' the entire crowd of officers and women stood up in recognition of it and sang the words. The entire assembly echoed their example and joined in with them. As the 'National Anthem' died away, Sergeant Cox raised a cheer by shouting:

"Three cheers for the commanding officer, and the king. Hip, hip..."

The sound of the troops cheering added to the occasion and the officers smiled in unison and cheered their leader.

The entire regiment embarked for France in two weeks.

A section of the regiment, a company with their own officers and NCOs, boarded the ship used as a floating training ship and a means of travel, after being met on the quayside. The lines of fully-equipped men carried their arms at the trail. Some of the soldiers shouldered coils of ammunition. The NCOs and officers carried small arms strapped around their stomachs.

At the rear of the columns there were several cars that held the ranking officers and their wives. A lorry loaded with a huge pile of kitbags and other paraphernalia, which bumped and jigged against the rest of the equipment, trailed behind.

"Company, company halt," sang Sergeant Cox, marching with the troops. He strode to the left of the company and shouted out, "Company, left turn."

The men dutifully complied and found themselves facing the dockside. Cox continued with the commands.

"Company, order arms," he yelled.

The men executed the order by transferring their rifle butts to the ground, then came the next order for which the men were waiting.

"Company, stand at ease, easy."

The lines of troops relaxed and ceased their rigidness. They strained their necks to get a look at the troopship and the surrounding dockside. They were dwarfed by huge cranes and dangling chains. The steel wires holding the ship to the quay tightened and relaxed as the seawater rose and fell. The ship echoed with groans and creaks as it moved.

For many of the men the sight of the sea was for the first time and as for them going for a short trip on a ship, it was a luxury they were unable to afford. The sea trip was, for some, to be the last short sea trip they were destined to take.

There were smiles all around, and even the officers and others had a smile to fit the occasion. The officers were the first to go aboard then the rank and file. As the men were led to the gangplank they looked back to catch the last sight of Blighty and the sea port of Dover.

The company took all of two hours to embark. They were all over the ship exploring every nook and cranny with their excited cries. While this was going on, several seagoing tugs were pushing the ship into position and getting it ready for the sea voyage. The ship burped its horn as each tug towed the monster, pushing and pulling, smoke stack billowing great globs of smoke that mixed with the steam of the tugs' whistles.

The walls of the ship were lined with the faces of the troops, some sad, but many laughing with the excitement of the occasion. With a final wail from the ship the tugs went their own way, answered with a poop from the little tugs as they lost their way in the ship's mighty rush to the sea.

As the ship started to dance with the action of the waves, the men started to thin out, many because of the chance of getting a meal, but a lot because of the action of the ship as it started to heel. This increased as the big waves started to take over and the ship pitched and tossed even on so short a trip across the English Channel. The ship was strangely quiet as the beginnings of seasickness took a quick hold on the men.

In addition to the troops, the ship was carrying small lorries and ambulances. The drivers of these vehicles were staying in the cabs, hoping for some relief from the seasickness. That did nothing to help, however, and they just had to suffer like the rest.

The troopship was joined by several other ships of the Royal Navy, guarding it from the attention of other foreign ships, perhaps German. They ringed the troopship with clouds of black smoke to hide it from the sight of the enemy. No such enemy appeared, so the ship was spared and made her way across the divisions of the channel to the shoreline of France, which soon appeared against the billowing dense clouds of smoke. Two destroyers ushered the huge troopship into the approaches of Calais port and waited as it anchored in the half-light of early morning. The ships exchanged signals by horn and waited as the troopship prepared to enter the harbour.

Two tugs appeared at the side of the troopship and waited to receive the towing ropes. They did the same as the other British tugs and towed it into position where a bevy of French longshoremen were waiting to tie up the ship to the shore with heavy wire ropes. The wailing of the troopship denoted that it was waiting to be tied to the quay.

As before, the soldiers were lined up on the main deck by the NCOs, who went through the same rigmarole of calling them to order and attention, and getting them ready to march off the deck. The gangplank was lowered and fastened to the quay with ropes and there it waited until the officers and their wives had disembarked first. It was then the turn of the lorries and supplies to be unloaded.

It was around two hours before the troops were shifted and allowed to wander down the gangplank, laden with kit and equipment, and wilting under the weight of their arms and ammunition. The full complement of soldiers took over three hours to shift. They passed down the gangplank one at a time, loaded with the equipment and other paraphernalia. On several occasions they became hooked up on the gangplank itself, which all took extra time.

The men lined up on the quayside one at a time, adding to the slowly growing bevy of soldiers, but as time dragged on, the waiting columns of men only increased by a few at a time. The NCOs waited, showing impatience with the slowness of the march down to the quay.

"Hurry up," muttered Sergeant Cox, agitated by the gradual slow speed of the men.

He turned to Gunn, who raised his shoulders to indicate it was the way it was when the men changed countries. As the last of the Tommies staggered down the gangway he watched him totter to the side of his mate and pull himself upright. He glanced at Gunn and nodded, tucking his swagger stick under one arm. He immediately straightened to attention and marched to the centre of the columns.

"Company, company *attention!*"

They obeyed the order.

"Slope arms. Straighten up at the centre there." Gunn repeated his order. "Order arms."

They dutifully did it and one hundred and fifty rifles crashed to the ground as one.

"Smartly now, slope arms," he tried again.

This time they all complied with a united action.

"That's better," he said, switching his swagger stick to the other arm. "Move to the left in fours," he shouted, and turned to the left to indicate the way to go.

The lines of men smartly turned left and waited as the order to march off was delayed.

"By the left, quick march," he yelled, and then kept time by saying, "left right, left right."

The columns of men marched off - all in time, all in unison.

13

THE TOWN OF CALAIS was packed with soldiers and French civilians. It was booming with riches, and the shops were crowded with shoppers all hurrying to get the last available supplies of food and other things on display in the stores.

The columns of soldiers never even caused a flutter of interest amongst the population; they just ignored them and carried on with their usual practices. In turn, the men of the Ninety-ninth disregarded them and marched upright and erect in formation.

They marched upwards of an hour until a bedraggled barracks building was in sight. The iron gates were opened and as the sentries gripped the two gates, they strode to the front of the building. Gunn called a halt to the columns and as they waited for the order to stand easy, they relaxed.

Another NCO, a sergeant, called out the names and assigned a barracks room to everyone. Smithers and Hartley were given a bed space next to each other, and after receiving a kitbag full of their possessions they wandered through the vast rooms of the barracks and found their room. They immediately grabbed vacant beds and laid out their kit in the way they had been shown.

Their next job was to visit the stores and get their bedclothes. After they had rolled up their blankets in the manner prescribed, they started to clean their rifles.

After supper they looked out through the dingy windows of the barracks room and decided to try Calais and what it had to offer in the way of entertainment.

"I've heard stories about those French birds and what they do for a chap when he has paid his money," said Hartley, with a smirk on his face.

"You have, *have* you?" said Smithers. "What if you get a dose of the pox? They say it is easy to catch it and hard to get rid of it, it can scar you for life."

"Yes," replied Hartley, rubbing the window with his elbow to see better, "but that is if she has the pox, she might not have it."

"Stick to beer, you can't go wrong there," advised Smithers firmly.

"I always do, except when I've had a few beers, which is where I make a mistake in choosing the woman. I've been lucky so far, but there is the possibility of getting the wrong woman. I live in hopes the same as you do."

"Yeah," persisted Smithers, "but as I said, stick to beer and you can't go wrong."

"Oh no, I wouldn't bet on it with some of the French beer. You could get sick on that as well."

Smithers pursed his lips and pursued the subject.

"Yeah, but that is with your stomach not with your doodah. It could be with you for life, it could even affect your wife if you had one."

They were let out that evening. They applied for a pass and to their astonishment it was awarded. It only remained for them to present it to the guardroom and once there it was just a step away from the pub.

They gleefully started to get ready for a night on the town and the night ladies. To top it all it was pay day as well, so they jangled a few French sous about in their pocket. They put on their best suits of khaki, and shined their boots.

As they were going out they winked at the rest of the lads and made a motion of drinking. They nodded and winked back.

"If you can't be good, be careful!" a tall lanky soldier yelled.

They grinned together and made an indecent gesture. They banged through the end doors and playfully tapped on the corporal's door. The door remained closed, so they banged a little bit harder. A noise was heard in the room and Gunn was suddenly framed in the doorway.

"What do you lads want?"

"We asked Sergeant Wilde if we could get a pass from him, just till midnight, he said yes and said to apply to our NCO."

"A bit sudden-like," said Corporal Gunn. "You only just got here to the barracks this afternoon."

"Yes, but I've got this toothache and its killing me," moaned Smithers, holding his jaw.

Gunn looked at the two men.

"You must know we don't have a dentist, so I've got to let you go. It beats me how the dentists work at night, but if you are in pain I'll have to allow you the pass." He vanished from sight for a minute as he signed the pass, then came back clutching the paper slip. "You pair of bastards, if you are trying it on I'll..." he said, the threat unsaid, just eyeing them with a gleam in his eye.

Smithers looked at the ceiling and avoided his gaze. They tried to keep a straight face as the door banged shut, then on the way to the guardroom they uttered gales of laughter about the way they had outfoxed the corporal.

The red-capped corporal at the guardroom looked suspiciously at the pass and at the two men. He ticked the pass with a red pencil then they were outside the barracks clutching the precious document.

Calais was a wide open town. It boasted a dozen or so nightclubs, a score of pubs and innumerable brothels, official and unofficial, with many prostitutes plying their trade.

The French soldiers were in evidence, not because of their swarthy nature, or of the rank of the individual, but of the different language they spoke. They frequented the shops and stores, purchasing everything in sight, anything from food to material. They were also avid in the way they packed the pubs and clubs, and partook of the sexual favours of the prostitutes with equal measure.

Although well paid in their own country, it was not on a par with the pay of the British troops. The French were so ill paid it amounted to starvation wages for the ordinary private. While the British spoke ill of their pay, in comparison the others all received a lot less.

Everybody seemed to have money to burn, and even the housewives with their meagre budget had more than enough to buy food and the essentials of the day. This attention to the food situation never eased the shortages though, the food never seeming to catch up with the demand.

The forces in the town were catered for by the various armies and were paid by each government, but the French housewife was left holding the bag with regard to the food situation. Every day they could be seen queuing at the big combines and waiting for someone to come to their aid and produce food.

The prostitutes survived on the money they received from the soldiers and increasingly that was how some housewives made ends meet. They just listened to the pros and joined them when the money or the food ran out. The children were the losers though, as they had nothing to pawn or exchange for sexual favours. The mothers, seeing this easy way of getting money and thus, food, just changed their lifestyle, donned their 'glad rags' and joined the army of prostitutes plying their trade with the soldiers .

Into this den of iniquity stepped Smithers and Hartley. They were ready and willing to enter into partnership with the café owner or prostitute. They could not afford both, so either it was booze or birds - when they had had a few beers they would not be able to tell the difference.

They had sex through an alcoholic daze and, apart from the end of the sexual satisfaction, fell asleep anyway.

"Look at that bird, she's lovely," expounded Smithers, eyeing the woman with an air of admiration in his voice. "She has got more paint and powder on her than I've got on my garden fence, but the smell and sight of it all has given me an erection. I'd like to give her one, and that's a certainty."

"A little while ago you were at me to avoid sex 'cause it will get you into trouble," said Hartley quickly. "Now you are doing the self same thing. You want to make up your mind, mate."

"Yeah, I know, but that was *then,* this is *now*, things change, as you know."

"And so do you, mate, you are changeable like the weather," said Hartley weakly.

They turned into as dingy café and, after counting up their meagre amount of French coins, decided they had only enough for three drinks each. They had a plentiful supply of tobacco and papers, which was the main thing.

"A smoke and a drink is all I ask out of life," Smithers said wistfully, "although a little bit of how's your father wouldn't go amiss if I can get it."

"Or *afford* it," added Hartley quickly.

"Especially that, mate, extra especially afford it," Smithers said pensively.

The proprietor-cum-barman was wiping the counter with a greasy cloth, and looked up.

"Yes, Sir, what you like?"

He spoke in broken English and the two men could hardly understand him.

"Two beers," ordered Hartley, looking all around the barroom with a corrugation of a frown on his face.

"Where is everybody tonight? The place is empty."

The barman raised his shoulders to indicate he did not understand English, and waited to be paid for the two beers. Hartley fished into his pocket and brought forth two of the French coins. He looked at them nestling in his hand and dropped them onto the counter with a swift motion. The Frenchman looked at the coins suspiciously and after a moment swept them into a drawer under the bar counter.

Smithers dipped his tongue into the flat surface of the beer and closed his eyes in rapture.

"At least it tastes like beer and it's got a small head, so it must be beer."

"That's a matter of opinion," said Hartley wryly, "just 'cause it looks like beer, it don't follow it *is* beer."

"I ain't here to argue the toss about the beer, "said Smithers darkly. "Where's the Judies?"

"Your guess is as good as mine," said Hartley quietly.

They sat down on a pair of dilapidated wooden chairs and gazed around the barroom with boredom. The door banged and two khaki-clad figures entered. The two British soldiers nodded to them and they did likewise. They just lounged at the bar and stood there drinking beer.

Smithers fished out the tobacco tin and started to make a fag. One of the newcomers turned around and addressed the two pals.

"Where's all the local talent, mate? I ain't seen a woman come in here for a while."

"Don't know. We was just saying the same thing," said Hartley with a smile.

"I heard those French birds are noted for giving you a good time, I only mentioned it because of what I've heard," said the shorter of the newcomers.

"Just like we heard," returned Hartley. "We came in here to see if it was true, looks like they are giving it a miss this time, must be the café or the beer."

"Could be you are right," the fat man replied, lighting up a fag. "One or the other." He looked all around and added, "The place is grotty, it's dirty and smells, the girls must be giving it a miss."

"I suppose so. They have a choice of either coming to this place or going up town to the high fashion places, what would you choose?"

"Yeah, I suppose so, but little Tommy is missing out. He has to get some loving someplace."

The two men drank their beer and with a nod banged out through the doorway.

Wonder of wonders, a woman entered the café about half an hour after they had departed. The barman started to play a record on the gramophone and the strains of 'Nellie Dean' echoed through the bar.

"Things are looking up," Smithers decided, grinning with relief and eyeing the woman.

Hartley was also smiling as he nodded to the woman. It was smiles all around, as the motion affected the barman as well.

14

Since his service in the Boer War, Sergeant Cox had seen many wars. There was the skirmish with South Africa after the affair at Transvaal between the immigrant gold prospectors and the British. There was also the fracas between the Boers and the frantic inclusion of British nationals to the African idiom. The South Africa problem also included the Depression of 1913 and the discriminatory laws between coloureds and English settlers. In all these battles Cox always excelled and left the combat with much acclaim, well be-medalled and wise in the ways of the leader of men.

The war of 1914-18 provided him with another ideal to join, and this he did with a lot of enthusiasm and zeal befitting other less able men. His upbringing was laced with middle class privilege provided by straight-laced parents, which was the way they were brought up. Their favourite saying was, 'What was good for them is good for us'. This they stuck to in the ruling and stood by, no matter what.

Young Cox went to school well versed in the ways of the privileged and well suited. He excelled at being a leader, especially when going into battle, his teacher hastened to add! He copied his father and his father before him, in achieving the rank of NCO.

His father acquired the rank of sergeant major, a rank he himself was offered, but turned down on condition of his advancing age bracket.

"I'm too old for that kind of rubbish, give the younger men a chance to get it, they might do a better job than me."

He was adamant in his denial and always followed the same ideal. That is why the men liked his way of dealing with them and openly said he was fair and above board with his judgement of their problems. His criticism of Corporal Gunn was that he did not want to join the men in his company or even his battalion in doing its best to earn each decoration or distinction for the good of the company or regiment. Gunn thought of the company as a unit, not as a integral part of a whole that ended on the fields of battle. That's where Gunn and Cox differed - Cox was for the men, Gunn offered nothing but discipline.

Cox had no criticism of the other NCOs because he did not have a lot to do with the other corporals, but he would hazard a guess that Gunn's record would be repeated at every opportunity. Gunn's life was littered with bad luck. He often complained about his ill fortune, but rarely when the boot was on the other foot. Cox had heard his unfortunate remarks to his underlings on numerous occasions, and he had had to pull him up on it many times, often with the raw recruits in mind.

Cox's grandfather died with the rank of sergeant on his sleeve. He was killed during one of the battles against the French, the Battle of Waterloo or some such fracas, he said when questioned. His parents were proud of the record of the relationship the family had with the army, and openly said so on every occasion. They were not warlike in their approach to the army, but respectful in mentioning the name of the family and their tradition with the force. The tradition extended from the time the family had entered the service seventy years or so before. They had a portrait of a family member who entered the army in Cromwell's time and was killed in one of those battles between the Roundheads and other factions.

Of course Cox liked the army. It had been his bread and butter for years and he looked upon it as so. He was a member of the local cadet force until his inception into the army. In a few years he rose to the exalted rank of boy corporal, and that rank stood until he entered the proper army as a raw recruit. Of course they took his years of being an NCO into consideration and, with his expertise to guide them, he soon gained a stripe to make him a lance corporal.

He had to wait until five years had elapsed before he got the second stripe. It was during the Boer War he achieved his third stripe, consequently, turning down his next promotion to sergeant major as a matter of course.

Thousands of raw recruits had passed from under his official wing and he watched their progress from novice to fully fledged soldier. He had time to spare for each man, even the lowest ranking recruit. He knew everybody and everybody knew him. He was familiar with what made the rookie tick because he used to be one.

Try as he might, Gunn could never understand why Cox had this gift. He wracked his brain searching for this ability, but it always managed to elude him. He even tried to copy the sergeant's ways, but his methods were beyond him. With a scowl he decided to give up the ambition to be like Cox and be himself. This brought an even bigger scowl to his face, something he was at home with though.

Beryl was one of those lost women. She had been a prostitute ever since she had left her employ with the state judiciary. Looking back over her life, she could not understand where her fortune and luck had overlapped and struck her a sharp blow in the face. She was sacked from her job at the ministry and her husband died within two weeks of her losing her job.

She drifted around looking for another position and on one of those aimless wanderings found herself in a bistro on the main street of Calais. She accidentally bumped into a dark-haired girl who was carrying a cup of coffee. They both apologised for it and when she turned around she found they had sat down on adjoining tables. They smiled at each other struck up a conversation in perfect English.

"What a lovely day," enthused Beryl, stirring her cup of coffee, "better than yesterday. I love the spring days, don't you?"

"Gorgeous," replied the dark-haired girl, sipping her coffee. She extended her hand in welcome. "I'm Louise, this is my 'ometown." She had a delightful French accent that hardly betrayed her nationality. "This your first time in Calais?" she asked, putting on a pair of dark glasses.

"Yes it is, Louise, but I have had a tragedy in the family. I just lost my husband to pneumonia a few weeks ago."

"Oh, I am so sorry, er-"

"Beryl, Beryl Simpson from London, England. I'm English, Louise."

"Did 'e suffer much, Beryl?"

"Not much really. He smoked a lot and that added to the illness."

Louise raised her shoulders in sympathy.

"Those things are a menace. I think they ought to be banned, don't you?"

Beryl nodded.

"They are all at it, especially now there's a war on. All the men are smoking in every country of the world."

"What are you going to do now that your 'usband has gone?"

"Probably get a job. I lost my position in England."

"Out of work eh? Why don't you follow my profession? There's plenty of money to be earned," suggested Louise with a smile.

"What's that?" Beryl asked, becoming interested.

"I'm on the game, a prostitute. I give what men want and they pay me - simple."

"Oh, I *couldn't* do that, I'm much too shy," said Beryl, going red.

"You try it. It's just like being married, only better. You get to choose your bed partner. If you don't like him you say no then wait for the next one. There's always the next person, 'e might be nicer too."

They had more coffee then Louise had to go, but not before she whispered to Beryl.

"I get plenty of money to live on. Once you get into it, it's all right, it's better than starving and you get to buy your own apartment as well. I 'ave been doing it for close on two years. There's money in the game, there's thousands of lovelorn men around, go out and grab one, bye."

She had then disappeared into the drifting crowds of Calais.

Freda was missing Corporal Gunn terribly. She had the café, and the sales of beer were on the up, but the shadow of the corporal still lingered in her mind,

He had asked her to marry him when the war was over and he could get a job. Although the army was his life he would be willing to give it all up for her, he had said so before he left for the front at the Somme. He must have been serious, for he had bought her an engagement ring and she was wearing it on her finger. She turned the gold band around on her finger and drifted into dreamland.

She often thought of Gunn as a husband and wondered what he would do in Civvy Street. He could help me, she thought, looking at the counter and picking up a rag. He could get the beer up from the cellar and tap it, he could do that. Her mind raced and he became the husband she wanted him to be. She progressed with her thoughts, and saw him as mine host, doling out the pints with a silver watch chain spread across his middle, which he would consult at closing time. He then called 'time' and opened the door to the street for the customers to use. After closing the café they would go upstairs and put their feet up for the night. In her imagination, Freda would often immerse herself in these fantastic dreams.

She sighed and looked at the front door, bolting the stout wooden door with the huge iron bolt that reached from side to side. She looked down to the mat and saw she had a letter. Curious, she stooped down and picked it up. She fingered the envelope and wondered who had written to her. She tossed it onto the counter, turned on the gramophone she turned the record over to play the other side.

Her mind wandered to the letter again and she took it up and opened it. It was from her boyfriend, Gunn, and she was treating it as though it was nothing at all. The first thing she looked for was the signature. It was from her boyfriend; she could see by his kisses on the bottom, then she read:

We are in the River Somme area. It is a pretty area with villages and forests. The bluebells are so colourful, making the countryside and valleys a forest of blue, in contrast to the scores of poppies showing through the grass and corn. It is a riot of colour, and movingly pretty.

The letter continued:

My darling Freda, I miss you so much. I yearn for the touch of your hand and your body. Your kisses are like fire and your caresses tender and warm. I wish I could be with you at this moment of time. I will make up for it the moment I return.

The letter continued in the same vein and touched on the war, how it was going and how he hoped to beat the Huns and return to her.

She turned the two pages.

I miss and adore you, wonderful Freda, and yearn to hold you once more in my arms, just like I did the night before returning to duty.

Her eyes misted over as she read the last line. I love and adore you, wonderful Freda, yours forever. He had signed it with his usual signature, adding five kisses at the end. There was no returning address. He had often said they were not allowed to give an address in case the enemy got information as to their whereabouts.

Freda picked up a broom and started to sweep the floor. The night before she had entertained several revellers and, apart from the usual cigarette ends and fag ash covering the floor, there was the odd spit mark to contend with where someone had emptied the contents of his mouth. She got the mop and washed the floor. The oilcloth, or linoleum as some called it, was getting thin in places were the iron-tipped boots of the soldiers scraped at it, especially where the bar started and they stood when ordering their beer. She examined the scuff marks and shook her head at the condition of the oilcloth.

It will need a new piece of lino to replace the old stuff, she thought. She got a hammer and started to tack it down in the bad places, hitting her finger twice and pricking her thumb on a sharp tack once. She then made a decision; she would use the piece of matting she normally stood on while serving the drinks. It meant she would be subject to drinks dripping down onto the floor from the beer taps.

"But what the hell if the beer does slop over from the barrel in the course of my duties," she muttered.

Using the hammer she yanked up the tacks holding the mat in place and, saving the tacks, carried the mat around to the bare place. She placed it on the bare patch and hammered the tacks into the wooden boards then she stood up, arms akimbo, eyeing the results of her labours.

As she surveyed the mat a knock came at the door. She opened it to see the French whore, Louise, staring at her.

"I knocked before," she explained, "but you were hammering something, you couldn't 'ave 'eard me."

Freda let her into the café and picked up the tools with a grunt.

"I was just getting the café to order. I was just sorting out a bit of floor where the boots scuff."

Louise smiled.

"I was just passing and I want to introduce my friend, Beryl. She's new to the game, so I said I would introduce 'er to you."

"Where is this woman?" enquired Freda, putting the tools away under the bar.

"She's outside. She's new to the game as I said, she 'asn't done it before."

"Well, I have a few moments to spare," said Freda, brushing her hair aside, "bring her in."

Louise grinned and opened the door, calling to Beryl. Red faced, Beryl stepped into the café, smiling apologetically at Freda. Freda tried to make her at home from the onset, holding out a hand of welcome to the woman.

"I'm Freda, the owner of the café, glad to meet you."

"I'm Beryl, I don't want to put you out, Freda, but Louise said it will be all right."

"Of course it is all right - you scratch my back and I'll scratch yours. You bring the customers in here to drink and I will let you meet them on the premises. You do me a service whilst plying your trade. They drink my beer and pay for it out of their earnings, simple."

With an apologetic shrug Beryl offered her thanks, commenting as she did so.

"You'll never know what you have done for me. I have had a run of bad luck in the past months and this is just what I need. I lost my job and since then I haven't known where to turn. You have my heartfelt thanks and I will play my part in the deal I promise, Freda."

Both women turned towards the door then looked back at Freda.

"We will be back this evening, Freda, so see you then, bye-bye."

They then disappeared from view along the pathway.

15

SMITHERS HAD HAD ENOUGH to drink. He had drunk his pint to which several the other men had treated him. He was feeling decidedly queasy and threw his cigarette away to ease the feeling. He teetered on the barside stool and looked through eyes that reflected the amount of alcohol he had got through.

He visited the lavatory and swayed as he peed into the pan. He staggered in the little room and buttoned up his flies with one hand. The lavatory boasted one mirror, and as he gazed into the scored and cracked surface, he noted the pale face and bleary eyes of the reflection. He fished through his uniform pockets and brought to light a blue comb. It had several teeth missing and he combed his thin locks, using the only remaining teeth. He dodged aside to get the clear side of the mirror, missing the cracked and warped side. As he pushed it back into his pocket again he straightened up to his full height and dusted down his uniform jacket with the other hand. He bleary eyed his image in the mirror and opened the lavatory door.

With eyes that missed the dark and stained walls of the passage, he staggered into the half-light of the barroom and found his stool again. The room was full of men in uniform, and women. Of course the females sitting with the soldiers were prostitutes. They made the soldiers drink the beer quickly, telling them their glasses were empty when they were still a quarter full. Of course, this plan was designed to make the men drink more. They even resorted to spilling the alcohol on several occasions, blaming the faulty legs of the table for the mishap.

With double vision now, Smithers was counting up his French coins on the counter, his finger edging from one coin to the other while his fuddled mind curled around each denomination. He turned on the stool to get a good view of Hartley. He was drinking the beer that other men had provided and was sitting at a table with one of the whores. His arm was around the woman's shoulder while his other hand was circling her left breast. She did not seem to notice his hand, or if she did, was ignoring it.

Smithers envied Hartley's ability to attract women. Although never mentioning it, he was secretly jealous of his way with the prostitutes. Smithers was the refined type and shy of the women of ill repute. He made a pretence of being accustomed to the ways of women, but was never at home with their ways. Although he did not like his own company, he was always after the women. He professed he was after sex, but secretly wanted their mothering as well.

Freda had an alarm clock on the counter to alert the soldiers that it was approaching eleven o'clock. It was designed to warn them that they must go soon or invite the wrath of the NCOs at their lateness.

Freda called to the men.

"Time to go home back to your barracks, the sergeant will be watching. He'll put you on a charge if you are late getting back."

She watched the men fidget in their chairs and prepare to return to the barracks. The women, used to the schedule, tipped their drinks down their throats and prepared to go. A couple of men began to question the time and pulled them back again. The women tried to coax them into returning home, and argued with them about the time. In the end they listened to reason and pulled on their uniform jackets. With voices raised in protest they let each woman lead them to the exit.

"That means us, Smithers," said Hartley, rising and approaching his mate.

"I suppose so," slurred Smithers, tipping his drink down his throat with a flourish. "Sod the army and sod Sergeant Cox."

"Well yes, Smithers, old son, but there are others just as bad."

"I suppose so, Hart, but he is in charge, so that makes him the enemy."

Smithers slipped down from the stool and, on unsteady legs, made his way to the door. He turned around to wave to Freda with uplifted hand, which dropped down to adjust his cap. As other soldiers went by them, he staggered to the door and into the street, stumbling on the broken pathway outside. With his arm around Smithers, Hartley stopped him from collapsing onto the pavement.

The next day, just before sunrise, the men were called at the usual time, and were told they were due to move up the line.

Smithers, with a headache through drink, suffered the most, and nursed a thick head for most of the morning. He waded through the kit inspection and the eventual early breakfast time and got his personal clothes up to scratch. He was just finishing the polishing for the morning inspection as the sergeant made a surprise visit.

Cox immediately got the rest of the barracks room on titivating the room to the standard that the commanding officer had come to expect from them.

"It's the last time we are doing this," Cox said to a group of recruits. "From this time on we will be making our way to the front line and the Germans."

They all fell silent as the import of the news suddenly hit them.

The inspection came and went, and as the retinue of officers passed by each bed space they departed quickly, knowing the scrutiny was the last for the company. The old man, knowing the meeting was the end for the men, went through the usual routine of wishing them the best in luck with their lives from now on. That meant they were going where their lives were at risk every day, now and for the foreseeable future.

They cheered him again and ended in the same manner of lining up, ready to march away - to where? The band cheered them on, blaring the lines of men onwards into the jaws of death and destruction. Every man was now conscious of the magnitude of the immense nature of the approaching confrontation.

Under his burden of back-breaking equipment, Smithers had his hangover to contend with. His rifle was carried at the trail instead of at the slope. The NCOs reckoned that was the way of easing the load of extra equipment the men had to carry.

As they passed they saw the results of past battles that had taken place. The villages and towns showed huge damage to the churches and other places of interest, which would take an immense effort to rectify. The roads were choked with traffic, each item of warfare, back to tip, all nearly touching as they growled on steaming engine amid clouds of choking smoke that had the soldiers coughing and retching for breath as the vehicles passed.

German aircraft occasionally came down to look at the trails of traffic and on one occasion a trio of enemy planes dipped down and strafed the moving columns. The German crosses were plainly etched on the body and the wings for all to see. The lorries tried to scatter to the outlying fields, but they were so hemmed in by other vehicles that they had to just increase speed and wait for the planes to run out of ammunition. Of course this happened, but not before a couple of vehicles had to suffer as a consequence. They burst into flames and, as the heat reached the ammunition they were carrying, exploded into a huge ball of smoke and fire.

The troops dodged around the flaming lorry and pulled the driver out of his cab. The company of troops, NCOs bawling their heads off, circled the blazing vehicles while their medical orderlies helped the injured drivers by carrying them to the side of the road.

The aircraft vanished to three tiny dots and disappeared behind a bank of grey clouds. The flames of the burning lorries reached up into the air surprisingly quickly. The ammunition had ceased to explode and the danger was over for the present.

Very soon it started to rain and the company pulled out their groundsheets and wrapped themselves in the dry folds. The burning lorries, enveloped in greasy smoke, were abandoned as the troops left the road and walked on grassy tracks.

The towns were becoming more frequent now. The harm to the buildings was more common as they passed by and circled each village and collection of houses as they appeared. The shellfire and aerial bombardment had reduced them to blackened stumps and skeletons of their former selves. They counted seven towns in a row that the war had obliterated. They were still smoking from the holocaust the war had created, even though the bombardment had passed them by.

The birds were singing in the trees weeks after the explosions had wrecked the towns. Even the flowers were still blooming, defying the wintry conditions and showing their colours amid the relentless rain. The grassy track bypassed a great depression in the road where a shell had exploded. Even the hole had blades of grass growing in the eruption of loose earth, the remains of withered poppies showing amongst the torn soil, looking so pathetic amid the earthen wreckage.

The countryside was pockmarked with shell holes, each one seemingly more recent as the company got nearer to the front line. The sounds of fighting got louder near the front line. The explosions of shells and bombs echoed through the countryside and reverberated on the scenery beyond. The soldiers even heard the pop of the individual bullet as it sped on its way across no-man's-land.

It all changed as the holding trench came into view. It started as a small incline on the lip of the trench and gradually descended down into the pit proper. As the men marched downwards they trailed along the muddy bottom of the trench and sunk their boots into a morass of water and soil. The entire column followed, even the small cars that carried the officers and drivers. The smaller lorries with the men's kitbags on board stopped at the beginnings of the pit, unable to continue into the confines of the trench. The tyres were bogged down in deep sandy earth and water. Try as they might, the engines roared and heaved, but still remained stuck in sticky filth.

A lone officer waved down the driver with a jerk of his hand.

"That's about as far as it will go," he said, looking at the spinning wheels. "Even the wheel grips won't help, they will only slide on the tyre walls. You will have to unload out here and get the kitbags to the men by hand."

The driver pulled the engine stop button and, with his mate, dropped down to the sodden ground below. They went around to the rear of the lorry and untied the ropes holding the canvas sheet to the lorry frame. One by one they heaved the kitbags from the vehicle and left them piled up in the road. The lorry lifted as the load lightened until the last item of kit was unloaded.

The column proper, ahead of the retinue of small cars and tiny lorries, had halted at the beginnings of the trench proper. Less than three or four hundred yards away a solitary shell buzzed in the air and exploded on the trench wall, ripping the lines of dirt-filled bags asunder. It scattered the ripped bags in all directions, dispersing the contents far and wide.

The sandbags lining the walls of the trench had two purposes; they gave strength to walls and added eighteen inches to the depth of the trench while providing protection for the soldiers. The lives of many a man was saved by this method of shelter.

In this area of the battle there were a few small gun emplacements scattered on the ground, all with artillery and manned by the Royal Artillery. They were firing small shells from these guns and shooting them at the unseen enemy. The resultant bang of the guns echoed around the countryside and the scenery.

Yelling at the men, the NCOs and officers directed them in the right direction. Slowly but surely they wound around the holding trench, avoiding the shell damage from the explosions.

Smithers and Hartley were about halfway along the lines of men, ducking instinctively as each shell exploded around, or on, the line of trenches. Several men had received minor scratches and one had a cut on his face that would merit stitches. The unfortunate soldier was dabbing at the wound with the sleeve of his shirt. A medical orderly was standing at his side, bag at the ready, rolling up a bandage. Now the din of battle was getting nearer the shells gaining in intensity.

"If it is always like this, I'm going home," muttered Smithers to Hartley, hitching up his rifle.

"Stop talking in the ranks," scowled Corporal Gunn, who was just behind them.

The company moved closer to the fighting, trying to present as small a target as possible. They hugged the earthen walls of the trench and flinched as another shell brought down a shower of earth and sandbag slivers. The vanguard of the company stepped over the fallen earth and shingle of the damaged trench and ducked as another explosion ripped the sandbags apart farther along the excavation.

The battle was getting louder and closer with each stride of the soldiers. The rattle of the machine guns could be heard in the morning air, as could the pinging of the enemy bullets as they replied to the onslaught.

Another fifty yards to go and then the trench opened out to the main channel and the trench nearest to the enemy - the fighting trench. Now as caution demanded, the leaders of the men hesitated as the corner came into view. Gunn, to set an example, walked to stand at the side of the leaders, ready to continue. He squared his shoulders and stepped from the safety of the holding trench and out into the fighting trench. After striding about the battle trench he waved to the men to come forwards. They replied by inching around the corner of the channel and gazing at the corporal. Gunn strode about the trench to show them that there was no danger in the move. He beckoned with his hand and watched the first man emerge.

Bolder now, they walked into the battle trench and the rest followed, still wary of what they would find in the new trench and of what it was like. They strode into the channel, bold as brass now they had a chance of seeing what they were faced with. The men, all with rifles swinging from the hand, started to laugh nervously with relief, but mostly from the realisation that they had survived.

They crowded into the new trench, fanning out until the new channel was choked with men. The NCOs then took over and shepherded them into groups for the doling out of accommodation. The battle trench housed cubbyholes cut into the walls, lined with corrugated iron and an assortment of cardboard boxes to keep out the damp and cold. The rat population was ever present and a few popped their heads up at frequent intervals. The men had to provide their own fire and cooking facilities whenever they were able.

Of course, Hartley and Smithers were billeted together again. Luck seemed to play it this way, or so it seemed, although Gunn had a hand in fortune by seeing he kept the two best con men where he could keep an eye on them.

Corporal Gunn immediately ordered an inspection to keep up the duty and moral of the troops. He marched into each area of accommodation before the men moved in and when they had moved in. They had to provide firewood and cleaning materials to buff up their kit, boot polish and Brasso to polish up their buttons and kit fasteners. They even had to buy floor polish to shine up the odd bits of oilcloth with which the dugouts were furnished. All this out of the six shillings a week pay they received from the army.

"Well, well," gloated Smithers when he saw his dugout, "we copped again, Hart."

"What do you mean?" asked Hartley, dumping his kit onto the floor.

"Gunn has put us together to keep an eye on us, he thinks we are stupid and don't know what he's up to."

"He may know we know. He's not such a fool as you think he is. He's a crafty man, that one."

"I'm beginning to see that, Hart, but we do our share of craftiness ourselves," said Smithers with a wink.

"Yeah, but he is in the driving seat with a great grasp of the reins," maintained Hartley, spreading out his bedclothes on the damp floor.

They spread their kit on the floor and made up their bunks. They never saw sheets, but slept between the blankets every night. The three biscuit mattresses kept them from sleeping on bare boards and served as an integral part of their equipment show during the day. The rest of their kit put on the biscuit mattresses or rolled around them to look neat and tidy when the inspection was being done.

They were just rolling up the bedclothes when Gunn made one of his surprise visits. He treated them to one of his leers of mistrust as he walked around the two beds. He wiped a finger around the shelves and looked at it.

"You ain't had enough time to dirty it, but I reckon you will in time," he remarked. He marched around the two bunks, eyeing the kit display. He poked the equipment with his swagger stick. "Do it again; the eating irons should be squarer." He walked up and down inspecting the floor. "As you haven't had enough time to move into the dugout, I'll let it go, but there must be an improvement of your personal kit and your dugout, the floor is a disgrace and so are your shelves. I'd hate to see what your rifles are like, but I'll leave them till next time." He neared the door before adding, "I'm moving one of your mates into this dugout. You know him, Private Willcox - dismiss."

They heard his boots grind on the scraper outside the dugout. They heard his voice bawling out to another soldier as a shell landed in the trench.

Hartley let out an enormous blast of air as Gunn's voice faded into the distance.

"That means we are doing the dugout this evening," moaned Smithers, dropping down to his bunk when he had shifted his kit aside.

"Don't forget we get another bod," commented Hartley from the wooden box he was using as a chair.

"Yeah, I was forgetting him. Willcox was his name, wasn't it?"

"Somethin' like that," returned Hartley, holding the nape of his neck with his folded fingers.

The teatime whistle sounded and they grabbed their mugs and went out to the trench. They joined the queue for tea and as another shell landed farther along, they ducked down to miss the flying splinters and scattering sandbags. They shivered in the cold weather. Smithers' teeth were chattering and he rubbed his hands together. The dugout was a bit warmer than the open air.

Surprise, surprise, the tea came up hot and sweet, and they gulped it down. They retreated to the dugout and sipped the hot liquid in the relative comfort of the billet. Smithers rolled a fag and scratched a match on the side of the box, breathing deeply into his lungs.

Regimental Sergeant Bliss twitched his moustache and poked his swagger stick under his arm. He had remonstrated many times to Regimental Sergeant Major Willcox, but none as serious as the last ten minutes or so. He had had this argument with the RSM before and now it was coming to a head. The same old subject was rearing its ugly head, and Bliss wanted an end to the matter.

Bliss's wife was sweet on Willcox and the attraction was getting stronger, so much so that she had openly admitted to the association after a row at the breakfast table one Sunday morning. It went back to the time when they were billeted together at the army training centre at Shalton. They were seen to play tennis together on the court at Telling Hardy, a suburb of Shalton.

The witness to the affair was a certain sergeant of the king's horse named Fox. He was having tea on the lawn at Telling Hardy when he pulled Bliss to one side and whispered into his ear.

"I think you should know that your wife is having a affair with RSM Willcox."

Bliss drew back in alarm.

"You and I have been friends for a good few years and you can tell me to mind my own

business, and on that understanding I will tell you that Patricia is having this thing with Willcox."

"Yes I know, George," muttered Bliss, reddening slightly, "but I have had a row about it with Patricia and she maintains there's nothing in it but friendship."

"Well, all right, Reg, but when I saw them together on the tennis court, no one kisses like they did when he won a point."

Later on when the dinner was on the table, Patricia was feeding their young son.

"I met George at the Melkshim club today and he said he saw you kissing RSM Willcox."

"I did," she admitted. "I do every time he beats me in a game. He is a good player and has been at it for years. Now what has he been saying about me?"

"Nothing except about the way you were kissing, he reckons you curled your leg around his as you kissed him, did you?"

"I may have done jokingly, but there's no harm done."

"Look, Patricia, we've been married for thirty years. You should be careful in the way you conduct yourself, you have a standard to keep. What's wrong with our marriage? Are you getting fed up with me, or what?"

"You are a bit of a bore, dear. It's getting so it is the same very day; getting up, feeding the baby, washing up and cooking your meals, the same day in and day out, the same old dreary drudgery without end."

"Well, it is the same for you and every other housewife," he maintained. "You should settle down and enjoy married life like other people do."

For a while Patricia fell silent, choosing to feed the baby with a boiled egg. Bliss had his marriage to save, so he carried on with the discussion.

"Have I kept you short of anything, money or sex?"

"I could do with a bit more money, the cost of living is leaping upwards, as for sex, I can do without that for the rest of my life, thank you very much."

"Then what is ruining our marriage, Patricia?"

She finished feeding the baby and wiped his mouth with the bib.

"I can make a suggestion," she said, folding the bib. "Remember it is only a suggestion and not a demand."

He looked at her with pleading eyes.

"Anything you say. If it is within my power I'll do it for you."

"Perhaps you can't afford it," she said with quizzical eyes on his face.

"Anything that will save my marriage from collapsing," he pleaded, with anxious eyes.

"You know that black dress in the window of Marks, the one on the dummy in the window?"

"I know it. The one priced at over three hundred pounds. You want that, it will take me three years to pay for it, Patricia."

"I want that," she said in a coy voice.

He lost his voice as he mentally calculated how long it would take to pay for the dress on his pay of twenty shillings per week, but he gulped and then nodded.

"All right, Patricia, the dress is yours. I'll start paying on it as soon as I get my next week's pay."

"You *will*?" she questioned incredulously. "It will take years to finish paying for it, darling."

"Nevertheless, if you want the dress you will have it, regardless of cost."

The baby started to cry and she picked him up, hanging him over one shoulder to pacify him. The baby burped up some wind and was sick on her shoulder. She wiped the sick off her frock and moved the baby to the other side of her body. With soft hands she tenderly laid the baby down in his carrycot and covered him over. Her hands tucked him in with gentle pushes then she gave him a dummy that he sucked in.

Straightening up, she turned around, faced her husband and took his hand. He responded by squeezing her hand and her ring finger. She smiled, and taking his arm in hers led the way upstairs to the bedroom.

The rat tried to escape Hartley's clutches. It ran up the walls, onto the shelves, into the cupboards and out again. It even tried to run under the bunks and into the kitbag, but there was no escaping the uplifted menace of the iron coal poker held in his hand. For an instant it seemed to see a way out of the threat by running to the door and escaping outside, but Smithers' form barred its way. He was there with uplifted rifle ready to crush the life out of the scabrous rodent.

The rat desperately tried to dodge Smithers. It slithered up the earthen walls and ran along the shelf, looking for a hole in which to hide. It was wild eyed and hopeless, trying to escape into somewhere safe, its ears flattened back in fear.

Hartley lunged with the blackened fire iron and crashed on the wooden surface of the shelf.

"Missed it," he growled, and readied himself for another swipe.

For a moment he lost it as the animal scampered under the bunks.

"There it is!" yelled Smithers, lunging with the rifle, "under the bed, there."

He followed up this warning by kicking at the terrified rat and poking the barrel of the rifle at the space under the bunk. For an instant they seemed to lose it as they stood in the bed space, listening for movement.

"Where'd it go?" Hartley questioned, lifting the edge of the blanket with the point of the poker.

"It went under the bed," cried Smithers, lifting the other side of the covering with the rifle.

"I saw it scuttle under the bunk," bellowed Hartley, lifting the blanket higher.

They both saw the rodent as it made a wild dash for the safety of the door. It was suddenly trapped by its tail as Smithers brought the butt of the rifle onto the tip. The rat then made a futile attempt to get away by gnawing at its tail. Smithers further compounded the issue by putting his muddy boot on the back legs of the rat then as he held it by the hind legs he lifted the wooden butt of the rifle and crushed the life out of the struggling rodent.

Using the poker, Hartley scooped up the dead body and carried it outside where he tossed it over the trench side and into the mud pools beyond.

"It was at our bully beef in the cupboard," Smithers said by way of an explanation. "It was eating the hard tack biscuits. I wonder it could eat them, they're that hard. I tried, but gave it up in the end."

"Yeah, I know what you mean, Smithy, I almost lost a tooth on those bloody biscuits myself."

Willcox decided to make an appearance then and as he brought his blankets and pillow into the dugout he commandeered the remaining bunk and dumped everything onto the wooden frame.

"All pals together," he crowed, lighting a cigarette and blowing the smoke into the air.

"How are you, Wilco?" Hartley said. "You just missed a bit of excitement, we just caught a big rat eating the biscuit ration. I just tossed it over the wall and left it there."

"I hate them things; they live on dead bodies and other offal. I usually shoot them bastards," said Willcox, waving the smoke away from his eyes.

"You'll be on watch this evening," said Smithers, taking his cup down from the shelf. "I'm on the twelve to four, you will follow me from four to eight. Watch Corporal Gunn; he will sneak up on you when you least expect it."

"I know about Corporal Gunn, we've met before," growled Willcox, coughing into the smoke.

That night the rain poured down on the trench as Hartley tramped the beat. He kept his rifle directed downwards to prevent it from rusting. The rainwater entered his groundsheet and ran down his trousers, soaking his puttees and boots as he walked in the quagmire. He lifted his steel helmet and loosened his chinstrap as the wet tightened the material.

He was only into his first half an hour by his watch and he looked forward to getting into the dugout to get out of the blasted rain. His breath frosted the air and he breathed out great clouds of hot air as the rain cooled it.

They, himself and the others, always patrolled the same stretch of ground, but nothing hardly ever happened in this kind of weather. It was when the rain came down in buckets that the enemy failed to appear.

Now and again, against the norm, a solitary shell exploded on the trench complex and caused it to collapse and bring down brown clay. Even the machine guns were silent, as they obviously did not like working in the rain. A solitary whiz-bang shell sheered overhead and landed far behind the front lines where it exploded in a crump and rain of sandbags and rocks.

Farther along the trench another solitary figure of a sentry walked the same beat, but more distant. Other men passed by his stretch of patrol, probably carrying orders of other moves or with other papers to deliver to the various section leaders. Hartley felt in his pocket for the bit of hard tack biscuit he had been gnawing. It was hard as a rock, so he was content in just sucking it. Little by little it dissolved in the warm saliva of his mouth.

The wind was still, but the groans of the mortally wounded and the dying, many hanging on the barbs of the rusty wire, rent the day asunder. The thunderous pounding of the guns with the screaming that accompanying it, was mixed with the constant cracking of rifle shots.

The Germans, clad in grey, swarmed across the field, firing as they went, bending down on one knee to get a better shot. The Huns scrambled across the field in their thousands, backed up by a vicious spew of hot slugs that wiped out the first wave of khaki-clad men with one fell burst and left them yelling in pain. The slaughter went on and another rank of men fell to the ground, dead, bleeding or mortally wounded.

The grey tide fell back and as if a signal was passed the guns opened up - heavy guns, light guns backed up by a brutal sweep of searching and killing bullets that opened up a wide swathe in the tight ranks of the Tommies. Many men tried to make it to the waiting trenches, but they tried it only to fail as they reached the wire. They tried it and failed as the cruel sweep of the machine gun reaped a huge harvest. Amid this surge of men the majority of them never made it to the next shell holes, and it was doubtful whether they made it to the blood-stained wire. If they did, they at once jumped into the many mud splattered shell holes that dotted the surface of the battlefield.

To do anything else but shelter from the hideous rain of death was inviting the opposition to bring him down with its constant shower of death-dealing slugs. A private clutched his breast and started to stem the fast flow of blood from his fractured arm. He had been hit with two rounds, one in his chest another in his arm. He tried stop the fast flow of hot blood, but only partially so. The scarlet liquid still escaped from the hole in his breast and ran down his arm as well.

Another sustained a deep cut in his forearm and the blood dripped from his wrist in sobs of crimson gore. The wound wept blood, running down the curvature of his arm and staining the trigger of the gun. His heart was still pumping out the blood and it pulsed and coagulated as it ran.

Overhead an aircraft joined in the fray and dropped its bombs on the British soldiers on the battlefield. One in particular, a certain Private Ball, saw the bombs fall from the bomber like balls of death. The gigantic bombs left the aircraft and began to fall. They emitted shrill whistling noises as they fell through the air and struck the ground. On the mud stained earth, Private Ball heard the whistle as they whirled through the powder puff smoke of the ground barrage, the guns screaming as they tried to outdo each other with the size of the racket, bursting into being as they exploded.

Ball instinctively ducked down to miss the bombs and in so doing escaped the ground barrage as well. His pulse pounded in his head and the wound he had sustained in a former battle beat at his temple in a wild and thumping tick. He edged higher, trying to claw a foothold on the shifting mud of the shell hole. His clothes were saturated by the constant rainwater. He looked skywards, trying to shut his eyes against the sting of the raindrops.

As he listened to the shrill noise of the falling bombs he turned his head away from where he imagined the bombs would strike. With an ear-shattering roar they hit the shell-marked ground and disintegrated. The muddy ground erupted into a roar and in the resulting explosion took with it a huge amount of brown earth. The stick of bombs opened up a series of bomb holes, taking with them not only the contents of the explosion, but other things like barbed wire, wooden posts and other indefinable objects. It also disturbed cadavers and other bits of dead bodies that were lying just below the surface of the field.

Trooper Ball lifted his steel helmet vision a little higher and saw a man's hand lying in the seething mud just three feet away. He turned his head away from the sight by lifting himself a little higher, and found he was gazing at the remains of a rifle that had lost its wooden butt.

The aircraft that had launched its bombs was droning away in the distance in company of other planes that had disappeared into the mist of the falling rain. Bits and pieces of everything were strewn across the ground. Bullets of all shapes and sizes lay haphazardly across every inch of spare ground. Pieces of metal of every distinction lay on the ground, in the ground and even peeping from the ground, the shiny brass reflecting the light on the surface of the war-torn battlefield.

For an instant the battle seemed to be easing and dying away. It seemed to lull for a time then the machine guns would start up again and stutter their lethal murmur. He had to escape the wild mantrap, but as he made every attempt to do so the rain of death would start all over again. He tried to put his foot in the soft mud, but only succeeded in bringing down more of the vile stuff. As he desperately strove to gain a foothold in the slime and filth of the oozing quagmire, he suddenly felt a solid foothold. His heart leaped when his boot touched something hard. He put his other boot on another one and used it to lever himself upwards. His senses leaped a lot higher; he was beginning to haul himself upwards then his second boot slipped on the first boot and he began to sink again.

Now, as he gazed down at the pool of water just below his left boot, he desperately fought to keep from sliding into the freezing water and madly tried to flail his way upwards once more. He mentally gauged how far he had to go before touching the surface of the rainwater below. He shivered with the expected cold, and swallowed. It was then his feet again contacted something solid and gained a fresh foothold on the sliding ooze. It was then that he looked down and decided it was too cold to enter it and struggled up to his former position just below the lip of the shell crater.

He decided that rather than fall into the water in the pit he would try to crawl over the edge of the crater. He tried for another foothold in the mud and touched another bit of hard ground. Now, if only he was able to haul himself over the edge of the shell hole. Before he started this superhuman effort he waited until the machine guns had ended their magazine total and fell silent as the operator stopped and came to the end of the magazine.

The bullets ended their shower of death-dealing rain. Bull knew what he had to do and leaped up onto the death ground, starting to inch forwards over the mud into the cover of an ancient bomb shelter.

Corporal Gunn looked through the field view finder and watched the progress of the soldier. Like so many of the latecomers, he was caught between the Devil and the deep blue sea by being the last to return to his own lines.

Gunn was not to know Ball was wounded and the exertion to lift himself from the shell hole had been nigh impossible to achieve. A shell splinter was the cause of his lack of strength. He could not feel the strike of the rain, owing to the fact that the shell splinter had gouged a great hole in his ankle. The wound had done hurting and his leg just dragged in the mud as the other one supplied the strength needed to force himself forwards, but wonder of wonders, he still managed to keep his grip on the rifle, testament to the fact that he had been taught to keep a tight hold of it at all times.

"That's Corporal Roy Ball," breathed Gunn. "He's been caught by the return fire of the Huns. Hope he makes it, he's a good man to lose."

Gunn stepped down from the firing step, just in time to witness Smithers hurrying into his dugout. He noted the time. Not time for his watch, now what's he up to? he thought. He followed the furtive figure with his stare, his mind wandering from the man in no-man's-land to Smithers. Now he was concerned with the actions of the amateur crook. Although he had pretended not to notice, he was well aware that Smithers was up to something - he was too shifty for Gunn to think otherwise. He resolved to keep a sharp eye on him and his mate, Hartley. For now though, his attention span was held by the man in no-man's-land.

Gunn stepped back up to the firing step and put his eye to the round glass hole of the view finder. The soldier, Corporal Ball, had moved during the time he had been watching Smithers. He appeared to be wounded by the way he was dragging his foot. He was about forty yards from the British front lines and the same from the sanctity of the British trench. Not far for a man to run normally, but a wide gulf for a man under fire, especially one suffering a wound in his leg.

Gunn dropped down to the bottom of the trench and onto the mud. He shrugged - it was not for him to clear the battlefield of soldiers, even if they were wounded. The medical orderlies were there for that purpose. This, of course, put another thought into his mind - he was responsible for the medical orderlies as well, although they had an officer doctor to guide them.

Hitching his gun higher onto his shoulder he strode along the trench, making for the dugout where Smithers was heading. On his way there he passed the place where the machine gun was housed. He saw with satisfaction Private Ehoe polishing the Vickers gun.

He was then at the dugout where Smithers had vanished. The three men jumped to attention as he made his entrance. Gunn's eyes swung immediately to where Smithers was rummaging in his locker. As Gunn made his appearance, he hastily shut the locker and secured it with an iron padlock. Gunn's suspicion was further aroused by the action of examining his rifle, which was standing on the corner of the bunk. He tapped the locker with the toe of his boot.

"What do you keep in here, Private Smithers? Not food, I hope, 'cause the keeping of food encourages rats. I hope you don't keep food in here."

"I know what the rules say," retorted Smithers sharply. He altered his tone of voice when he saw Gunn frown with annoyance. "If you don't mind, Corp," he added hastily.

"What you got Smithers, a picture of a naked lady?"

Smithers simpered to himself.

"Nothing like that," he said with a smile.

"Open up," ordered Gunn, tapping the locker with the toe of his boot. "I don't believe you, Private Smithers."

He protested by standing at the locker and seeming to refuse.

"Open it up or you will be on a charge, Private Smithers," demanded Gunn hotly.

Reluctantly Smithers bent down and unlocked the padlock, standing to one side as he pulled it off the metal hasp.

"Open it fully," ordered Gunn, indicating the locker with a sharp nod of his head.

Smithers turned an eye on Hartley and opened the locker. Gunn undid a rag-rolled bundle and brought to light a German Luger revolver.

"What's this, Private Smithers?" he enquired, holding up the pistol with the tip of his swagger stick. "It's not regulation arms, what are you doing with it?"

Smithers cast another look at Hartley and spoke with his eyes averted to the floor of the dugout.

"I got it in exchange for a tin of bully. I was hoping to sell it to someone else."

"Well," retorted Gunn, "there's no law in collecting mementos, even if they are kept for sale. See that you get rid of it as soon as possible, Private Smithers."

"I will, I will, Corporal Gunn."

Gunn made a pretence of inspecting the dugout and commented as he exited.

"Your kit is laid out all right this time. Keep it up all three of you. Your rifles are something to be desired, though. Keep the metal part of your gun well greased and free from any rust pockets - dismiss."

Gunn pulled the sacking aside and dropped it as he left.

"There you are," said Smithers to Hartley, "I was right; he had seen me carrying the gun. He must have eyes in the back of his arse to notice me bringing it in. You heard him, there are no regulations forbidding the collection of enemy guns, so I'm in the clear."

"If the Germans catch you with the gun in your possession they will shoot you," said Hartley.

"They've got to catch me first," said Smithers, holding it up.

It was a Luger automatic, one of the older type. It was minus a bit of the barrel and the magazine was missing as well. He fingered the barrel.

"Looks like a bullet hit it," he mused.

He rewrapped the gun in its rag smock and returned it to its place in the locker. With one motion he dropped the key into his breast pocket.

Private Willcox started the fire and got the meat ready for the midday meal. He broke the wooden sticks into thin kindling and, spending a match, set fire to the thinnest part of the firewood. The wood caught and very soon the flame built up into enough to start the coal pieces. The warmth of the coal was soon felt as it burst into regal flame. He waited as the cast iron top of the stove got red hot before he put on an old battered kettle. He waited, warming his hands as the heat of the stove increased. He cut the meat into strips and transferred them to the frying pan.

As he was cooking the dinner a whiz-bang shell flew over the dug-out and landed close by, dislodging several layers of dust from the shelf above. As for the men, they never paid it any heed, calmly going about their business in the same old way. Another shell whizzed over the trench and exploded several hundred yards to the rear. Their attitude was that if it flies over and lands on another position all well and good, if it scores a direct hit on the dugout then it's all up with them - goodbye hell, hello heaven.

16

THE NINETY-NINTH HAD AN air force arm. This fledgling force was only just beginning to show on the statistics, and everything was new and just born in its advanced infancy. It only boasted two pilots, a mechanic, a fuel station and a woman who made the tea and cooked meals for the men daily.

This infant force, only six months old, was commanded by a pilot lieutenant and a sergeant. The aircraft they used were two Sopwith Pup fighters and a single Sopwith Camel. They were mainly employed as mail carriers, ferrying personnel and, in an emergency, as defense and attack aircraft. Today they were employed as bombers and were busy being loaded with HE bombs attached to the wings of the aircraft with quick release levers and other devices.

The second in command, Sergeant Hollis, was a stickler for accuracy, and a harsh disciplinarian. He maintained a clean aircraft was a good aircraft and got the men on jankers to wash and dry each plane to his satisfaction. One of these men was Private Smithers, who had been given fourteen days for using objects prejudicial to army orders, to wit, one enemy revolver that he offered for sale to an unknown person etc. He was currently employed by Sergeant Hollis to wash and brush up a dirty and airworn Sopwith Camel that had seen better days.

Smithers was without his 'oppo', Hartley, to offer him support for two weeks. He sloshed the soapy water over the aircraft's hull, over the wings and the RAF emblem of red, white and blue circles. Unbeknown to the sergeant, he had sat in the pilot's seat and felt the stick for the first time. In addition, he had felt around the machine gun that sat on the space forward of the pilot's seat, pressing an empty gun trigger and getting the feel of fighting the battles of the air against the enemy pilots.

For Smithers this was the first introduction he had to flying, and he was enjoying it. As he slewed the stick around on its axis, trying to imagine himself against an enemy pilot, he sighted through the gun sight and shot down an enemy plane. It meant death or injury for the other man in the opposing plane, but he chose to ignore this course of events. To him it was no more than shooting at a Hun across no-man's-land.

As he pressed the pedals and jiggled the stick he caught sight of the sergeant talking to one of the other 'jankees', and jumped out of the cockpit. When the sergeant came around the corner of the sergeants' mess, Smithers was hard at work on the plane.

"That's the ticket, Smithers," the sergeant said, "you're doing a fine job of cleaning the plane." He strode around the aircraft looking at Smithers' work. "Don't forget to check the plane's ailerons for any damage enemy pilots have done, and washing the wings will remove any foreign object that it might have picked up from contact with the ground. The pilots have said washing the filth from the aircraft prolongs its life. Keep up the good work."

Of course, Smithers only worked hard when authority reared its ugly head. When the sergeant had gone he relaxed and fell into his regular pace - dead slow. He enjoyed these 'little jaunts' as he called them. He watched the sergeant go around the corner then climbed back into the cockpit.

He held the stick once again and tried to imagine himself flying the aircraft. The machine gun was cold and hard in his grip. He fingered the empty magazine and ran his fingers around the curvature of the machine gun. The rest he could not do; the firing of the gun, the shooting down of the enemy planes. He could only imagine the rest, but he had a good brain and thought about the rest of it as it entered his dream of what he could do if only Lady Luck was kind to him.

Smithers was dreaming again. He pulled the stick back as far as it would go and watched the wing flaps dance up and down. He tried the foot pedals and saw the tail plane wave. Now he had some idea of what guided the plane, and imagined what would happen if the wings were uplifted by the wind.

The mechanic came to inspect the engine and Smithers stopped washing the fuselage to let him look at it. The mechanic swung the propeller and, with Smithers' help in switching on the engine, soon had it tuned to perfection. He shouted above the roar of the engine.

"*Increase revs.*"

Smithers pushed the lever over to full and felt the engine start to lift off. He watched the air mechanic and as he signalled by sliding his finger around his throat, cut the engine noise to just idling. It dropped down to a lower note and just ticked over. The air mechanic signalled for Smithers to stop it, he pulled the lever and it puffed to a close.

"Seems all right," he remarked, looking at Smithers and smiling. "Might need petrol though, it's due for a visit to the station to get more. The next move is shoving it closer to the filling station to fill up."

He and his helpers pushed the aircraft a few yards farther down the airfield to the filling station; a collection of metal drums lying in a small heap in the corner. Smithers helped by inserting a pump into the upright drum and pumping fuel to the waiting plane. The air mechanic watched the fuel gauge on the aircraft instrument panel and as he did so, raised a thumb to indicate full. Smithers stopped pumping and the fuel pipe slackened. The mechanic seemed to lose interest in the proceedings then, and eased himself out of the cockpit and down onto the grass runway, where he pulled a sweat rag from his pocket and wiped his hands free of oil.

As the refuelling of the Sopwith Camel came to an end Sergeant Hollis returned, and spoke, pointing to another one of the planes and to the bucket of soapy water Smithers had abandoned.

"Now you can get cracking on another, since you did such a good job on the Camel. When you have finished there is another one to do. You can get your 'Smoke ho' when you have done." He pointed to the bucket and to a water pipe dripping a slow dribble onto the grass. "There's more water and more soap if you need it."

He produced a big bar of yellow Sunlight soap and dropped it onto the grass next to the dripping pipe.

———

Across the airfield another aircraft was being loaded with bombs under its wings, and the machine guns were being loaded with .303 gauge rounds that glittered in the weak sunshine.

The pilot of the aircraft was overseeing the reloading of the guns and pointing out to the armourers how best to do it with the breech open. As the men were new to the job they listened with interest. The pilot, uniform bedecked with several campaign medals, was sporting a pair of goggles and a leather flying helmet. He laughed as they asked his advice on how to arm the machine gun and load the bombs the right way up.

"Don't pull that trigger will you, lads, it will spray you with rounds before shooting off into the air."

His hoarse laugh echoed across the airfield and disturbed a flock of pigeons as they picked at the crumbs one of the men had thrown at them. One of the men laughed at a chance remark of the pilot. The noise seemed to frighten the birds, causing them to flutter away from the sound. They flew a few feet away then returned to the feast.

Within the next half an hour the bomber began to move away from the preparing area and into the take-off zone. The note of the engines rose higher and the aircraft began to pitch on the uneven surface. The roar of the engines broke into the midmorning air of the landing strip. Several uniformed figures climbed aboard and strapped themselves in. They were in heavy flying gear, and masked with goggles and leather helmets. As they jumped into the open cockpit of the bomber they pulled the lever of the engine opener and it instantly roared into a higher register.

In response to this demand for more power the propellers spun faster and louder. The noise tore the relatively peaceful atmosphere of the aerodrome apart and echoed around the cluster of small buildings. The bomber, moving in its own shadow, turned left in its own slipstream and began to enter the take-off area, preparing for take-off. A figure with two indicators waved to the pilot and he opened up the engine power to full. The aircraft answered by moving forwards. The aircraft overseer dodged out of the way of the bomber, leaving it to taxi forwards. He waved to the pilot, indicating he was satisfied with the progress of the aircraft by waving it through.

The plane stopped in its tracks while the pilot adjusted his goggles and helmet. The observer on the balcony of the flight counter, pressed a torch and watched as the bomber roared into life and began its primary bombing take-off. The aircraft shuddered in preparation of its initial take-off and in seconds was approaching the required speed.

The wind indicator, the air sock, was stretched right out as the aircraft left the ground. The wheels were spinning with the force of the speed and only just beginning to slow. In the midmorning mist the plane lifted from the end of the runway just as the airport fence passed under its black shadow.

In his job of washing the aircraft, Smithers watched the big bomber take off. He saw the bombs fixed to its wings and was aware of the heavy note of the engines.

"Wonder where that lot is heading for," he muttered to himself, "the enemy trenches at the Somme, I'll be bound."

He plunged his mop into the soapy water and lifted it out, letting it just drip for an instant before he splashed it onto the aircraft body. The treatment was as before. The recognition roundels of red, white and blue were given special washing by him then he dried them with the rag Sergeant Hollis had given him. The bullet holes in the body fabric were left as he found them. He laughed as he imagined sewing up the fabric with a needle and cotton. Imagine me as a mender of aeroplanes. They'll have me sewing up women's dresses next, he thought, with a grin.

The sergeant made his rounds, eyeing Smithers' work with a critical stare.

"Keep it up, Private Smithers," he enthused, "you are doing a good job."

"Good to know I am appreciated, better'n that Corporal Gunn who had me on report for owning an enemy revolver. Why can't he mind his own fucking business?" Smithers muttered as the sergeant moved away.

He viciously slapped the mop on the roundels, imagining it to be Gunn's face.

––––––––––––

In contrast to Smithers, Hartley was at his old job of getting the tea to the waiting troops, only this time it was with the other trooper, Private Willcox.

They were doing the usual practice of slopping the tea over the sides of the tea urn. As much as they tried to stop it, it always happened.

"Why can't you be more careful?" whined Hartley. "Wind your sling around the handle of the tea urn. That way we can save it."

Even though he did as Hartley had urged, Willcox still managed to spill it.

"It's no new thing," said Hartley, "we always did spill it, me and

Smithers. We couldn't help it no matter what we did, it's the mud what does it, it lets you down when you slip in it, it also trips you up as you are carrying it."

Slowly and painfully they carried the tea urn to the waiting men. Willcox eyed them as they waited for the tea, rattling their mugs on metal rims of mess tins, which showed how impatient they were. This rattle of mess tins was in contrast to the racket of the enemy missiles that constantly hit the walls of the trench and buried themselves in the clay and sandbags.

Willcox slipped on the muddy surface and uttered a curse as the hot tea scalded his hand.

"Bugger that for a lark," he said, holding his hand, "that was bloody hot."

He got a new grip on the tea urn by lifting the container higher as a trench mortar, whirling on a message of death, crashed on a part of the trench and showered them with mud and stones. A big lump of watery soil splashed the tea urn with muddy drips. Willcox stopped and cleaned the leather strap of his rifle.

"Sod the tea, the rifle comes first. You ask Corporal Gunn why."

As usual the NCOs were first in the queue. They staggered the last few paces to where they were queuing and set the tea urn in its place in the alcove of the trench. Someone had knocked up a small table for the tea and they edged the tea urn into place on the table.

"Your mate's on jankers as you know," commented Gunn, blowing on his tea. "It seems it is an offence to use nothing but the firearms you were issued with." He treated Hartley to a smile of sympathy and added, "If it was me I'd let him have it, but you know what the top brass are like; they just make up the rules as they go along."

Later that evening, marching his stretch of the trench, Willcox heard a whiz-bang shell fly over and explode in a section past his area of watch. He watched the sparks fly as the shell exploded with a devastating roar, momentarily lighting up the night sky. He was relieved it had flown over, bypassing his trench and finishing up a hundred yards in the rear

Another one to the good, he thought, hearing the shell splinter as another was heading his way. It seems it was always this way - one gone, another coming his way. The Huns are trying to wear us down with attrition, he thought. The rifle sling was rubbing at his shoulder, so he changed shoulders.

It was early morning and the company was forming up in the deep mud of the trench, ready to make another foray into enemy held territory. Great wads of frightened perspiration steam arose from the packed ranks of the assembly and the sweat rolled down their faces and into open mouths. A hundred tongues licked dry lips and ran around a hundred mouths.

Hartley, minus his mate Smithers, clipped his bayonet into place. He felt the keen edge of his blade with the edge of his thumb, running it down the shining bayonet until it brushed the wooden hilt.

Everywhere the men waited, closing their eyes in silent prayer, or muttering the Lord's Prayer through firm lips, or even both. Ranks of men, from privates to NCOs lined the foremost extremes of the trench, facing forwards into the clay skin of the earth and the sacks of sandbags. A captain, his metallic pips gleaming in the half-light and shining like stars in heaven, stood at the rear of the men, a glittering whistle held between clenched jaws, ready to blow.

Above the men the enemy bullets danced a rapid tattoo along the rear of the trench walls, causing bits of earth and stones to shower down to the foot of the trench. The minutes dragged by, every second felt by the waiting men like eternity in waiting, bereft of any emotion except dread, then the whisper rang around the massed ranks:

"Get ready."

The men steeled themselves, crossing themselves with trembling fingers. A few kissed the St Christopher crosses around their necks, whispering quick words of prayer to heaven. They were grouped around scaling ladders, with the first man ready to ascend the first rung of the wooden steps - to perdition, wherever that might be.

An enemy shell burst amid the rear of the assembly, the resulting explosion bringing down one of the dugouts, showering the soldiers, a mud-splattered cacophony of bits and pieces. They just brushed the bits aside, ignoring them with hardly a glance.

The seconds ticked by and the tension heightened, accompanied by the audible prayers of the men. The captain produced a big pocket watch and held it up to the shaft of light provided by a small torch. He was still gripping the whistle with his clenched jaws, then another officer nodded and he blew a loud blast on the whistle - the attack was in progress.

One by one the men climbed the ladder, gripping the handle and holding onto their rifles with the sling. As they disappeared over the edge of the trench, Hartley dropped down into a crouched position, emulating his previous behaviour. He kept as low as possible, hearing the bullets thudding on the sandbags. As he dropped into a shallow shell hole he heard a trench mortar whizz by and land in a group of men doing the same thing ten yards farther on. The crack of the projectile threw out its slices of metal at the men and as they screamed in agony was drowned out by another shell exploding a few feet away. He shook his head as a shell fragment hit the top of his helmet, knocking it across his face.

The men who had been caught by the trench mortar were much quieter now and one of them was moaning quietly. Hartley had to shut his ears to the sound and look around for his own protection. He had hardly enough shell hole to afford him any sort of safety. Lifting his head a little more he saw a deeper shell hole several yards away from where he was sheltering. It looked a lot safer with the soil displacement more pronounced.

Now is the time, he thought, hearing the whistle of the bullets passing by over head. He slithered over the inhospitable mud, pushing his rifle on before him. Just how much he was able to dodge the shower of slugs was brought home to him by a low bullet that just skimmed along the top of his helmet. It was only a slight impact, but it brought it home to him how low he had to be. He was swimming in the mud with his legs pushing him forwards, a frog-like action that had him getting nearer to the shell hole. He was partially sheltered by the soil displacement as it stopped the rain of bullets.

Hartley had no idea where Willcox was. He supposed he had done likewise and was hiding in a shell hole. He might have got farther than the barbed wire. Hartley was now in the lee of the shell, and slithered over the lip of the hole and down into comparative safety. He was now in the shell hole and had no intention of going any farther.

"I will go no farther than I am. I'm no hero. I will wait until the coast is clear and try to get back to the safety of the trench," he muttered into his helmet straps.

He gazed at the early morning stars shining in the grey sky. He saw the dark outline of a blackbird crossing the sky between him and the stars, and wondered what kind of bird it was that risked life and wing crossing the battlefield. He was in a quandary; he was slipping to the bottom of the shell hole, which, as usual, was partly full of cold rain-water. He noted it was freezing cold water that filled both his boots from the moment he stepped into it.

The stars faded into the sky as the light broadened, and as he peeped over the rim of the shell hole he was able to make out his position in the battlefield. The barbed wire, already decorated with the corpses of dead men, stretched into the distance and beyond. It was supported with wooden stakes driven deep into the ground. As far as he was able to make out, it was hung with dead soldiers who had got caught in the first wave of men. There were several wounded troopers on the ground, some screaming for help. Hartley steeled himself to turn a deaf ear to their cries and hung his head in shame, as he was forced to deny them his help

The bullets ceased in a lull in the battle, which was filled by a few shells that crashed into the battlefield. Hartley turned around, expecting to see his mate, Smithers, until he remembered he was not in the charge. Willcox was probably sheltering in one of the many shell holes and was not expected to show himself to anyone.

An hour dragged by and his arms were getting tired of supporting his body. He tipped his steel helmet downwards to avoid the splash of muddy water thrown up by a close by shell. His hearing was affected by the close proximity of the shells and every time one crashed near him he winced in agony as the sound assailed his ears.

Others of the company slithered past him, but when they saw the water in the shell hole they turned away to search for a drier refuge. Hartley glanced at them and watched them slide away.

"Can't stand a little cold water," he muttered to himself, 'but I could do with a little less cold water myself.'

He pulled his rifle to his chest and laid it on the lip of the shell hole. He opened his breast cartridge case and loaded his gun. His hands were cold and the metal case was freezing.

Another half an hour went by and he knew he had to get out or risk getting a cold bath in the pool down below. He lay down below the rain of bullets, and as they sailed over his slithering body he made for the comparative safety of a derelict foxhole. He stood up to ease his frozen body and a machine gun bullet pinged off the sides of the concrete bunker, which made him think how exposed he was.

Now what would I do if I was in his place? he mused. Why, I would aim for the bunker with one of my shells. That decided it for Hartley. Rather than providing an easy target for a lucky gunner to shoot at, he would quit the foxhole for the dubious safety of the ground, and continue his slide in the watery mud and partial safety. He had barely gone fifteen yards when he heard an enormous crash. The bunker erupted in an explosion.

"I was right," he grated to himself, smiling at the luck of the gunner. "He *did* target the foxhole, lucky bastard. He must've seen me enter for shelter and gave it one - lucky for me as well."

All around him the other men were doing the same thing. The rain of shells was too much for them to bear. They were getting back to the safety of their own lines, and the shells that prompted them onwards had made the decision for them.

In another incident Hartley heard another shell burst in the vicinity of a group of soldiers. He was just sliding into another earth fracture amid the holocaust, shielding his face from the mud and shell splinters, when another shell exploded into the centre of the sliding men. A spasm of pity for the men shivered through his vitals, but he had to look after himself and shut his ears to the screams of agony that radiated from the incident. Suddenly there was no sound from the site of the explosion and he assumed they were all dead.

There you are, he thought, one minute they were a moving phalanx of human beings, the next, nothing. The shell whizzed into the space occupied by them and they disappeared with hardly a trace left of them.

The puff of smoke the shell had left drifted in the slight wind. Farther on, after another shell had crashed onto the field, Hartley heard the cries of the wounded once more, knowing full well he could do nothing for them. The shells eased their pressure and fell way, but the cries for help went on for some minutes. Someone called for water and he fingered his water bottle, but knew it was almost impossible to get to the wounded man.

The reaping of human beings by the steel monsters continued unabated then, as he held his fingers in his ears for the umpteenth time, it all suddenly stopped. Hartley's ears were bleeding with the pressure of the blasts and he ducked below the earthen rim of the shell hole to avoid the resultant explosion. This timely cessation of the explosions caused him to look up and view the scene of the carnage.

He felt like castigating himself for his lack of help. He almost hoisted his body out of the shell hole, almost, but not quite. He was in the process of cocking his leg over the tortured lip of the hole when the shelling suddenly resumed. He physically shrugged his shoulders and dropped back to his previous safe position. His body slipped into the mud and he covered his ears with his flattened palms.

Later on as the cries faded away to nothing, a light rain began to fall, running down his face and saturating his filthy clothes. The watery sun vanished from sight in a solid wall of grey-black clouds.

His only hope of keeping the enemy in check was taken by sliding over the ruptured hole of the shell damage. His complement of equipment was dragging him down, but he inwardly blessed it for the protection it gave his back. By the same token, his other equipment slowed him down a lot. He thought of discarding the crossed webbing of his other things, but even though the NCOs were absent and it was during the battle, he still had a vision of the corporal and others deriding him for losing his valuable paraphernalia. Hartley laughed, but bitterly resented the imposition of Corporal Gunn and his vision of duty. He was duty bound to kill the enemy primarily, but if he was alive at the end it was his duty to answer the roll call when called.

His body slid over the muddy water. It was bitterly cold and the icy chill of the liquid froze his bones to the core. To make matters worse the rain beat down on his prostrate body and trickled down his steel helmet. He was making strokes like swimming actions. He reached out his hands to claw for space and followed up with his legs, which were splayed like a frog. He felt comfortable doing these strokes, which fitted the bill as far as escape to the British lines was concerned.

His mind wandered to the absent Smithers.

"Where is he at the moment? In some cushy job where the work is missing, trust him to fall on his feet in a crisis," he muttered, answering himself. His senses broadened as he realised his dugout friend was missing. "Where's Willcox? He's been missing for over two hours and there's no sign of him."

His brain reacted when he realised that perhaps he had been killed in the primary charge across no-man's-land. Nobody would know until roll call was called and his name was crossed off or ticked off as the case may be.

The sandbags of the British trench were getting closer. He was down under the lethal barrage of bullets that kept thudding into the wall of the trench. Ahead of him a wall of dancing slugs stitched a pattern of instant death. In his imagination he saw Corporal Gunn looking at him with the optical glass of the field viewer. He was not on duty in the battlefield, and Hartley was sure he was watching events as they unfolded. He envied him his rank; those stripes saved him from being killed or wounded. They also assured he got a better rate of pay than Hartley, something he was able to recall amidst the heat of battle.

Another stroke, another foot nearer. His arms and legs worked overtime, swimming the mud and rainwater in strokes that edged him forwards. Another frog-like motion and he was a yard closer to the British trench and safety. His bid for salvation was crowned with the wish for self-preservation, and it was definitely working.

His mind harked back to Smithers and what he was doing right now to avoid manual labour. Hartley had no idea what his mate was doing at that moment. He only supposed, but he was right that any work involving Smithers was pure fiction - except for things that interested him, like now. His new interest was laced with a new idea; flying and what it involved. Hartley had doubted if Smithers could be really interested in anything, but he was wrong; Smithers was really engrossed in flying.

Although he was only cleaning the flying machines he harboured the desire to get up in a plane and give the other pilot the trouncing of his life. His cleaning of the aircraft and other attentions were second in his mind.

To Hartley and the short distance he had to cover, the remaining stretch of ground seemed enormous. The trench and its sanctity was the goal for which he was aiming. He averaged about six inches or a foot in a good snatch, but as the bullets wanged overhead and banged into the clay of the trench walls, he had the satisfaction of noting they were getting closer with every slide he mustered.

Private Willcox was hale and hearty, and never felt better, although his foray into enemy occupied territory was one he could do without. He copied the movements of Hartley and dived into the welcome embrace of the nearest shell hole.

The troops had their first glimpse of an airship as one dodged between the heavy clouds and showed for an instant. As the clouds passed and hid its distinct cigar shape from view, it was able to hide in the angry billowing formation. It was obviously searching for an opportunity to bomb the British trench, and the first they knew of it was when the bombs whistled down and exploded on it.

Now a new and devastating dimension was added to the war. The airship cruised through the clouds, happy in the supposed knowledge that it was safe - safe, that is, until the Royal Air Force came on the scene. They found a new way of scotching this form of warfare and they went at it with a will.

It was only a few hours before this method of aerial warfare was fully appreciated. The counterbalance of this mode was swiftly set and the RAF declared war on all known German airships. The fighter planes attacked the blimps and very soon controlled the skies. Although the airships were equipped with machine guns, and fired back at the planes, the nippy little fighter planes soon shot the airship down and saw it crash in flames. These actions were the result of this gallant band of airmen who challenged the might of the German Air Force.

The bombs continued to fall on the British troops, courtesy of other big bombing planes. The Huns introduced the firepower of accompanying fighter planes, but they were so high up in the atmosphere it was difficult to breathe. They only protected the airships as a last resort in this turn of events.

Pilot Officer Skinner was one of the pilots who helped to shoot the airship down. He and Lieutenant Claud Jeff claimed half the title each of destroying the airship. This was later attested by a survivor, a German lieutenant named Skell. He was travelling with the airship at the time and was taken prisoner when he fell as it plunged downwards in a ball of fire. He said the RAF had attacked the airship and caused it to burst into flames. He even described the two pilots who had engineered the attack; one blonde while the other was dark and sported a dark moustache. With these descriptions he was able to pinpoint the successful attack on the airship.

17

Gunn was one of the recipients of the bombing attack. In company with others he had his first sight of the airship accompanied by a stick of bombs that was allowed to fall from the big blimp. This included the familiar whistle of the falling bombs.

Instinctively he ducked to avoid the resulting explosion.

"Another way of doing warfare," he grated, expecting another fall of bombs to hit the trench. "Let's hope the RAF has an answer to this kind of fighting."

He was overheard by a trooper who had seen the new dimension begin,

"My thoughts entirely, Corp," said the private, holding his ears against the sound of the blast.

He was crouching down, pressed against the surface of the trench walls. He straightened up, looking up at the sky, waiting for the next salvo.

This method of waging a war was new to Gunn, and he shook his fist at the cigar shaped airship sliding by overhead. He expected another stick of bombs to be released, but he waited in vain. The sky was completely empty. He eyed the clear atmosphere, issuing a big sigh, wiping the expectant sheen of sweat from his face with one hand. He then noticed the soldier, hard against the earthen wall of the trench, with his fingers in his ears.

This won't do, he told himself, a corporal showing fear to a common private. He eyed the soldier and snarled.

"Ain't you seen bombs before? Don't you know they are as dangerous as high explosive shells?" He fixed the man with staring eyes, adding, "And where is your rifle, soldier? Don't you know you must carry it at all times? What's your name, Private?"

The confused man shifted his gaze from the area above the trench.

"Sorry about that, Corp, must've slipped my mind when the airship came over. It won't happen again."

"Make sure it doesn't," grated Gunn, approaching the unfortunate man. "There might come a time when you desperately need it, so keep it by your side at all times."

Now the danger of falling bombs was over for the present, the private grinned, showing his teeth. Gunn just sniffed and stumped away, treating the free fresh air to a look of relief as he left.

The airship slipped away above the clouds, followed by the German aircraft trailing the planes of the RAF. The British planes lost the airship in the low clouds, and despite searching the skyline and the clouds beyond, they never saw the blimp again.

———————————

Smithers was enjoying a cigarette. The sergeant was away at the sergeants' mess drinking his daily pint of mild and bitter. He always enjoyed his beer and, good weather or bad, he was there to drink the pint.

This lull in duty enabled Smithers to snatch a crafty smoke of a roll-up. While the going was good he took the time to sit on an upturned bucket and indulge himself. He was always wary though, for if he was caught slacking by the sergeant or someone in authority, he risked that person's wrath, even though he was a good worker and did his work faithfully - when the NCO was watching! Although he hated overseers and tried to avoid them when he could, he was always careful to take note of the one in charge, who could be liable to make it hot for him.

As far as Corporal Gunn was concerned, Private Smithers was always unlucky; a trait he was born with and no matter how hard he tried to alter it, it would always remain so. The only answer to this problem was to keep out of his way as much as possible. In such confines as the British trenches it was, more or less, impossible to do this, so he had to use his wits and avoid him by being one step ahead of him at all times.

During his time in the British Army, Smithers had learned to avoid authority, not because of his respect for the individual, but of the ability they had to administer punishment. No matter how he ranted and raved about the matter, his luck never changed; it was always in the negative.

"It's my luck, mate," he was always at pains to say. "It is always at a low ebb, like a low tide that never seems to return to the shore."

It never altered his friendship with Hartley though, possibly because of the luck situation of his friend. He was normal and never complained about the bad luck he encountered. Smithers was fortunate in his friendship with Hartley, and Hartley saw something in him of which he was not aware.

Another airship was sliding through the lowering clouds, hoping to catch the RAF unawares.

This was Smithers' first sighting of an airship, and his eyes goggled at the apparition. His hair literally stood on end at the sight of the cigar shaped cylinder that wove in and out of the grey sky. The great blimp, propellers racing, was being chased by two RAF fighters, and he faintly heard their machine guns rattle as the aerial battle took place before his wondering eyes. The note changed as the defences of the airship replied in kind, the chattering machine guns of the enemy answering by blasting at the RAF planes. The guns of the RAF were getting the best of the exchange though, and being quick as well as smaller, they darted in and out of the airship's return fire. The only thing that saved it from being shot out of the sky was the speed of its engines. The RAF planes shot in and out of the battle area of interplay and thudded a spasm of armour-piercing bullets into the huge girth of the giant airship.

It was during one of the frequent exchanges of gunfire that the airship dropped its lethal load. It shrilled down to the airstrip and, amid running figures who made a dive for the nearest cover, exploded on the surface of the grass runway.

As Smithers watched from his position behind the sergeants' mess he was able to see the aerial battle unfold and witness what the last of the bombs did. The last one of the stick of bombs hit one of the planes on which he was working.

"Just my luck it got the cleaned one. Now, why couldn't it be the dirty one that copped it?"

Although being over two or three hundred yards from the impacts he was able to see the results of the bombing. There were gigantic holes in the surface of the aerodrome, leaving it with huge craters on the centre of the airstrip. One of the buildings that housed the movement of the aircraft and the wireless reception, was obliterated. All that remained of it was a huge heap of bricks and concrete, from which a pall of smoke and dust was slowly rising.

In the distance the bell of an ambulance was shrilling, getting louder as the white painted vehicle drew nearer. From another direction a big fire brigade lorry leaped into view, tolling another, but deeper, bell as it hove into view. Smithers' eyes shifted back to the airship and he was just in time to witness the destruction of the bomber as it burst into flames. Soon it was burning from nose to tail, and several figures were falling from the wreckage. They cartwheeled through the air and crashed to the ground. There was no movement from the figures after that.

The big lorry rapidly disgorged three or four men, who started to fill in the bomb holes using shovels. Another two men lifted a big container and turned it over, where it poured out other brick materials into the big craters left by the bomb explosions. The ambulance stopped at the bombed building, throwing out several figures, who started to search the smoking building for survivors. As Smithers watched, he was able to make out a lone man being carried out on a stretcher to the waiting ambulance.

The sergeant returned and Smithers had to get back to his initial task of cleaning the one remaining plane. He was upbraided for neglecting his job.

"It happens all the time," he said, handing him a bucket of cold water. "They bomb us and we fill in the result. Just get on with your work, Private Smithers."

He made a start on the dirty plane, muttering under his breath about Germans and airships with bombs. In the distance he was able to see the glow of the burning airship. The flames lit up the sky and the surrounding countryside, reflecting on the clouds hundreds of feet above.

Already the bomb craters were almost filled and the tops were smoothed over. Smithers wondered at the hard work being done by the men of the RAF. They shifted over to allow for the landing of a flight of Sopwith Pups aircraft coming onto the tarmac after a sortie in no-man's-land. The aircraft ran over the place where the bombs had struck the landing ground, the wheels bumping and rocking on the disturbed ground, and stood there roaring with a noise of propeller blades and blasting exhausts that echoed around the aerodrome and the encircling Royal Air Force buildings.

The pilots vacated the cockpits and slid down the fabric of the war-beaten planes. They slapped each other on the back to indicate their good luck in returning hale and hearty, with no added injuries to worry about. Their nervous laughter was heard above the normal aerodrome sounds.

Pilot Officer Potts eased back on the stick and felt the plane respond to his touch. He liked the plane so much that he had named it Wendy, after his girlfriend, Wendy Gill. It was fitting, he decided. It was synonymous with Wendy's gentle nature and her liking for red lipstick, being of a light touch and red colour. He liked blue because she always chose blue, the colour of her eyes. As he broadened his mind he thought of her most often.

Potts was a member of the aerial arm of Ninety-ninth Company of Foot. He thought of himself as air force - he flew RAF planes, wore RAF-type uniform, he ate in the mess halls of the RAF with aces of distinction and he even copied their style of painting the amount of kills on the side of their aircraft. To date he had only two successful kills to his credit. He was flying the wonderful Sopwith Pup fighter and he was so confident of his skill with the aircraft, he always carried a tin of black paint with which to add to his total.

He pushed back the aerial goggles to the top of his forehead and gazed through the windscreen. The Vickers machine gun was ahead of his view and he crooked his head to see if there were any other aircraft in sight. He had a rear-view mirror, but he had little faith in its small area of vision and always screwed himself around to see if there was any other plane following. He knew the enemy planes had only one direction from which to catch the other pilot unawares, from underneath, and carried it out to the letter. If they could sneak up on you with one of their bursts of fire from beneath, with the sun shining in your eyes they were in seventh heaven.

Most times he was aware they went for this distinction and in return he did the same to them. He was near ceiling zero with the

Sopwith Pup and he always flew high to gain this advantage. He knew it had its limit though, with regard to its performance, and the air was rarefied, but to get to this advantage he had to suffer some sort of discomfort. In both his kills the enemy planes had caught fire and crashed into the ground below. After that, his mind was too full to wonder to worry about the fate of the pilot. He had his own life to consider after the confrontation in the air.

He glanced at the instrument panel and noted the fuel gauge. About another half an hour's flying time, he calculated. The oil pressure was ticking on 'good' and the air speed indicator was nearly at one hundred and three miles per hour. It's time to throttle back, he thought. The only thing to note was the height indicator, which was swinging from one position to another. He mentally decided to get the gauge seen to at the next opportunity when he touched down at the airport.

Potts jogged the gauge and hit it to make it register properly. He partially shifted it and had some success when the needle registered the correct height. He jigged it once more and the needle jumped again. He was just about to try it again when a volley of bullets stitched a line across the windscreen.

Too late! He had not done what he had always maintained was vital; to keep a sharp lookout at all times. Now it was up to him to nurse the aircraft until it crashed. He caught sight of the enemy pilot as he saluted with a wave of his hand. He saw the height indicator register properly as he plunged lower.

"*Now* it does its job," he breathed, preparing for the crash.

The aircraft turned faster and gradually developed into a spin. That was when fortune favoured him. The plane skimmed the waving stalks of golden corn and ended up, upside down in a field of flowing poppies and yellow daisies. So far, as the reek of petrol rent the air, the smoke of unlit fumes just lifted into the atmosphere, but it was just a matter of minutes before the aircraft would be aflame. He struggled with his leather restraint and managed to unbuckle it. He was feverishly racing against time he knew as the smell of petrol grew stronger. Desperately he tore at the straps and fell into the corn growths. The fuel started to drip onto his face as he lay there, wetting his head. His next problem was to get away from the aircraft as soon as he was able, although his arm was twisted behind his bulk. He straightened it up and scrambled away, wiping the petrol from his head as he made his dash to safety.

18

HE STOOD UP ABOUT thirty feet from the wreckage, waiting for the plane to burst into flame.

The enemy plane had vanished and no sound of it remained. The silence reigned until the rest of the German squadron made an appearance and followed in its wake. One of the enemy aircraft detached from the group to have a look at Potts' crashed plane. It also disappeared from the scene after viewing the downed aircraft.

The Sopwith Pup never caught fire though, and after a while the petrol stopped dripping. Potts was staunching the flow of blood from his arm when the absence of petrol fumes was noted. He struggled up from his sitting stance and onto a path at the side of the cornfield. After giving the downed plane a cursory glance he followed the path to a deserted road.

He hid in the shelter of a blackberry bush just in time to escape from a lorry load of German troops out to find the crashed English pilot. After they had passed by he stepped back onto the road and, giving the empty space a wide grin, staggered along the dirt track. He had no idea were he was, possibly five or ten miles from the aerodrome in his estimation. It looked like enemy territory by the presence of the German soldiers.

The track branched and came to a crossroads where a sign pointed. The lettering was almost erased, but he could just note the name, Poitres, on the cross member. It also said two kilometres, so he decided to take the right fork to the village.

He was just passing another cornfield when he saw a bicycle leaning against a stile. He looked all around for the owner, grabbed the cycle and felt the tyres. The wheels were fully inflated and felt hard beneath his fingers. He looked around furtively before jumping astride it. He pressed hard on the pedals and cycled away down a small incline in the road towards a village.

The local people eyed his flying clothes and pulled him into the shelter of a farmhouse as a lorry load of German troops passed them by. They shook their heads and spoke in French.

"Boche no good."

The rain drizzled down from a grim sky. It was late autumn and the harvest would be gathered late. Using sign language, he thanked the French family for their meal of potatoes and beans. He noted the poverty of the farmhouse and the missing furniture. It was evident this was the case when they took it in turns to sit at the table.

The housewife shrugged her shoulders to indicate the chairs were missing because of a German raid. She smiled and spoke in broken English.

"Boche no good."

Potts took it to mean the Huns had taken away the family's stock of furniture and did not intend returning it. When he turned to go he kissed her on both cheeks and shook the farmer by the hand.

"Thank you both for your kindness, you are so kind. *Vive la France!*"

They shook their heads at the first part of his speech and laughed at his attempts to speak French. Before he slipped away from the farmhouse they first went outside to see if there were any Germans around.

"*Au revoir, bon chance*," the farmer said as he returned.

Potts had gone, riding down the slope of the hill, heading for God knows where. To make matters easier he rode in the opposite direction to where the Germans were heading. He had forgotten to ask where the British lines were, mainly because he could not speak French and decided to forget it and find out for himself.

The village was deserted because it was a farming community and the villagers were working in the fields. He rode into the decline and was about to climb uphill when he heard the noise of an approaching vehicle. Quick as a flash he threw the bike over the hedge and jumped over after it. He buried his head in the bushes and lay there panting, his chest heaving with his exertions. He raised one side of his face and caught sight of a lorry load of Germans going down the hill. Through the stalk blades he saw the lorry brake as it felt the incline. It increased gear and roared away into the village proper. He waited until it had gone before putting the bike back onto the road.

"Have to watch things," he muttered to himself, swinging his leg over the saddle. "Lots of activity around here, wonder what the Huns are planning."

The road flattened at the top and he passed over wheat fields, giving him a wide view of the road ahead and other lorries that might be travelling along it. It was while cycling along the road that he heard the sound of engines overhead and was pleased to see a lone British aeroplane heading for the distant horizon, so he judged it might have been flying to or from its base. He had to decide which way. He tossed a coin he had in his pocket and turned to the left at the crossroads.

He could see other vehicles hundreds of yards ahead, but he was relying on the fact that his image was smaller and they wouldn't see him. As he breasted another rise, he was able to see the waters of the River Somme in the distance. When he saw that he knew where he was and within an hour was pedalling into the aerodrome.

The guards on duty at the front gate saw a pilot in flying gear with a leather helmet attached, tipped with the usual goggles that flashed in the weak sunshine.

A small shell landed some yards away from Hartley and rained down watery earth. For a moment prior to this it lay there fizzing and spluttering before bursting in a small explosion.

Hartley was in another shell hole. He had sheltered in a small eruption less than forty yards from the British trenches. His usually immaculate khaki uniform was caked with mud and running with dirty water. He was coated with dirt from his face to his knees, with the rounded material of his puttees hanging in tatters around his boots. His steel-tipped leather soles were scrambling for perches on the sliding mud of the shell hole.

He gazed at the trench so far away and bent his head to the wall of machine gun bullets scything from the German position. He lifted his head to see the flash of the machine gun as it tolled out death-dealing rounds that were either lost in the thick mud of the killing fields or flew over the British positions. He was waiting for the lull that followed the onslaught, a reminder that the Red Cross was due to cross the field and collect the dead or dying. The firing slackened and stopped, allowing both sides the time to bring in the casualties. It was unofficial, but both sides allowed this time.

Hartley slithered from the slimy confines of the shell hole, half-heartedly aware of the other men of his company, who were doing likewise and quitting their means of shelter. The barbed wire of no-man's-land hung with the bodies of his mates, stood out. The Red Cross orderlies could be seen running across the pockmarked ground, intent on rescuing the dead and injured alike. Athough not fully trusting the opposition not to open fire, the orderlies braved the condition retrieved the fallen.

Hartley crawled along the ground avoiding the deep mud and also the shell and bullet fragments buried deep in it. This time he fell into the eager hands of the other soldiers who had managed to make it back to the trench. Some of these men were suffering wounds of their own and were coated with a heavy skin of black mud.

Hartley's first reaction was to go into his dugout and strip naked. He heated up a tin bath of water then languished in it luxuriously. He finished his attempts to clean himself by dousing his filthy uniform in the same water and hanging it out to dry on a long length of frayed rope.

He had only been clean for an hour when Smithers walked in. He was smoking as usual, and was full of stories about flying machines and what he had been doing on jankers.

"Look at you," he said, looking at him and the uniform he had hung up. "Nice and clean in your dugout, while I was washing planes at the aerodrome. I nearly got clobbered with a bomb when a fucking great big German airship came over. It dropped its bombs on the airstrip and nearly stopped it operating 'cause a bleeding great big bastard bomb almost landed on me and hit a plane I had been cleaning. It got the one plane I had been cleaning. Boy, was I choked. It couldn't be the one left, oh no, it had to be the one I had cleaned and worked on until the sweat poured down my face. The sergeant never had time to see if I had done what he had told me as well." He bit on the cigarette in his annoyance. "I'm looking forward to a little peace and quiet, you been doing anything in your neck of the woods?"

After his session in no-man's-land, Hartley's attempt at an explanation choked in his throat. His endeavour to crown his mate's escapade at the airport looked superficial to the extreme. He decided to forget his experiences on the battlefield and put it all down to the luck of the draw.

In the meantime, Smithers was making himself comfortable. He sank into the inviting arms of his bed springs, arms crossed under his head, legs crossed, and smoking like a chimney with the flu blocked. He still praised the virtues of the fighter pilots who were knocking the enemy planes from the sky at every opportunity presented.

"They all deserved a medal for their bravery," he enthused, the fag waving with his words. "No less than the Victoria Cross, every man jack of them."

Willcox was on guard duties patrolling his stretch of his duty. It was his turn to miss cooking the meal and it fell to Hartley to do the cooking in Smithers' absence.

After his venture into the battlefield it was positive heaven to play cook. He cut the blocks of bully beef into squares and diced the onions and potatoes ready for the frying pan. After cooking the food on the cherry red of the stove, they got down to eating it in virtual silence.

As they were chewing the food the entry curtains were pulled aside to admit the mail carrier. He handed over two letters to Smithers and a small package to Hartley. Smithers slit open the larger of the envelopes and took out a two-page letter. The other contained a black and white photo of his mother and father.

The letter was from his mother and father wishing him all possible safety in his chosen job and life in the Ninety-ninth Company of Foot. They also said his bicycle was still in its place beside the cat's entry flap in the front door. They both missed him and spoke of the shortages of food in the village because of the war in Europe. His mother hoped he liked the photos, saying his father was going bald on top and sporting grey on the sides of his head.

Hartley opened his package and was surprised to see a cross and chain in a small cardboard box. He lifted it from its bed of cotton wool and dangled it before Smithers' gaze. Beneath the box was a bill for six shillings from the local cleaners, warning him that they would keep the overcoat to defray the cost of cleaning it if he did not pay his bill. He relayed the message to Smithers.

"It was going out of fashion anyway, so let them keep it." He dangled the cross before Smithers' eyes again. "Nice cross, hope it works for me the same as it did for me a few hours ago in no-man's-land."

He lifted his shirt collar to reveal another St Christopher under the wool of his shirt. Smithers' head was raised at the news.

"Been across there, eh mate? Been mooching on the fight site?"

"Got safely across the shell stretch, must've been the power of the cross wot helped me," commented Hartley, swinging the chain. "That and the time taken in collecting the casualties of war by the Red Cross," he added. "I knew I was wearing the St Christopher though, which helped me through the shot and shell." He hung the second cross around his neck. "Might as well have another one to add to the fluence and its power, might bring me that extra bit of luck that got me through my recent spell in the battlefield."

Outside another whiz-bang exploded in the air above the British trenches, bringing the dust of ages down from the wooden shelves and dislodging a cup from its bent nail hook on the woodwork. Smithers tried to catch it, but it fell to his boots and rattled against the bed frame. He shifted the fag to the other side of his mouth and stood the steel mug next to his prostate body. He picked his teeth with the spent match and swallowed the result. As if in celebration of his dinner, he lifted one of his buttock cheeks and farted.

"That's better," he said through the smoke haze. "Better out than in, I say." He then sniffed, crying, "Whatever have I been eating? It stinks to high heaven!"

"Like your bleeding feet." Hartley sighed. "When did you last have a bath, Smithy?"

"When did *you*?" countered Smithers, straining for another fart.

"Only just now," he replied as Smithers broke wind again.

"I can't help it," he complained. "It's me stomach. I get it every time I eat fish, just one of those things I have to live with I suppose. I suffer every time I eat fish, and I had some this morning. It repeats on me something cruel. I get it every time I have fish and chips, I like them too."

He lay back on his blanket roll as he dreamed of his favourite meal.

19

CORPORAL GUNN ENTERED THE dugout quickly, mainly to inspect it, but also to catch the sqaddies as they lounged around the earthen rooms.

Smithers grabbed his rifle and started cleaning it, all the time signalling for Hartley to see the corporal as he entered. For a moment Gunn surveyed the dugout, watching Hartley drying his socks at the stove, after giving Smithers a look to show his attempts of warning had been noted.

Gunn coughed and as Hartley turned to see him, he immediately dropped the socks and the poker he had been using to hold them.

"Carry on with what you were doing, Private Hartley," he said surprisingly, and as Hartley did as he was told, Gunn stepped over to the fire and warmed his hands. "I saw you out in no-man's-land this morning," he remarked, turning his hands to the fire, so that the back of them got the benefit. "You did right in using the unofficial wounded recovery system time to gain the last few yards to our trench. You showed an unusual know-how of the system, and I am saying you would never have made it back here without showing initiative." He twisted around. "See you are back in our midst, Private Smithers, did you like working at the airport?"

"Yes, Corp," said Smithers, pulling the brass end of the pull-through out of the barrel so that it landed on the oilcloth with a dull plop.

He noted the corporal was watching him with half-closed eyes, so to impress him he lifted his rifle and eyed through the barrel, using the reflected lightness of his thumbnail to light up the gun's winding interior.

"How is it?" questioned Gunn over his shoulder then he grabbed the rifle to have a look for himself. "Ah, good, Private Smithers, the rifle is satisfactory, you are learning at long last." He cast his eyes around the dugout and added the rejoinder, "Your billet is also satisfactory. That little stint at the air force base did you a lot of good. It will keep you in trim for the work in maintaining this dugout in the same manner. Keep it up both of you, it will go on your record for future recommendation - dismiss."

Smithers waited for him to go through the sacking door before giving his departing form the two-fingered sign.

"All right, Corporal Gunn," he mimicked after him. "Clean your rifle, Private Smithers, that is satisfactory, Private Smithers, did you a lot of good, Private Smithers. Wipe your arse, Private Smithers – *bullshit*." He sat on the bed still mumbling softly to himself. "You're nothing but a rerun of Sergeant Cox." He lit another fag and eyed his mate, Hartley. "He's always spying on you through that spyglass atop the trench walls. I bet you he even eyes the Hun soldiers to see if they are properly dressed. There's also another thing; that officer that reported me for the revolver was seen with a German helmet by one of his orderlies. Bet he don't get done for keeping enemy equipment like I was."

He kicked the bottom of his bunk in his temper and blew a great cloud of tobacco smoke across the dugout.

Across the trench, Private Ehoe was again cleaning his Vickers machine gun. He kept the live rounds in a metal box beside the gun and patted it to reassure himself it was in the right position for firing. He was rubbing the mechanism, trying to erase a slight bit of rust that had appeared on the barrel. He was forever trying to get rid of such imperfections, first with a rag dipped in oil then without oil, to see if that would make any difference. No matter how he tried it was still there, even after firing a few rounds.

In his job as machine-gunner's mate he lifted the bandolier of bullets around his neck so that it would not jam. The entry gate of the firing pin was apt to slip if the round was difficult. The gate was so delicate the slightest difference of thickness of the round had to be just right, or it could cause a blockage in the mechanism. Any slight difference might cause it to back up and jam in the ammunition casing. There are cases where a slight bend in the barrel has caused a bullet to fly in another direction entirely.

Of course, when the stream of bullets came out of the barrel, who would notice a single round that came out off course? The NCO in charge of the machine gun, Corporal Doust, saw to it that the rain of bullets rang true and unaffected. He personally pressed the trigger so that it did so.

The dugout housing the machine gun was hit by several star shells to ferret out the machine gun fire. As he fired, Corporal Doust aimed to stop as many of the enemy as possible. When his underling, Private Ehoe, took over the firing he tried to copy his example, being careful to do the same thing and try to bring down the enemy.

Although not liking killing, Ehoe was just doing his duty in annihilating the enemy. After all, he mused, was it not total war, and in such situations anything goes? It was just a case of pressing the trigger and directing the bullet burst. He was not concerned where the bullet shower went, as long as he was doing his duty and fighting the Germans. Someone had to oppose them or they would march across Europe, grinding every nation into dust before their jack boots. Ehoe had to perform his job and stop the German hordes from crushing the little states into oblivion.

He was oiling the mechanism prior to his firing the machine gun when the word went around that the Germans were trying to mount a surprise attack. They were due to make their move and it looked like it was nearing the moment.

The trenches of the British troops were teeming with Tommies, and the mixed sections of other Commonwealth soldiers as well as the English were intermingled with the Ninety-ninth to swell their ranks. The newer members of the opposing ranks were black men, who came from the colonies of Africa by way of Jamaica, and other members of the Commonwealth who had joined the Ninety-ninth at the call for help. They were new to the fighting and just in from the troopship that had brought them over from their home in the Caribbean Sea. There were even as few Inuits from Baffin Bay in Northern Canada.

This assemblage of men gathered in the well of the trench and awaited for the Germans to make their entrance in the bloody battle of the River Somme.

20

F REDA SWEPT THE BAR of its collection of cigarette ends, smashed glasses and other paraphernalia. She was alone in her work, but it never bothered her. She employed a young girl to help with things like washing glasses and cooking her meals, or any odd job she might want doing. The main concern was left to her when it came to serving the customers with beer. It was done by her and she jealously guarded it because not only was it difficult, but it involved taking money from the customers.

The girl had a good heart and did her work well, cheerfully wishing everybody good morning etc. She had an aged mother to support and needed the work to keep herself and the old woman. She had a ginger cat as well and until recently it had a habit of following her to work every day, which Freda discouraged.

"Cats and bar work don't mix. Either he stops coming or you, Lottee, will have to go."

He eventually stopped coming when a female cat moved in next door.

To date, Freda had received two letters from Corporal Gunn, but she searched the mat daily in case he wrote another one. Gunn was never one to do much letter writing and he found it hard going to pen one every six months or so. The men in the trenches also had this trait. They all excelled in such things as weaponry, but when they picked up a tiny pen or pencil they were more or less speechless.

Freda had a tin of blue paint and was touching up a small section of the barroom. She was on her knees brushing off the peeling paint with a small hand brush. She worked with her tongue pressed hard against her lower teeth and occasionally licked her lips in exasperation. She just could not get it right. She brushed on paint and in the process got a paintbrush full of hard bits. She tried wiping the paintbrush on the lip of the lid and only succeeded in making more blue bits. She then had a brainwave - she would get Lottee to take over.

"You might make a better job than me; you've got a lighter touch. I just can't seem to get it right."

Lottee did do a better job than Freda, and finished it in quick time. She went up in Freda's estimation and was given a day off in recognition of her good work.

There were plenty of things to do in the bar. Freda was washing the windows free of ingrained grime from the previous owner, which was proving to be a hard job. She had to hurry though, as the first customer of the day was outside looking through the window she was washing, shading his eyes and pointing to a little smudge.

"This needs a little bit of polishing," he mouthed silently.

She humoured him and polished the glass free of the small mark. As she got down from her chair she slid the bolt, opened the door wide and grinned to him as he entered the room.

"Morning, Fred," she greeted him.

Private Fred Chester replied by answering and showing his teeth in a smile.

"Morning, Freda love, you *are* doing a good job there. I'd help you, but my teeth are sticking to me lip with thirst."

"As long as you pay for it you can have what you like, which is almost anything."

"How about a big sloppy kiss then?" he asked, puckering his lips.

"I said *almost* anything, so that is out for a start," she said, avoiding his grab for her waist. "What will your wife say?" she added, making for the bar and safety.

As she slipped a record on and turned on the gramophone the dulcet strains of 'La Vien Rose' echoed through the empty barroom. Other people slipped into the bar and sat at the various stools that graced the smoke-begrimed walls of the public house. Freda swept the coins from the counter top as the men paid for each glass of flat beer. She only had two kinds of beer - mild and bitter - mild for the cash-strapped privates or troopers; a better class of beer for the corporals or senior NCOs. Slowly, bit by bit, the pub increased its complement of customers. It was payday for the troops and they were celebrating by drinking their earnings as fast as they were able. The barroom was thick with cigarette smoke, wreathing up into the ceiling and parting as a lone figure stood up and disturbed it.

Freda was serving as fast as she was capable and she often spilled the contents of the jug with the speed of her service. The barrels were housed under the counter and she filled the jug with beer from the barrel. She finished by transferring the beer to each waiting glass. Added to this task was the right payment for the beer; their right kind of beer and the change given, if any. She was used to the work and actually liked working as a barmaid and being the owner of the pub. It made her independent and mistress of her own finances.

As she was pouring out the beer, the record finished and danced on the end line. Seeing as there was a lull in the drinking procedure she turned the record over and played the other side. As Freda dipped a glass into the bucket of cold water she hummed to the melody.

As the day progressed, the rest of the regular customers put in an appearance. Troops went in and out singing the praises of the beer and mine host, and slightly swaying with the potency of Freda's beer, but happy in getting what they wanted.

Freda was busy counting up the day's takings. She jotted a few lines on a piece of paper and mentally added up the amount she had made in the course of the day. She added to the amount she had saved up with the result that she had more than two hundred pounds saved, a huge sum she thought, enough to retire on if she had a mind to call it a day. I have no interest in retiring or calling it a day, though, she thought, listening to the music and humming along with its central theme.

Her thoughts went out to Gunn and his life at the front. Like others, she had no idea what life was like at the front line and what they were going through. Just firing the rifles they were fond of carrying, and fighting the enemy, she supposed.

The pub she ran was as typical working man's pub. She had mostly privates and senior NCOs for her clientele and hardly ever entertained officers or their class of girlfriends. She preferred the lower ranks though; they had no pretence about them and were more or less as they were born, happy-go-lucky or serious as God made them. Not like the upper class twits, who were pretentious or infected with class distinction.

Freda sighed and poured a flat pint, holding the liquid up to gaze at the brown beer that was meant to make her fortune. Still, two hundred pounds in total is a great deal in this day and age, she thought, especially for a woman to save up in several weeks.

The lines of men swelled to several thousands and the crowds were cheek by jowl, pressed against each other as they waited for the whistle to climb up the ladders. The black contingent of soldiers had exchanged their preferred form of headwear and donned the protection of a steel helmet. The rest of their uniform was composed of khaki, puttees and steel-tipped boots.

The forest of steel bayonets stood up like a band of iron that matched the steel edge of their heavy boots. Now and again a nervous finger twitched on a ready trigger and banged off a round into the air above the heads of the packed ranks. The tension was mounting and affected all the men with its stiffness and rigidity. From the highest in rank to the lowest, it brought out the rank sweat of fear and caused them to steam with the perspiration of induced heat.

At the rear of the men the officers waited with mouths clenched around the silver barrels of their whistles ready to blast the frenzied air into the instrument and set the men into motion.

The ranks of the men stretched hundreds of yards into the distance and gave them the look of thousands of intense wriggling snakes. The packed ranks of snakes waited for the head snake to spit into the whistle and define their life cycle.

21

The two pals were together again, with their other friend, Private Willcox.

Willcox gripped his teeth together and licked a dry mouth. It was only the second time he had taken part in a maximum effort wave assault by thousands of troops and the first time such numbers of men were engaged in the initial wave of the attack. Although this fact should have heartened him, it did not and it still brought him out in a cold sweat. The prospect of putting his life on the line was off-putting, and he still had that niggle of doubt that somewhere along the line something had to go wrong, and radically so.

At the back of the sweating lines of Tommies was a senior officer of high rank equipped with a pair of headphones clipped to his head with leather straps. He was engrossed in his job, trying to concentrate on what the other voice was saying. The hubbub of the men was so loud he had trouble hearing the orders coming down the headphones. He shushed as loud as he was able, but the noise around still prevented him from hearing. He had to press the instrument hard against his head to hear the voice of the other man.

Willcox eyed the major with sweat rolling down his face. It just kept coming and stung his eyeballs so that the tears joined the stream and caused more tears. Farther along the line Smithers was hunched against the mud of the trench wall, clinging grimly to his rifle and bemoaning his lot, calling his superiors vile names and questioning the likelihood of them being born into wedlock.

"Bastards, all of them, from one stripe upwards, no idea of running a fucking army, no idea at all. Put 'em here where the fight is and they are lost, the lot of them. I'd put them in a great big field and let 'em battle it out between themselves. I'd make them pay for getting me killed. Dirty bastards ain't got a bit of guts between them."

Because of his recent foray into no-man's-land, Hartley had been excused duties and put on a different job. He was assigned to latrine duties and liked it not one little bit, but he liked the duties on the battlefield less.

In the trench the men were getting restless. They were weighed down with equipment and other things, and were leaning against each other for support. A quick shell buzzed its fizzing journey across the waiting ranks of the men, followed by a burst of bullets that shot off a layer of clay and stones. The men instinctively ducked to avoid the missiles and packed harder against each other, as they ricocheted from the many stones that packed the top of the trench walls. In addition, a whiz-bang exploded in the air and spewed out its lethal load of death-dealing iron pieces in all directions.

The whistle for them to start the attack came suddenly, but was not unnoticed. The officer blew his instrument, and ushered the huge ranks forwards with a further blast on his whistle. The men, carrying big loads of equipment, leaped on the homemade ladders and scrambled up them into the opposing fire of the Huns. A big soldier, weighed down with equipment, fell down into the crowd, bleeding from a wound in the face. He was gently left to sink down onto the trench floor and left to another man dressed as a Red Cross orderly.

Smithers quickly sank into his usual mode of survival and made for the nearest shelter, a shell hole. He was too crafty to do anything else, and slipped into the mud to dodge the bullets and shells. This time he was accompanied by the slithering form of Corporal Gunn, who had followed him in his bid to dodge the issue.

"Not this time, Smithers," he breathed into his ear as they crouched in the shell hole.

"Corporal Gunn!" exclaimed a surprised Smithers, clutching his rifle to himself.

Gunn gave him a shallow grin and dipped his head as a shell landed close by.

"Surprise, surprise," said Gunn, eyeing him. "You thought you would get rid of me, Smithers. You ought to know I can't be got rid of as easy as that, I am a trier and I stick like shit to a blanket."

Smithers gave a shallow grin at this observation.

"I was only getting shelter from the enemy fire," he argued. "It is really dangerous out there; that machine-gunner has our range in his sights, especially shell holes where we go."

"Then you should know he has you for his victim and you should do the obvious and not drop into the first pothole you see," Gunn snarled, fixing him in his eagle-like gaze. "You know I always keep an eye on my boys no matter what they do out here. That's why I am here with you now. You know, I always look at you with my optical gazer, and that is why I'm one step ahead of you when you get out here in no-man's-land."

"Is that what you do, Corp? I would never guess," Smithers lied, spitting out a glob of mud that had splashed into his mouth.

"Yes," said Gunn unbelievingly, eyeing him with suspicion, "I think you are being a big liar, but I can't prove it. I know you often saw me with the optical viewer, so don't bother to lie to me."

An extra big bullet hit the surrounding shell hole spoils and sprayed the two people with muddy earth. The stony ground was swept up in a sudden burst of earth and other things that showered them with sharp pebbles.

"He has certainly got our number with his machine gun," muttered Gunn, after dipping his head for the third time. "We've got to get out of this hole in the ground and get farther along."

"Just what I was thinking," bleated Smithers as he bent his head as well.

Gunn took the initiative and waited for the machine-gunner to reload the weapon.

"Here we go!" he shouted, and leaped out of the hole and under the bullet stream depth.

Smithers was caught by surprise for an instant and almost left his rifle behind. He quickly recovered himself though, and was soon skidding through the potholes. Seemingly their shift of position did something to the rest of the company and they collected other men as they went past them sheltering from the enemy onslaught. Very soon hundreds of soldiers were slithering through the shell holes to the barbed wire coils stretching to the end of the battlefield and out of sight in the thick mist.

Several shells burst in the air to catch the vulnerable men, but helped them by destroying the wire coils and wooden stakes supporting the barbed wire. The remaining men could hardly believe their luck and, as one, they all made for this gap in the fence. In the mist the hordes of khaki-clad men made the fractured fence and went through the coils with measured delight. They wriggled through the remainder of the barbed wire and rested on the other side, panting with the effort of crossing the obstacle.

Gunn had progressed with the rest of the troops and was slightly ahead of Smithers. Slowly they approached the enemy trench and stopped just short of it in the shelter of a shell hole. They were accompanied by dozens of others who were sheltering from the enemy fire. They judged they were about thirty or forty yards away from the enemy trench and in one of the many destroyed pillboxes that dotted the line of the German defences. They couldn't stay there though, because of the threat of shells shot at them when they were observed.

Gunn, sensing this possibility, nodded to Smithers to follow him and snaked out of the pillbox into the slime once more. The rest of the men copied his actions and started to slide towards the enemy trench. They had another great slice of luck, as the mist was thicker on the edges of the enemy trenches, masking their moves to the enemy positions.

Smithers could see shadowy movement in the German trench and steeled himself in readiness for the battle to come. Unmanned rifles were poking out from the sandbags and were covered with the mud of the field. The mist was so thick it was almost rain and the pair of soldiers could hear the German soldiers talking to each other as they waited for the British attack to begin. The rain, or a combination of the two, was the probable cause of the Germans failing to hear the British approach their trench. In some cases it was their final hour because the first wave of British troops was going over the sides of the trench and executing slaughter on a grand scale.

Smithers could feel his bayonet on the end of his rifle through the folds of his greatcoat. His pulse was rising in his temple and he breathed with difficulty as a result. He was sweating profusely and it dripped from his sharp nose. He was worming his way through the sandbags, and used his bayonet to hack a way through the sides of the trench. One more hack and he was through the sacking, ready to defend himself at all times. He fell through the line of sandbags and lay there on the mud of the trench floor, clutching his rifle to his breast.

To the right of him a German soldier was looking at him, thunderstruck with surprise, his rifle leaning up against the sides of the trench and out of reach. The astonished man made a quick grab for his weapon just as Smithers pushed a bayonet through his stomach. He uttered a cry of amazement and pain, and slobbered on a great gush of blood that came quickly to his mouth.

Another man wearing the grey uniform of a German trooper made a desperate lunge at Smithers, and paid the final price with Smithers' bloody bayonet in his throat. Smithers shot the third man to attack him, and slammed another bullet in the breech as the smoke died away on the grey mist. He beat away the bayonet of the next man and caught him in the arm with the tip of his bayonet. The German dropped his rifle and screamed with fear. His high-pitched cry so unnerved Smithers that he stood back and looked at him with surprise. The German looked so frightened he let the man go.

Smithers was alone and looking for Gunn. He was around the corner of the trench apprehended by two German troopers. Smithers immediately hit the nearest one a whack with the butt of his rifle and tripped up the second with his outstretched leg. Gunn was just bayoneting the third one, who had come out of a nearby dugout.

Together they stood there breathing hard with heavy breaths stretching their khaki coats. As others of the company joined them they grinned at each other with a shallow grin. It seemed to be a complete victory and as they congratulated each other on their survival they fanned out and took over the entire trench.

22

Hartley rolled over on his bunk with comparative ease and gazed at the earth ceiling of the dugout. He was smoking a cigarette and he watched the smoke whirls rise up into the air. He noticed how the smoke ascended easily, untroubled by any draught or passage of air. He watched a small spider cross the expanse of the clay roof and stop as it encountered the cigarette smoke. It seemed to meet the cloud and examine it before continuing with its journey.

His mind ran to the thought of Smithers, and in his mind's eye he could see what he was going through in the battlefield beyond the trench.

"Good luck to him," he breathed. "He will need all the luck he is entitled to and more besides."

He got up and began to make a cup of tea, before he thought of the optical viewer and its survey of the scene. Outside I could use that, he thought, as long as Gunn doesn't see me. He frowned on any other ranks using it; it was for NCOs and others above, he had maintained, when caught eyeing the field. He was aware the corporal was otherwise engaged and that left the way open for him to use the instrument. He was still thinking along these lines as he sipped the hot tea and spat out a tea leaf.

Outside the trench rocked with the sudden explosion of a whiz-bang, and the container he had used to make the tea edged over to the lip of the stove. The bang of the shell was followed by a sudden burst of machine gun fire that rattled the slugs on the metal the corrugated iron sheets covering the outside of the dugout. With one accord he got up from his seat on the orange box and peeped out into the trench.

It was deserted, of course, and the optical viewer was showing on top of the trench head. He looked all around before jumping on the step to the trench head. The optical viewer was open to view before his eyes and its metal protector was hanging down, waving in the gentle wind that blew in the trench. He gazed into the viewer and, screwing the lens of the instrument, brought the field into sharp relief.

Except for the bursting shells that exploded on the mud it was empty of any living person and only showed the twisting barbed wire and the dead men attached to it. Disappointed, he rolled the viewer around the site to all directions, trying to see if there was anyone alive in the field. He thought he saw a movement in a crowd of wounded men, but he never saw the stripes of a corporal in the movement or anything remotely like the shape of his mate, Smithers.

"Then he must've made the German trenches. Good boy! I only hope he is giving those Hun bastards what for."

Smithers wiped his nose on his jacket sleeve and gave Gunn a wide grin.

"What about that then, Corp?" he said, feeling the edge of his bayonet with the flat of his thumb.

Gunn returned the grin with a smile of his own.

"You'll do, Smithers, you did your best, *over* your best in beating those Germans. So those words of mine *did* sink in before forgetting 'em, good man."

The rest of the company made sure there were no more Huns in the former German trench, and proceeded to occupy it. They searched it for anything of value like food or guns, finding very little in the way of food. Even water was scarce, with very little in the water barrels in the dugouts lining the firing trench and other connecting trenches. What food they found was cooked up in the stoves and other cooking implements. The men managed to rustle up a glorious cook up of German sausage and sauerkraut, followed with lashings of cream. This was considered 'off' by the main body of the troops, and many left the dessert for fear of food poisoning. The wine was plentiful as was the beer, and the British troops had a good time until every drop was downed.

The company began to withdraw when the shells began to fall on the former German trench. The machine guns opened up, falling on the British troops as they prepared to quit the trench and go back to their own lines. The depleted ranks of the company streamed over the battered sandbags, taking with it the many ladders and hop-ups the Huns had abandoned in their haste.

Gunn and Smithers had a relatively easy job in coming from the German lines for a while until the Huns had time to collect themselves and brought a new selection of guns into play, taking potshots at their retreating backs. They immediately reverted to their old tricks and dropped down to the shelter of the mud and water. The trench mortars and smaller shells took a little longer and it was a quarter of an hour before they had moved their ordinance, got the range and readjusted themselves to the new distance. Gunn and Smithers took full advantage of this shift in their fortunes and managed to put some distance between themselves and the Germans. They were almost home before the enemy recovered and started their onslaught again.

With one concerted rush the two men fell into the British lines and slithered down the sides of the trench into a pool of muddy water that had collected at the bottom. Smithers' chest heaved as he gasped with the exertion and he had to lean against the earthen wall for a minute to regain his breath. Gunn was out of breath as well and leaned against the barrel of his rifle, blowing hard. Other men came over the sandbags and did the same, all out of breath. One of them clutched a badly bleeding wound in his arm, which he suddenly held to his chest.

The machine guns had started their earthen razor cut and were stitching a line of red hot slugs along the rim of the trench, dislodging shards of sacking and stones in their stride. For a moment Smithers was breathing in sharply until his heart slowed to a slower beat. He gathered up his steel helmet from where it had fallen, and collected his rifle. He nodded to Gunn and tottered his way to his dugout nearby. Once there he gave a quick nod to Hartley and dropped on his bunk with a great sigh.

"Good God, am I glad that is all over," he said to Hartley, who was just mashing the tea. "Any chance of a good cup of hot tea?" he asked. "My tongue has got hairs on it with dryness."

The pilot of the Fokker monoplane never saw the Sopwith Camel that shot him out of the sky on that day in 1916. The pilot of the Camel shot up under the enemy plane and riddled the underbelly of the Fokker with slugs that tore through the fragile fabric like a hot knife through butter.

Captain Francis Ball of the aerial branch of the Ninety-ninth Company of Foot, white silk scarf streaming out through the slipstream of the Sopwith Camel, waved in salute as the Fokker smoked and caught fire. The enemy pilot battled with the controls of his machine and with the fire that soon tore over his monoplane.

Ball, seeing the enemy plane was a goner, held his hand over the firing pin of the Vickers machine gun, brushing his thumb on the hand grip and wondering whether it had enough bullets to make it crash. He gave the enemy pilot another wave of salute and watched the orange smoke surge out of the body of the enemy plane. The Fokker carved a wide circle of smoke in the autumn air and crashed in a field of waving vegetables. Ball dipped the Camel down to the field and saw the blazing plane, looking for any sign of the pilot. There was none, and he watched the blazing monoplane erupt into a ball of exploding metal.

Ball was accompanied by three of his mates and he lifted to rejoin them in tight formation. This flight of fighter planes was stooging around, looking for other enemy planes that might be in the vicinity with the same thing in mind, only with the reverse intended. Captain Mike Train, in command of the wing of Camels, waved to him as he joined the other two. They had bagged two other German aircraft and this one made the total for the morning at three.

A good morning's work, mused Train with a grin at the Camel coming into formation. He waved to Ball to acknowledge his part in the recent confrontation between the Fokker and the Camel and thrust his thumb into the air to see that Ball had come off successfully. Ball returned his wave and nodded. The trio of planes thrust through the circle of light clouds and vanished into the sunlight.

Down on the ground the furious fight for ground area was going on in the Somme Valley. Hordes of grey-clad Hun soldiers were pouring out of their trenches and flooding the battlefield with their charging masses. In contrast to the quietness of the Tommies they emitted wild whoops of frenzy, hoping to drive fear into the ranks of the British with the ferocity of their charge.

The coolness of the British reply was to answer this attack with massed guns, big and small, which reduced the charge by almost fifty per cent. The Hun soldiers fell under this avalanche of power, like chaff hit by a storm, melting away and falling into the mud before them.

So much for the mighty German war machine, thought every British soldier who poured down hot lead on the swelled ranks of the Hun supreme being.

———————————

Smithers was bitching as usual and furiously smoking a roll-up that dangled from the corner of his mouth like some over-fat darning needle. He added to this the spent match with which he had lit the fag and sucked the two articles as one from his tight lips.

"There we were," he was saying to his mate, who was lying on his bunk, "surrounded by these Germans soldiers - must've been a dozen or more in number. Me and the corporal, with just one cartridge case full of bullets and my bayonet. I gave him one in the belly and he bled like a stuck pig. I turned around and just caught a Hun making for me. We tussled around, trying to outfox each other. He was a big man and he punched my bayonet away as I drove it at him, then he made one mistake by falling over a large stone in the bottom of the pit. I had him then, and gave 'im one in the guts."

He took out the match, collapsed on his bunk, took out the roll-up, blew out a big cloud of blue smoke and watched it drift into the air above him.

"I watched you through the optical viewer," said Hartley, quietly. "I tried to see you, but couldn't because of all that fog."

"I was in the German trench by that time, fighting for my life, I might say."

Hartley shifted in his bunk and rolled over to face Smithers.

"I guessed that, Smithy. It was the same as when I was there. We did all those things and more. We got back by the skin of our teeth, I almost thought we were not going to make it, things were that close."

"Yeah, I know it, we got the same feeling as we fought, me and Gunn. I said to 'im afterwards, there was a time when I thought he would 'ave me, that was the time I fell over the same rock he did. Lucky that I managed to keep my balance when I did, must've been all that bike riding I did when I was a nipper."

Smithers blew out another cloud of cigarette smoke and put the spent match into his mouth again. He crossed one leg over the other and gently pushed the bent metal of the bed with his boot.

"Wonder why they don't give you a wooden bed like the ones they do in the barracks? Maybe it's because of bed bugs or fleas," he said, answering the question himself. "I don't mind them myself, it's the rats I don't like. They live off you and eat human flesh. Makes my skin fair crawl, that does."

"Suppose they've got to live," opined Hartley, twisting over and regaining his feet, "but they've got to eat human flesh instead of other things like rabbits or mice."

"Plenty of human flesh around here," said Smithers, remembering his recent battle with the Huns. "Extra plenty, if you ask me. Dozens of men dying all the time, especially when we have a push."

"Yeah, we helped as well," said Hartley, striding to the stove and stirring up the black ashes. "Don't forget that, Smithy, we helped an awful lot."

"With regard to me, Hart, it was 'im or me. He would have done the same to me if I'd given 'im the chance. Just think of it, I might've been lying out there in that Hun trench, or I might've been lying in a puddle of blood after he had bayoneted me. Rather him than me."

Smithers was indignant at the thought.

Hartley got a glow of red out of the fire with his breath and, after putting on a couple of wood shavings, managed to coax the flame into a roaring mass. He explored the tea tin.

"We're running out of tea," he said with a sigh, "where's that packet of tea I gave you?"

Smithers shot out a stream of cigarette smoke.

"You must be getting me mixed up with Willcox," he replied from the corner of his mouth. "You didn't give *me* any tea"

"Didn't I? I must be losing me marbles, I thought it was you I gave it to."

Hartley sat down on his bunk and waited for the rusty kettle to boil. Outside a shell banged at the side of the trench and brought down a cloud of dust. He caught a tin mug that had been dislodged, and replaced it on its nail.

Sergeant Cox dipped down beneath the sheltering wall of the trench and stepped aside as a whiz-bang shell exploded into pieces farther up the pit. He was currently carrying an important item of information and he didn't want it destroyed by enemy action. Although he did not know what the message was, he could guess its contents with certainty. Another attack by the company, he was sure.

"And in the near future," he mumbled to himself.

He knew the men were tired and deserved a rest; a rest away from the continual confrontation between the warring factions. They needed a few hours' leave, a brief respite from bloody battle. Away from the sight and sound of continual fighting that seemed to go on for weeks at a time without end. As well as the next attack message there was an order that all ranks were to be given one week's paid leave, to be taken by them in the next month.

A small smile played around Cox's mouth when he thought of the leave.

"That should warm the cockles of their hearts," he mumbled to himself. "It's just the ticket for the lads, especially after doing a signal job stopping the Huns."

Cox was just rounding the corner of the trench when he bumped into Corporal Gunn. He stopped the corporal's progress with his swagger stick.

"Corporal Gunn, the very man. You will be the bearer of good news and bad news. The bad news is tomorrow we continue the push we started at the first part of the week and do the same thing we did then.

We will overrun the nearest German trench and capture as many prisoners as possible before returning to our own positions again. We have it on good authority that a couple of high ranking German officials will be visiting the Hun trenches in the near future. We are to capture them and enough of the other ranks to make it worthwhile."

Gunn eyed his superior with some suspicion.

"I hear you, Sergeant, I will convey the news of the attack as soon as possible, and the *good news*, Sergeant?"

Cox broke into a smile.

"All ranks below the rank of sergeant major will get paid leave after the attack. That's an order, Corporal Gunn, effective immediately, all right?"

"Yes, Sergeant Cox, I will tell them just after the push. It will be something to look forward to after the battle with the Huns, might even fill them with firmer resolve to beat them and do the job you demand."

"Good show, Corporal. I know I can depend on you and the lads to make a show. I will make the necessary paperwork available for the attack and the leave. All in one, like you like to see it, all official, above board and Bristol fashion, just the way you like it, Corporal, eh?"

Gunn left Cox by the side of the trench with the official news and dodged aside as another shell thudded into the next slit trench. He spat out a mouthful of mud and soil as he made his way into the dugouts lining the battle trench and crossed into the nearest foxhole. After making himself heard by shouting at the rigid occupants, he marched into the dugout occupied by Smithers and Hartley.

The first thing heard by the dodgy pair was the voice of Gunn remonstrating with the sentry on duty. They immediately shot off their bunks and grabbed a pull-through, which they used. When Gunn finally shot into their dugout they were hard at work on their rifles.

23

"WELL, I *AM* SURPRISED," said Gunn, when he saw the two men cleaning their rifles with such gusto. "Could be you were warned by others that I was coming in on inspection. Of course, *that* wouldn't happen," he jeered, "not to you pair of bludging bastards. You wouldn't do such an underhand thing to me, not Smithers and Hartley, not them, me old muckers. Not much," he added under his breath.

"Yes, Sir," muttered Hartley, pulling the pull-through from the barrel of his gun and looking down the barrel.

Gunn, used to their way of doing things to impress him, decided to run along with the impression and fall in with the effect their way.

"All right?" he commented, when the barrel was tipped up in his direction.

Hartley said that hopefully it was and rubbed at the ammunition holder furiously. Smithers just kept on working, his eyes glued to his rifle, trying not to see the corporal eyeing him.

"Well, you can stop work while I talk to you," the corporal declared, pulling the paper from his pocket.

The two men were surprised to hear this and looked at each other questioningly.

"No, there's nothing wrong," Gunn said when he saw the looks. "You ain't done nothing wrong or anything, so you can rest easy."

In reply they both dropped their cleaning rags and eyed the corporal with scepticism. Gunn ignored the looks.

"We are dropping our usual mode of operation and letting you know something in advance. We have it on good authority that instead of just capturing prisoners as we do, we are altering the usual by going in and getting the top brass of the Germans. The two high ranking officers who we hope to capture are a major and a colonel, which we know because of intelligence. We hope to capture these officers when you once again are ordered to storm the enemy trench. These are your orders and we wish you good luck. When this part of the war is over, your leaders announce that you are due a substantial amount of leave. This will be taken in the next month by all ranks up to the rank of sergeant major, apart from defaulters. It will last for one week and no more - dismiss."

"Just a case of scratch your back and we'll claw yours," said Hartley as Gunn exited through the sacking door. "If we do as he says, a lot of men will be killed, injured or both in the push."

Willcox returned off guard duties and learned the news.

"Not another basinful of fighting," he grumbled, dropping his rifle onto his bunk. "What more do they want - blood?"

"Yeah, your blood, brother," snarled Smithers acidly. "Seems they want us to mount an attack on the Hun trench and get a couple of German officers who are visiting the enemy troops; a dead liberty, I tell you."

"What you gonna do, revolt?" asked Willcox, lighting a fag. "The last man who did that ended up being shot for disobedience. If they don't get you one way they'll get you another, make no mistake about that, man."

Smithers slapped a huge chunk of bully beef into the frying pan and held it over the flame.

It was dark outside the dugout and Hartley was doing his stretch of sentry duty in the trench.

Just for a change, Smithers added cabbage to the mess and smelled the cooking food with satisfaction.

"Fit for a king," he mumbled, shaking salt and pepper into the pan and stirring the contents.

Willcox was snoring gently on his rumpled bed and mumbled something in his sleep. His bulk was showing beneath the brown blankets, breathing slowly.

For a little while the shelling had ceased, but the small arms fire continued. The single crack of a sniper echoed on the night air as Hartley caught a movement in the trench. The ground was slushy beneath his boots as he ended his walk and turned to retrace his well-worn steps. He stopped when he heard a sound. The noise was repeated and suddenly a fat German soldier dropped over the wall of the trench and, with others of the same mind, confronted Hartley with bayonet outstretched.

Hartley immediately adopted a crouch, with his rifle directed at the German troops. As he faced the enemy soldiers he backed away and managed to fumble a shot from his rifle. The resultant sound echoed on the night and for a few minutes it outplayed the shellfire that had moved to another area of the trenches. Suddenly the trench came alive as other British troops arrived on the scene. Guttural shouts were mixed with curses as they engaged in mortal combat.

Until he became aware of the fighting in the trench when he heard a shot, Smithers was still on cooking duty. He was in the middle of adding potatoes to the mixture and cooking them together.

The shells had stopped and the trench was quiet for a change, he noticed. A shot rang out and outside shouts disturbed the quiet that had started to reign. Smithers raced outside to see his mate, Hartley, surrounded by fully six German soldiers, who were edging closer as they advanced. He grabbed his rifle from its place at the side of his bunk and was instantly joined by the awakened Willcox.

They attacked the group from the rear and caught the fighting Huns in a trap between the two factions. The upshot of the action was when the Germans saw they were heavily outnumbered they surrendered to the British troops and were marched away to face eventual interment in a British prison camp.

"Will you look at that then," Smithers proclaimed to Willcox after the incident.

He was looking at the meal he had been cooking. The food had burned on the stove and

was curled over like dog's tail. The frying pan had blackened and was running into the bully beef. To his utter despair he turned the pan over and saw the hole in the bottom.

"Now we need a new frying pan, more expense. We'll just have to pool our money and buy a new one from company stores, that's what we will do, we'll just have to chip in and get another one."

"I ain't got no money," said Willcox, making a roll from a battered tobacco tin and putting it into his mouth. "I will have to owe you the money until next payday. You should've been more careful in the first place."

"Oh yeah, I should have put the stove out beforehand!" exclaimed Smithers. "You know what happened; I was busy fighting the Huns, you saw it, you were there as well as me, I even had to go back for my rifle, never mind the stove. You are to blame as well as me, Willcox, it was your supper I was cooking, so be fair."

Hartley's place on guard was taken by another soldier from the next dugout. He marched into the dugout to hear the last stages of the argument between the other two.

"Where's the supper?" he demanded of Smithers, then espied the damage to the frying pan. "What happened to the stove? Look at the hole in the pan, we'll have to get another one to replace it, more fucking expense, just on payday tomorrow as well. What happened to it?"

"He left it on the red hot stove," complained Willcox, "during the fracas with the Huns. It's a wonder the bloody place wasn't burnt down."

"It couldn't be helped," moaned Smithers. "I was otherwise engaged fighting the Germans, you *saw* me, I was one of the backup group that cornered the Huns. That must've been when it got burnt. It was a pure accident and nothing else."

The incident was soon forgotten and for a couple of hours there was peace.

The Germans who operated the guns must have heard of the capture of the raiding party because they started up their peppering of the British positions with the same ordinance.

They had to make do with a cold supper. It was cold outside and Hartley stood at the stove warming his hands. Slowly but surely the stove did its allotted duty and began to warm the dugout. Hartley felt his bones begin to heat up, and stepped back to his bunk nearby.

"Just the job," he announced, sitting on his bunk and easing over onto his back. "Those Hun soldiers were surrounding me, it was nearly curtains for me, I can tell you, mates. That big German with a skull and crossbones on his helmet was pointing his bayonet at my guts. The others were all around me, good job they never fired a shot otherwise I would be dead by now. They must've been saving their ammo and relying on cold steel to finish me off."

Smithers was heating the water to do the washing up. He had the drying up rag over his right shoulder and felt the water a few times, testing it for heat.

"I think it is my birthday," Hartley announced, gazing at the soil ceiling. "If it is the tenth, as I think it is, it *is* my birthday. I forgot my own birthday and I got no mail from my mother. She must've forgotten it too; she didn't send me a card or nothing. Fancy your own mother forgetting the day she gave birth to you." He turned around on the bunk. "Raining too, must mean something when it rains on your birthday. Probably bad luck when it rains on your birthday, which fits me to a tee."

"If it is, then many happy returns of the day," chimed the other two.

"What, no birthday present?" said Hartley, sucking at a cigarette end. "I told you no luck, not even a card from my own parents, and raining too. Roll on demob and a good job with real money."

"There's no work in Civvy Street. The politicians have cornered the market in money to pay for the war," said Willcox. "If there is a job to be had it will be for low wages and hard conditions. As usual it will be for the rich and not the poor. If you've got it then hide 'cause they will only take it away from you in the long run."

Smithers tipped the tepid water into a tin can and dipped the dirty plates into it. He positioned them on the shelf above the stove where they dripped down to the hot iron cover. With a sigh he dropped the piece of rag and sat on his bunk, lighting a roll of tobacco.

"Where you going on leave?" he enquired, watching the smoke rise.

"It's a dead cert you can't make it to home or Calais, so it will have to be somewhere in France, behind the lines somewhere, where the Judies are almost naked and wanting sex," Hartley replied.

"Here we go again," said Smithers, winking at the recumbent Willcox. "Beer, birds and the other, especially the other, that's my motto."

"When's this leave gonna be from?" questioned Smithers, looking at Hartley.

"Just after we risk our lives in trying to take the German trench, only this time we have to capture a couple of German officers into the bargain. That is all that is wanted of us," returned Hartley.

"*All*? That's enough," said Smithers. "If I remember correctly, in the last lot I not only risked my life, but on other occasions as well, fighting the Hun on his own doorstep and winning the fight into the bargain."

"Now you gotta do it all over again," said Hartley, with a wry grin, "only this time we gotta bring back a couple of German officers as well as other ranks."

"They want a lot for their little bit of leave," commented Willcox.

"A whole lot more," spat Smithers, "much too much for me to do."

"What you gonna do, go absent without leave?" asked Hartley. "There's a law against desertion."

"Others who have tried it have ended up against a wall to be shot," warned Willcox.

"That won't be me," said Smithers, "anyway, I have done my duty by crossing no-man's-land to the enemy trenches. They can't ask for anything more, at any time."

"Can't they? They pay you for your services and they want their money's worth, no matter how much they pay," returned Hartley.

"They can keep their five bob, stick it up their arse with my blessing," said Smithers.

"Me too," echoed Hartley, for once agreeing with his mate.

As the attack neared the start, a crowd of soldiers pressed hard against each other. The sweat of fear was imprinted on each brow as the hour approached. They each gripped an assortment of weapons to their chest, and the equipment creaked as they moved. In the half-light of early morning the eerie scene took on a ghostly shape as the light of day fell across each sweating man.

When the whistle sounded, one by one the mass of men hesitated on the first rung of the ladder, before daring to brave the test of the unknown. The lines of profusely perspiring men were suddenly active as the whistle shrilled that morning. The first of the sweating ranks topped the head of the ladder and stepped forwards into uncertainty. Almost as regular as clockwork the first line of the Tommies fell backwards into the trench nearly into the arms of the next line of waiting troops.

Their breath frosting the morning air, the two pals were in the rear of the bunch of men. Smithers carried his rifle on his thin shoulder, with the addition of a cross bandolier of ammunition. He was nervously biting his lip and a tic of worry edged his face. The two men never talked to each other as they waited for the line to ease. Hartley hitched his rifle higher up his shoulder and felt the outline of the magazine against his thigh. He sniffed and catching the eye of Smithers, gave a quick wink. The other caught the action and raised his eyes in disgust.

Smithers was the first to step onto the ladder and, hitching his bullet bandolier higher, achieved the second step before jerking it higher onto his shoulder. The machine guns chattered their message of death and loudly stitched a line of tracer bullets along the lip of a line of sandbags that graced the wall of the trench. He could feel the presence of Hartley, his greatcoat fanning the two bandoliers. Now he was feeling the heat of battle and saw other men fall to the mud with bullet wounds. Miraculously he survived the first onslaught as he dipped below the depth of the bullet storm. This he was familiar with, drawing on other things he had done in the face of danger and won through.

He felt rather than saw Hartley do as he was doing, and prostrated himself on the watery mud. He knew he was dodging the shower of bullets and wondered why he didn't cop one like the rest of the wounded. I must have a good guardian angel up there looking after me, he thought. A bullet chipped a hole in the brim of his steel helmet and dislodged it, the force of the impact nearly knocking him cross-eyed. He shook his head to clear it. He sensed Hartley was at his rear and was thankful he had managed to live through the initial stages.

Now the next move in the operation had to be initiated. Never mind what the British brass wanted in getting German prisoners, he was only interested in one thing, self-preservation, and nothing else mattered. The mud was clinging to his uniform as he swam forwards into the next shell hole, which contained three soldiers who filled it up to capacity.

Events were looking exceedingly gloomy as he carried on sliding under the metal curtain of bullets. He noted with satisfaction the amount of expended shell holes in the region and gratefully accepted their shelter from death with pleasure. He slid into a slimy hole and held the mud close to him, waiting for a few moments until daring to raise his head above the earth overfill. Through the slot provided by his steel helmet he was able to see the movements of his mate, Hartley.

"So they didn't get him!" He whooped and shouted above the noise of the battle. "Come on, Hart, come on, lad!"

Hartley could be seen slithering through the muck and grime, swimming towards the shell hole, inching his rifle with him and sliding it before him as he moved. He raised his head above the rain of bullets and caught sight of the steel helmet above the shell hole.

In Smithers' imagination he could see the look of delight on Hartley's face as he saw his salvation.

24

FREDA LOCKED THE FRONT door of her café bar and, grabbing the bass broom, started to sweep up. The place was a mess, she decided, after the birthday party a man had been celebrating the night before. He was a young recruit who had only been in the unit for a couple of weeks. The rest of the squad had grabbed him and given him a bump for every year of his young life, and made him drink a pint to go with each year as well. All together they paid for and consumed the better part of a barrel of ale and got gloriously plastered. Eventually they had to carry him back to the barracks and to his bunk.

She sweated in the heat of the room and the difficulty of her work-load. The sun was streaming around the corners of her draw blind and into the barroom. She made her way around the counter and drew off a bucket of cold water. As she was cleaning the main window she heard the door knocker bang.

The daily girl was at the door and Freda smiled in welcome as she let her enter. Without any to-do she strode across to the counter and started to get stuck in.

"I just saw Beryl," she said as she started to wash the glasses, "and that other prostitute, Louise. They've got a small room at Chalons-sur-Mer on the outskirts of town. Seems they got it for a song too. Half the rent they usually charge and furnished as well." She was rinsing up the glasses and lining them up on the counter to dry. "The only thing they had to buy was a bed and a couple of blankets," she continued. "That Louise must be lucky; the chance of getting a room in Calais and at a cheap rent is unheard of, especially in this day and age."

"Did they mention when they would be coming around?" enquired Freda, grabbing a tea towel with a big hole in the middle. "Louise and Beryl made a date with one of the boys and he was asking when Beryl would be here. Looks like he has the hots for her, I'm thinking."

The girl laughed as she clunked a glass onto the counter.

"That Beryl is a good-looking girl," she said. "I wouldn't blame a man for falling for her."

"Yes, but I'm only interested in her as an investment if she pulls in the customers and they spend their pay on my premises. The squaddies won't come into my barroom unless they have something to entice them, and the two ladies of easy virtue are the attraction. As I have said before, the only reason I have them here is because of the lads in khaki. I don't charge them anything as you know. The only thing I have is the lads' pay, so if the lads are happy with it then I'm happy, it's as simple as that."

Freda went out back to her little drawing room and lit the gas stove. She had a small joint of lamb in the oven and added a couple of potatoes to the dinner. It was a frugal meal and only meant for one. Her mother had always said the addition of green stuff such as a cabbage was the ideal way of rounding off the dinner. She had cut up the cabbage just before she started work in the bar.

While the meat was cooking she returned to the barroom and the young girl.

"You can open the front door and admit the first of our customers," she said, watching as he repeated what he had been doing for the last four months.

"Morning Freda," said Private Fred Chester as he stepped into the barroom. "I'll have the usual pint of mild ale," he said, and made for the table he had made his own.

Freda gave him a big wide smile and readily accepted the few coins he had shoved into her hand.

Today was the day she was opening a new barrel, and it stood in place behind the bar counter. The foam of the beer rose up and frothed over the end of the barrel. The mild beer emitted a heady smell, something with which she was familiar. It amounted to her day's takings and was the cheapest beer she sold. The record came on as the gramophone was switched on and the strains of 'La Vein Rose' wafted to the ceiling, joining the smoke of the cigarette that Private Fred Chester had lit.

Freda counted the coins into the tin she kept behind the counter. The few copper coins rattled in the tin every time she shook it. She liked the sound the coins made and wished the tin was full to the brim with money. She almost never had a note of any description, and had to examine the money for any foreign coins that a chancer had managed to slip in between the right currency. Only the night before a soldier had managed to pay for his beer with a foreign coin. In the heat of the moment and she had not noticed the difference between the small coins. The lads knew she had to pay for the beer herself and the wholesalers wouldn't accept any other currency but French. Still, she had to rely on the honesty of the army lads, but to make sure she examined each coin to see if it was acceptable.

The music was nearing its cut-off line and jumped as a crack went under the needle. She lifted up her stack of records and quickly selected another one. Some of the records were on the serious side, but she rejected them for the ones the soldiers liked. She took pot luck and dropped on one she thought she knew. As the strains of the

'National Anthem' rang through the building she quickly changed it
for another.

The sergeant major's orderly, Harry Ward, breathed on the glass and
held it up to the light. He saw a spot on the clear glass and polished
it off. The boss, his boss, the sergeant major, had a guest and did not
want him to see a dirty glass.

Ward selected another dirty glass, dipped it into the washing up
water and as he examined it saw the faint traces of red lipstick, and
knew the sergeant major had been entertaining a lady friend. Probably
the mousy-haired lady I saw entering the mess last night, he thought.
Usually female guests were frowned on by the rest of the club. One
had got through the net. Not my type, he thought, holding up the glass
after scrubbing the red mark from the rim, too much of a lady for me
and apt to be a bit bossy in her ways.

Ward emptied the water down the sink and watched the suds drain
away. He was more of an orderly batman and served the members
with their daily meals. After the job with the glasses he straightened
a white serviette and added a fork. He grabbed the utensil and, after
giving it a polish for luck, laid it in its place beside the rest of the
cutlery. He moved around the edge of the table, doing the same thing.
Next came the seats. He spat on his hand and rubbed a mark off the
back of a chair.

The room housed three round tables, three members to a table,
some nine in all, and when they came into the mess they all brought
their favourite drinks with them. Ward knew them by the bottles
they carried. There's so-and-so, he drinks plain water mixed with a
faint trace of salt; an odd taste, but to his liking, he would think as
he entered. There's what's his name, he drinks Scotch whisky, I know
'cause I had some when he left his bottle on the table one morning
after breakfast. The third one to come in was always a fat sergeant
called Bliss, who carried a bottle under his arm, which Ward knew

was wine, it also having also been tasted by the orderly after dinner one evening.

Ward kept the mess nice and clean, and never had any complaint regarding its cleanliness. It was better than risking his life like the other squaddies. They carried a gun and did the fighting for him. He wondered if he was a bit of a coward, hiding in the mess and not joining the rest of the mob. He only wondered for a bit then deleted it from his mind as the thought went away. They have their job to do and I've got mine. Admittedly, they have the most dangerous one, but that's how it goes, he thought.

He tried to look like a waiter as he held a towel over his arm and waited for the first of the evening to enter. It was the sergeant major, who sported a large moustache that twitched as he spoke.

"Good evening, Ward," he twitched. "What have we got this evening?"

"The usual Thursday evening fare, Sir; roast beef of old England and roast potatoes to go with it."

"Good, I'm as hungry as a hunter, bring it on." Ward had to carry the plateful of food from the mess kitchen outside to the tables. He had

managed to carry the big dinner plate in his hand to the table, balancing it. Several times he had burned his hand on hot plates and now he used the napkin to shield his flesh from the heat. Now he held the plate out sufficiently laden with hot food and laid it down on the nearest table. As he did so the next two NCOs entered the room and sat down at the farthest table.

They exchanged quick repartee with the sergeant major.

"What's for scoff tonight, Sarn't Major?"

Sergeant Major Willcox pulled a newspaper out of his pocket before answering.

"Roast beef and roast spuds," he said, flattening out the broadsheet and starting to read.

"How's the weather going, Jim? Looks like rain coming over," enquired the elder of the two men.

For a minute Willcox read the front page of the newspaper before answering him.

"Look at the politicians, all of them saying we must do more to finish the war with the Germans, and at the same time asking for less money to do it. I ask you, Bill, what right have they to expect me to do my job on less pay? I'm on rock bottom pay and can hardly afford to pay my mess bill, money is that tight."

The mess orderly listened to the discourse and thought of his own bad wages.

"If I didn't get the halfpenny or penny tip they usually leave under the plate I wouldn't be able survive," he muttered.

He rattled the three pennies in his side pocket and wished for more. If he made sixpence extra in a week he considered himself lucky. With his army pay he made seven and four pence last week, the most he had ever made. Still, there are others who survive on a lot less, he thought. I have a full belly with what I get in leftovers, and anything else I use I give to my girlfriend, Elsie, after that the cat gets the rest. That cat is getting fat on the scraps we give him.

He came out of his reverie as the last of the diners came into the dining hall.

A great big shell landed fifty yards from Smithers and peppered his helmet with stones and dirty water. Hartley had managed to make it to the shell hole and comparative safety. His gas mask had taken most of the shock and his backpack saved his back from the stones. Around the shell hole others copied his action and sheltered from the leaden rain.

Farther on, the barbed wire ran through the shell holes and vanished from sight where the holding posts had been blown up. For once the wire was free of its complement of dead bodies, and the absence stood out stark and real.

"We've got to get those prisoners, especially the officers," said

Hartley, snorting through his nose as he tried to get rid of a piece of mud that had got under his helmet. "That way we can get the leave they promised us."

"I know that," returned Smithers, daring to look over the parapet of the shell hole.

"That means we gotta get out of here and go and capture 'em," grated Hartley.

"I know that too."

"That means *now* and not later."

"It's still a bit dangerous, but if you lead on I'll follow you," sniffed Smithers from under his steel helmet.

Hartley gazed at the scene before him and tried to follow the shell pattern. He noticed it had a certain rhythm to the explosions and after a series of bursts it waited for a while as the shells were loaded into the gun before firing again. He was quick to see the importance of the change and seized on the difference as a way of quitting the shell hole for something better.

"When I go, you go," he said, dipping his head down low. "After the next one we go, remember that, after the next one we hop out and make for the next shell hole, get it?"

Smithers nodded under his helmet and pulled his rifle up to his chin and over his head.

"You sound like you know something. You must've been counting the bangs, Hart."

"Something like that, there's the next one to go," he said as a shell landed close by.

The rain of mud was followed by an interval before the next shell exploded farther up the field.

"*Now!*" he shouted, and leaped from the hole, followed closely by a scrambling Smithers.

Others who had noticed the interval between the shell shots did exactly as he did, taking the opportunity to change their shelter for another one. Sliding men criss-crossed each other's trails, all with the same purpose of heading for the German trench, and the end of their mission. Of course, they had to dodge the machine gun fire, and a lot of them shuddered to a halt as the leaden slugs met their mark on the slithering forms.

Soon the barbed wire loomed up before them and they wriggled underneath the rusty coils with ease. Although their backpacks somewhat hampered their movements they managed to worm their way around the barbed wire until free.

Smithers gazed up at a bright day, and freed his gas mask from snagging on the barbs. From his position past the wire he could just see the observation post of the Hun trench and the flash of field glasses as they were trained on the British attack. He turned his eyes on the form of Hartley who was ahead of him by several yards. He was making good headway as he wriggled past the second line of barbed wire and the start of the anti-personnel mines that dotted the line of enemy trenches. He watched the clouds scudding across the sky and a flight of birds that flew dark against the blue sky.

For an instant the image of his cat came to him chasing the birds from his home in England. As an afterthought, his mother came into his imagination, chasing the cat after the birds. A bullet pinged off his steel helmet and jerked him out of his daydream back to reality. It was good he did so, for just under his right elbow the shining steel nose of an anti-personnel mine was just where he was about to put it. He swallowed a large glob of sputum and changed the direction of his slide for another, slipping past the murderous weapon.

His mates were all around him, by the side of him, even ahead of him, surging forwards, making for the wall of sandbags that guarded the top of the German forward trench. There were upwards of half a company of men attacking the German positions, while the rest of the company lay fallen on the first half of the thrust forward.

Hartley's heart was beating like a hammer in his temple as he neared the Hun trench. He saw a movement in the fallen sacking of the sandbags and heard a bullet as it smacked into the mud before him. So they have me in their sights, he mused, gazing at the spot where the slug had vanished. He hid behind the trunk of a splintered tree and heard another bullet wang into the thin trunk with a soft thwack. So the Hun bastard has his measure and is content to throw lead at me without end.

Luck then kissed him with its fickle ways and it began to rain. He twisted around to see if Smithers was near, and shot at the figure firing at him. He had to clear the way to the trench, the only way open to him. With one click he shoved a slug in the breech and waited as the figure moved. The trigger moved under his pressure and he felt the rifle kick against his shoulder. For a few seconds he gazed at the fissure where the German was, and the shooting stopped

"Looks like I may have got the bastard," he muttered as Smithers slid up beside him.

"There're plenty more," growled Smithers into his earhole.

The two men wormed their way past the tree and up to the wall of sandbags. They were met by other members of the company who had accompanied them. As the swarms of soldiers clambered over the ramparts of the enemy trench, the cries of yelling Germans could be heard.

25

SEVERAL MEN WERE TRYING to clear a path through the wall of the trench by lobbing a few hand grenades over the sandbags to gain access to the German trench. They had succeeded in their goal with one of the grenades, and were now pouring into the hole.

The two friends shifted their position and squirmed to the ready-made hole, scrambling over the fallen sandbags to the trench behind.

Behind the ramparts all hell was breaking loose as both sides met, striving for victory. The bloodbath was horrendous and a lot of men were killed in the battle, but Smithers and Hartley managed to survive. They played a big part in capturing the officers they had been sent to capture, plus a crowd of other ranks that made up the giant haul of Hun prisoners.

When the two men finally got back across no-man's-land they met Corporal Gunn outside their dugout. He was beaming with pleasure about the operation and the amount of prisoners they had brought back, especially the high ranking officers they had captured.

"Report to my office later to collect the passes I have promised you," he said.

After they had done so, they were the proud owners of a pair of week-long passes, effective from the next day. The jubilant pair waved the passes in the face of Private Willcox.

"We got them at long last, the promised day has arrived, we start tomorrow and for a week we will do nothing but eat and drink, and give the ladies a right royal seeing too."

"Me too," enjoined the other man, "where are you going to get this treatment?"

Where indeed? Until now the thought of where they were going to enjoy these excesses had never come up in the conversation.

"Where are we going, Hart?" posed the curious Smithers. "And what we gonna do for money when we get there?"

Hartley thought hard for the answer and suddenly came up with it.

"We will sell something," he said after some serious thought.

"Sell what?" asked Smithers, after a pause. "What've we got to sell?"

Hartley picked his lip in thought and muttered in a low voice as he walked up and down.

"What've we got that's legally ours? Something that will pay for the night out and for the ladies as well."

They turned out their kit and were left with Hartley's silver St Christopher.

"That's all we've got of any value, so it will have to go," said Hartley firmly.

Smithers had to agree, and together they set out from the dugout armed with their rifles and the little silver St Christopher they hoped would pay for their leave.

After showing the pass to the redcaps several times they trooped up the sloping entry trench and were free for a week, but in reality until their money ran out.

The shining waters of the River Somme showed them the way forward and as the miles disappeared beneath their feet they came to a junction in the road and made a decision.

"I feel lucky," said Hartley, sitting down on a spur of grass that was left after a nearby shell had blasted the farmhouse that nestled in the corner of the garden.

They ate jam sandwiches they had brought with them and took a long pull at their water bottles.

"What do you mean?" questioned Smithers, lighting up a cigarette after eating his sandwich. "I suggest we turn right here and head for the river again."

"What makes you think we are heading for the river again, we ain't seen it for the past hour?" Smithers argued, letting out a long blast of cigarette smoke.

"I feel it," said Hartley, then a thought came to him. "I wonder if there are any vegetables left in the garden."

Someone had beaten them to it and found the vegetables before them. A tree had shed a few apples on the ground and, after pulling out the worms that had burrowed into them, they ate the rest of the fruit. After having another rest and another smoke they turned right into where Hartley had imagined the river was, and trooped up a small rise in the dirt road. They passed by a forest leading to another higher rise that had them blowing with the effort. By mutual consent they sat on the grass verge and drank a long draft out of their water bottles. As usual, Smithers had lit up and was blowing the smoke into a cool wind that had followed them up the hill.

"How long do we have to do this?" he said. "You said you feel lucky and will reach the river before long. Seems to me we've been walking for hours and I've got a hole in my sock an' I can feel it."

"Stop bitching, I've got the same as you. I said we will see the river when we get to the top of this hill, it's a well known fact what goes up must come down, which means the river must be down the hill in the valley below."

Hartley was right in his summation and as they crested the rise the river was glinting in the sunlight.

"There you are; it's right before your very eyes," said Hartley triumphantly.

More to the point, there was a small town nestling in the hook of the river, and with hoops of delight they headed for the town and the proposed delights that might lie there. Within half an hour at every turn they were viewing the small war-torn town and the blasted streets. They were just turning a corner when the silvery tinkle of a piano met their eager ears.

"Where there's music there's beer and where there is beer there are birds. We've landed, Smithy boy, and copped the lot," said a delighted Hartley.

They turned into the main square of the town and followed the sound of music. As they got nearer it grew louder until they halted at a shell-damaged building at the edge of the square. The piano music was accompanied by the high pitched laugh of a female.

With a wide beam of pleasure on his face, Smithers entered the building, followed by Hartley. As they crossed the threshold, a large pall of cigarette smoke hung in the air and a wall of silence descended on the large room. One of the girls in the corner of the room stopped in mid-laugh, and gazed at the two Tommies. Even the man playing the piano stopped at the interruption.

Hartley marched up to the counter and, turning, took in all that was happening with a quick glance. The girls changed the expressions on their faces as the pianist pinged out 'Rule Britannia'. Now they were all smiles as they sensed that something was about to change for the better and lift their fortunes a little bit higher.

Hartley fingered the St Christopher in his breast pocket as he spoke to the woman behind the bar.

"Would you be interested in buying a St Christopher? It's solid silver and worth a lot of money."

The woman replied in excellent English and held out her hand for the keepsake.

"Let's have a look at it first."

Hartley dropped the St Christopher onto the counter and waited as she picked it up. Without any preamble she gazed at it and spoke.

"I'll give you two francs for it."

Hartley, who was expecting five, had to make up his mind on the spur of the moment then nodded at her offer. The two drinks cost twenty centimes and he nodded at the girls who had quickly finished their drinks.

Smithers took the flat top off his beer with his dry tongue and eyed the bigger-breasted girl with a quick leer.

"Would you girls like a drink?" he offered as the pianist changed the tune.

Would they not? The girls pouted prettily and nodded in unison. Smithers put the drinks on the table and sat down beside the three girls. Hartley joined the others and leaned over to whisper in Smithers' ear.

"Cheese it. We've only got enough money for one drink. It will only be one for you and one for me, mate, one of them will have to get their own."

One of the girls made it easier for them by jumping up and sitting near the piano player. That cuts the odds down a little bit, breathed Hartley as he carried the drinks over to the girls' table. They all smoked, so they had to make four cigarettes out of Smithers' tin of tobacco.

"Make 'em a bit thinner," said Smithers. "That one you just made, you can get two out of it."

"Make 'em last," grimaced Hartley, gently sipping his beer.

"Good job they are sticking to the cheap beer," whispered Smithers back at him.

One thing about Smithers was the ability he had to talk, and when he found something to talk about he was in his element.

"I live on a farm in my country. We have a few chickens and a couple of ducks on the stream at the bottom of the garden. We live on the vegetables from our garden, all fresh and picked every day by my mother. We also have a dog and a cat, which was alive at the time of asking. The cat is black and white and enters by the cat flap we cut in the front door. In one letter I got from my mum, the dog had been poorly and had a bad cough. She feared for him and he nearly pegged out one morning. I barely remember him 'cause he was a lot younger when I left England for the war."

He came to an end with a gasp of air. The girls were staggered, mainly because he had not given them a chance to chip in, but really because his English was too fast for them to understand. They smiled at him and talked among themselves in French. Hartley took the opportunity to break into the conversation with a question of his own.

"Do you Mademoiselles live around here?"

After the session with Smithers the two girls talked more slowly and managed to make themselves understood.

"I live two kilometres from this place. I live in a small 'ouse with my father and mother. We are living in a shell-hit 'ouse and we 'ave to live on what we earn from prostitution. There is no work for us, so we come in 'ere 'oping to meet a man to get married."

Hartley smiled at the girl.

"You can see what *we* are. We are back from the trenches after fighting the Huns. We only get poor pay and we are both privates."

The other girl tried to make herself understood.

"I saw you sell your keepsake to the bartender. I am sorry about your St Christopher, can I buy you a beer, Monsieur?"

Hartley was so taken aback by this offer that he was struck dumb for a minute and could only look at his mate with wonder. He shook his head.

"Perhaps later. What's your name, darling, mine's Hartley, just call me Hart."

"Corinne," said the girl. "We both live in a shell-torn street. In case you want to know, her name's Angelique."

"I'm Smithers, you'll always remember me by my long hair. The corporal is always telling me to get it off and I always forget to get it cut."

"You said you were a prostitute?" questioned Hartley. "I could use you, but I have only got a franc left."

She pursed her lips and shrugged her shoulders.

"C'est la guerre, Monsieur."

"What's that mean, Corinne?"

"Hard luck, come back later when you *do* 'ave money, Hart. I can't pay my way with nothing."

"I realise you have to earn your keep, but I have nothing but my meagre pay, so I say, forget it," returned Hartley, sipping his drink and looking at Smithers with a meaningful look.

Smithers then continued with his spiel, and addressed the other girl.

"Look, if I do use your services if you agree, can't I do it and pay you later, like on the never-never we have back home?"

The two girls argued in French and, with a multitude of finger and hand waving, held some sort of conversation. They were speaking so quickly that the boys were baffled by the heat of the argument. Corinne translated into English what they were saying.

"She said rather than waiting 'ere we should accept your offer and give you what you want. We only 'ave a little money, like you; we only get our money to live on by being prostitutes. We 'ave a room where we do it. This 'as to be paid for by us to a man who lets us use it - you understand what I am saying?"

She was hard put to make them understand her meaning and stumbled over the words with difficulty. Eagerly they nodded their heads and gulped their drinks faster. The girls started to talk in their native tongue, laced with more finger waving and gesticulations.

"Looks like we've struck lucky," Hartley whispered in Smithers' ear. "They might do it for free, like you said, Smithy, or rather on the never-never like you offered."

Smithers laughed at the thought.

"First time I ever offered a pro on the book. It's laughable."

26

THE NAKED BODY OF the girl looked brown against the white sheet of the bed. She was lithe and thin, and except for the narrow scar of brown tissue that marred it, her skin was pretty in a sort of way.

Smithers tried to avoid the scar and let his hand miss it as he kneaded her flesh.

"What's the scar?" he enquired, kissing her on the lips and holding her tight with his legs wrapped around her thin frame.

"Another man; he try to 'ave sex. I try to get my money first. He attack me after he got it. I got his coat to get to 'is money. He pulled a knife and slashed me with it."

"I won't do that to you, ducks," Smithers said as he entered her. "I always pay my debts," he said, "especially to you girls on the game. We all have to live, so I say let live and die happy."

The girl did her best in supplying him with sex and, when he was satisfied, she smiled at him.

"I only 'ope the Monsieur is 'appy and will return with the money he owes me."

Smithers winked at her, climbed into his uniform and fastened the belt.

"You can be sure that I will get the money to you even if I have to borrow or steal it, that's the way I am, it's a debt of honour that I mean to repay."

He passed his mate, Hartley, with the other girl and winked at him as they entered the room.

Smithers was drinking a small glass of weak beer as Hartley entered the beer hall. There was a great big smile across his face as he sat down on the chair opposite his mate.

"No need to ask you if you enjoyed it, it's written all over your face. Was she good though," asked a grinning Smithers, handing him a small glass of beer.

Later on the two girls returned to the beer hall, wearing huge grins and laughing together. They gossiped with each other, but the pianist and the other girl were missing.

"Good, she was excellent," replied Hartley. "The best for many a long while."

Within a few minutes the piano man came back and very soon the tune of 'Keep the Home Fires Burning' was dancing on the cigarette clouds. Men came and went, the majority of the population being of rough appearance and using their valuable money sparingly. They were mostly old country people, with just a smattering of French soldiers wearing the French uniform. They husbanded their money carefully and only showed it when it was exchanged for a drink.

The hours went by and it got dark. The pals knew they had to return to the dugout and danger. They trooped out, knowing they had to face the long walk home, or sleep in the woods surrounding the town. The night was cold and threatened rain, so they buttoned up their overcoats and set out.

It was well past midnight when Smithers and Hartley finally arrived at the dugout. When they got there they flopped out on their bunks and slept the sleep of the exhausted.

Willcox was away and they had the dugout to themselves, so the only thing they had to contend with was the occasional shell that flew overhead and landed farther back on the trench complement.

"Did you enjoy last night, Hart?" was the first thing Smithers had to say as he woke up. "That one of mine had a scar on her neck where somebody had slashed her with a knife, but apart from that I enjoyed the night."

"So did I," confessed Hartley. "She had a lovely body when I stripped her off, like a model I once knew. I had a stand all night long, but she knew her onions when she saw me, and more than satisfied me."

"We owe them four francs, two for me and two for you, but it was worth it." Smithers licked his lips as he recalled the moment of sexual lust and in his mind's eye saw again the naked body of the prostitute. "Forgetting the scar," he uttered quietly, "I could do it again with her, it's been so long I barely remember when I had it before. Yes, sir, I could do with her again at this very moment," he repeated quietly.

Hartley finally got up and put on his boots. He was just going to tie up his laces when a shout outside brought him to the sacking door. He looked out just as an enemy plane shot over the British trench and dropped a bomb on a group of soldiers, killing two of them and seriously injuring six.

The two men ran to aid the stricken and helped carry the stretcher away to the ambulance. Later on they learned the lone aircraft was shot down by anti-aircraft fire from a machine gun aimed at the German. The pilot was killed as the aircraft crashed to the ground, enveloping flames swallowing the plane and burning it to a cinder.

On the second day of their leave the two pals again left the trench, only this time they borrowed a big chunk of bully beef from the next dugout and two francs to pay for one night's entertainment with the ladies of the night.

"It's to pay for last night's frolic with the ladies," Smithers said as he pocketed the notes. "Best to pay them something of what we owe; they can have a franc each as one payment and another when we get it."

"You never know what they will do in the future, we might have another like last night on account."

He roared with laughter and stepped out, making for the town by the river and another beer. This time a couple of lorries were travelling their way and they managed to hitch a lift. They rattled on the old vehicle that had had its last days at the front and was falling to bits. They watched as a bit of the tailboard parted company from its hinges and fell into the road with a clunk.

The lorry left them at the edge of town and, hitching their rifles higher on their shoulders, they set forth down the main street and into the square. The building was quiet as somewhere close by a bell tolled the time of day. They counted the time as eleven o'clock and rattled the front door. The house was silent and deserted, and the building creaked as a wind hit the woodwork.

"They can't be up yet," said Smithers, trying the lock. "P'raps we are too early for them."

The two men sat on a shell-damaged house wall and ate their rations.

"You know we ain't got no money to buy beer," pointed out Smithers as he paraded the two franc notes before his friend's eyes. "I vote we only give them one franc note to share with each other, that way we can get a couple of beers at the same time, what say you, Hart?"

Hartley was swallowing a bit of the bully beef and just nodded.

"Good idea, Smithy." He suddenly remembered the few sous remaining in his trouser pocket. "We might get a small loaf of bread to help this bully down, with these coins."

The two girls wandered into the area of his sight. They were coming from the same place where they had all been the night before, only this time they were accompanied by a dark man who looked suspiciously at the pair sitting on the wall. The two pals returned the look and nodded as the two girls neared.

"Hello, girls," said Hartley, waving at them, "how are you this morning?"

"How early you are, we did not get up till ten," one said, looking at them.

"We get up with the lark every morning, the corporal sees to it we are out of bed before six," replied Smithers, treating the dark man to a scowl.

Just as he was speaking the front doors of the bar squeaked as they opened to admit the two girls. They both pushed the doors open and held them for the men to enter.

"You're all early this morning," repeated the woman behind the bar. "We don't keep army time here; we don't go to bed until after one in the morning."

"As it is," the one known as Corinne said with a wide yawn, "we are early this morning. We don't usually wake until well past midday."

She turned to the dark man as if confirming it. Smithers plonked the franc note onto the counter and ordered two beers. He gave the other note to the girls with a nod.

"This is your first payment. The rest will come when we get our pay. It might take a few weeks, but you can be sure of getting it."

The girls gave a laugh of surprise when they saw the money.

"Well, it's good to see such 'onesty," said an astounded Corinne. "To tell you the truth, we didn't expect to see you again. Most men treat us something bad, but we see it as a service and expect our clients to pay for the pleasure. Thank you, it is a treat to know you two men."

"There you are," said Smithers, carrying the beers over to the table and sitting down. "Nice ladies for whores, they are anybody's, but nice girls all the same."

Hartley was rummaging around in his knapsack and brought
to light a picture album with a black and white photograph of his
mother.

"I always have it in there, it's something I always carry," he explained.
"I had one of my father, but it got lost in the past movements, I'm
thinking of getting one of him-"

He was interrupted by Smithers grabbing the album and examining the frame.

"This is silver!" he exclaimed, holding the frame and eyeing it with
enthusiasm. "I thought you said you ain't got nuffink of any value, we
could get a lot for this, might get roaring pissed with the money."

Hartley grabbed the frame back from him.

"This is my mother's picture in the frame. It's the only one I've got
of her and I ain't gonna get rid of it," he said angrily.

"Well, that's it then," said Smithers in a quiet vioce. "After these
drinks go we ain't got no more money to pay for any more, so we
might as well pack it in and go back to camp for all the good we are
doing. We ain't got no more money for no more beer."

Hartley showed some signs of relenting.

"Do you think it's valuable? I could take out the picture and keep it
in my pocket. It would be just as safe in there."

"Of course it would be, safe as houses. If you are serious we could
find a shop that deals in silver like the St Christopher you had – here,
you might sell it to her behind the bar!"

"And get a pittance for it like the last time. The St Christopher was
worth double she gave," exploded Hartley, cuddling the picture to his
chest. "She'd give me nothing like its true worth, probably want it for
a song or a couple of drinks."

"Where're we going to sell it then?"

"How the hell would I know? We might find a jewellers or something in this town."

"We don't speak no French to bargain with the shop. We might get cheated out of the money if they see you don't understand the language," said Smithers firmly.

"We've got to risk that," returned Hartley, slipping the picture out of the frame and putting it into his breast pocket.

For a moment Smithers was silent and just sipped his drink. Hartley fingered the silver frame with his other hand stroking his upper lip. He reached for his glass of beer and drained it to the dregs.

"We gonna do it?" asked Smithers softly, looking at the girls, who were chatting quietly.

"Looks like it," replied Hartley as he slipped the frame into his jacket pocket and patted it.

27

Outside they walked slowly, eyeing the buildings of the square for a sign of anywhere they could sell the frame. In the centre of the town they passed half a dozen businesses, but no jewellers.

They stopped to sit on a heap of shell-blasted bricks and finish off the bully beef. They drunk the water in their water bottles and eyed the few stragglers who passed them with hardly a glance.

"We're not getting nowhere sitting here," said Hartley, putting his bottle in place at his side.

"Where're we going to sell the frame then?" asked Smithers, tipping his cap back on his forehead.

"Look for something I suppose, some shop, like I said."

"I've been looking at every shop I see, there just ain't no shop that sells rings and things."

"Keep looking, like I said before," said Hartley.

Smithers kicked a brick in his way and stood up.

"This place is just a ruin. We've been looking for an hour and we ain't no nearer to selling it to anyone for any price. We should've sold it to the bar woman while we had the chance."

They continued to walk and eye the damage to the town. The few people around included a French soldier who walked with the aid of a stick. He hobbled forwards, barged into the two and apologised in broken English.

"You up line at Somme?" he asked with a little salute. "I just come out 'ospital, got shell splinters in leg, much pain, Monsieur."

They regarded him with sympathy and gave him the small square of bully beef they were saving for later.

"There you are, mate," Smithers said with a smile. "Hope you enjoy it, it's the last we have, so eat slowly."

The soldier took the meat and chewed it with delicate movements of his jaws, and as they watched he swallowed it.

"I 'ave wife back, Paris, she do not like me in army, you like to see picture of my wife,

Louise?"

They exchanged photos; one of his wife and one of Hartley's mother. He produced the folded up photo and the silver frame, now separate. The French soldier glanced at the frame and his photo fitted it exactly.

"I'm trying to sell it," Hartley told the soldier, and when the Frenchman quoted a figure he readily accepted it.

Smithers was delighted, and said so.

"How much did you get?" he asked.

"Twelve francs," replied Hartley, stuffing the notes into his pocket.

"*Twelve* francs, wee, we're rich!" yelled Smithers.

The people passing them, startled, eyed them as they started forwards to the barroom.

"I've never had so much money, how much is that in English money?"

"Don't ask me, I ain't no froggie, all I know is we sold the frame," said Hartley, cock-a-hoop.

Back in the barroom they ordered a couple of pints and sat behind the two girls. Corinne winked at them and waved as they arrived. The other girl, Angelique, also waved and greeted them in French.

The man playing the piano arrived and straight away started to play. After a few drinks Smithers started to sing 'Nellie Dean' and as he did, the pianist followed him with the melody. Hartley tried to sing as well, but gave up after a few bars. He looked at Smithers as he reached the high notes with no difficulty. The rest of the drinkers clapped as he came to the end of the song.

"I didn't know you could sing so well," said Hartley, quaffing his pint.

"There'a lot you don't know about me. For a start, I had my own business in Blighty."

"What kind of business?"

"Towards the end, before I joined the army, I had a profitable green grocery round."

"Did you make it pay?"

"I did until others decided to undercut my prices with the same idea."

"Hard luck, there's always others doing that."

"I almost started in on bread delivery, but when I saw others doing it too, I packed it all in."

"That when you joined the army?"

"About the same time, the work situation was getting as grim as others told me."

Hartley drew in a big breath.

"I was doing the same line, but not so well. I was just thinking of starting my own business, but the war came along and stopped me doing it."

The conversation lagged as Smithers downed his drink and began to make a cigarette. Hartley watched him as he licked the gum and rolled it into a tight roll. He offered it to Hartley and made another one. Others passing by caused a current of air that whirled the tobacco cloud with their passage. Hartley, with the comfort of the money in his pocket, got up and replenished the drinks.

The piano player started on another tune and very soon the strains of 'There's An Old Mill by the Stream', rang out. This prompted Smithers to lapse into the song with a rendering of his own. This time his voice was joined by others. Even the two girls joined in with the melody.

The two men were hard pushed to walk the distance back to their dugout. They both had an overload of beer, and the weak moonlight just managed to guide them on the road.

"No chance of a lift tonight," said Hartley, hawking up a big throat full of sputum and spitting it out.

Smithers sat on a milestone and tried to read it upside down.

"W-ass it say, I can't read the f-fucking thing, it's all Greek to me?"

"You're reading it upside down and it's French anyway, not Greek."

"Well, French then, they're both double Dutch to me."

Smithers laughed to himself.

"I bet that bastard Gunn is tucked up nice and warm in his little beddy byes. I hope he has nasty dreams an' all that."

"Don't mention 'im, we've got enough bad luck without 'im."

"It was bad luck when he got corporal over me, I hate his guts," blew Smithers as he got up to go.

The two soldiers heaved themselves from the cold seat and started up the road to their warm beds. They were drifting over the roadway when they were pinpointed by a dim light on the road. The light drew nearer and they were just going to flag it down when it turned into a side road. The dim light was extinguished by a group of tall trees, and faded away.

"I thought we might be lucky and get a lift," said Hartley, tramping forwards "This damned haversack is rubbing my arms raw with its movement, be glad to get it off my back tonight."

Smithers cursed as he kicked a large stone aside.

"Talk about your knapsack, what about my feet? These boots are hurting terrible, I bet I've got a big blister on my heel when we get there," moaned Smithers. "Before long I'll have to take it off and have a rest."

"Yeah, but stick it for a while," said Hartley, heaving his rifle up on his back. "At least we get to sleep in tomorrow, that's one thing we've got to look forward to."

The moon lit their way forwards as they struggled along the road, Hartley with his back trouble and the other limping along the road with his feet trouble.

A couple of hours later they were entering the first of the trenches to the tune of the star shells that illuminated the sky with their light, and the accompanying thuds of the shells as they exploded in the first trench.

The alcohol had worn off and the burn of the different wounds was becoming unbearable. The last two hundred yards were an effort and they arrived at the dugout in a lot of pain.

———————————

They decided to have a day off from walking, and when they awoke the following day they examined the previous night's damage. Smithers had reddened blisters on his heel as well as his big toe. Hartley just had red marks on his back caused by the large pack.

Smithers sat on his bunk and bathed his feet in cold water, adding a little drop of Vaseline to the liquid for luck as he dipped his toes in it.

"Aah!" he cried as the cool water touched his skin. "That's better; I can feel the pain easing." He wrapped a rag around his heel and secured it by tying it around his big toe. "I never thought I would make it last night!" he exclaimed, trying his foot by leaning on it and touching the floor. "My feet must be getting soft, not like they were when we were square marching. They were hard and firm, not like now - soft and flabby."

He tried his boot and donned it tenderly after winding the puttee around his leg and tucking it in. After he allowed his weight to settle on his foot he stamped it softly on the oilcloth.

A crash sounded outside and brought them to the sacking door. Willcox joined them outside as the cause of the crash was revealed. They heard, rather than saw, a dark shape through the optical viewer and immediately thought it was a foray from the enemy. On further examination it seemed to be a giant metal box that was moving around the ground of no-man's-land, making a deafening roar.

"What on earth is it?" asked Smithers, stepping back to let Hartley see.

"It is some giant metal box on rollers with machine guns poking out through the sides."

The metal monster roared and puffed, shooting out great globs of smoke from its tail. It was clad all over with huge rivets that dotted its iron casing, and was shooting the guns from its metal sides, the noise echoing through the countryside with the rattle of the machine guns that were directed at the Hun trenches in the mist of the morning.

"At least it's one of ours," marvelled Hartley, looking at the metal monster. "It is shooting at the German side and causing an uproar."

Willcox took the viewer over and gave an accurate description of the vehicle.

"It's like a tank thing on caterpillar tracks. It has four machine guns, two on either side, and they are blazing away at the enemy side, so they must be on our side."

He watched the metal tank dip down on the shell-blown contours of the mud, and it easily crossed the shell holes with one motion. First it vanished then reappeared, crossing the hole and topping the disturbance with one easy movement, then reappeared once more nearer the enemy defences.

"Well, I'll be..." said Hartley as he watched it dive into another shell hole. "It must be some sort of secret weapon we have invented. I bet it disturbed the Germans when they saw it, frightening too."

"This must be the turning point of the war," declared Willcox. "All we need is a dozen of these machines and the Huns will run away for half a mile. I'm glad it has been invented by us and is on our side."

Others were trying for the optical viewer and edging the three aside, wanting to see the phenomena for themselves. The tank was near the Hun trenches and still pouring machine gun fire at them.

Very soon he three mates were pushed to the rear of the group and decided they had seen enough. Smithers hobbled to the door of the dugout and threw himself onto his bunk.

"Did you ever see such a sight?" he said, lighting up a thin cigarette. "I thought I must be seeing things. Bet them Germans nearly shit themselves when they first saw it."

"Better than lying out in no-man's-land waiting for the bullets to get you," said Hartley, from his bed.

"All that steel around you, it must be as safe as houses," said Smithers with a cough.

A huge shell exploded on the area near the tank and the metal monster withdrew to a safer distance. The man looking through the viewer saw the explosion that blew one of the tracks off the tank.

Later on as it grew dark, many men crossed into no-man's-land and sweated to get the tank back onto the tracks and move it beyond the reach and firepower of the Huns. The three men watched the enormous vehicle pull the tank onto its plates. Several men tied the vehicle to its trailer with wire ropes and covered it with canvas covers.

"So much for the tank," declared Hartley. "I thought it would be the saving of thousands of lives, but one lucky shell dislodges the track and it's kaput."

"They will take it back and make it better, make it safer with more armour, so it will resist the shell fire," declared Willcox from the comfort of his bunk. "Mark my words, they *will* improve it. This may be the start of something new in warfare. It might be the salvation of the human race, preventing it from killing by confrontation as now - it might even save it from self-destruction.

"You've got to be joking," said Smithers, "there'll always be wars. We were raised in wars and we will die in wars, that's how it is in this world, more's the pity."

The sacking parted to reveal Corporal Gunn with a big smile on his face.

"Seen that abortion on its trailer? One shot from the Germans and it falls apart. You can't beat men to fight a war, and that has been the favourite way for hundreds of years."

All too soon their leave came to an end and they were back on duty once more.

It was five o'clock in the morning when Gunn breezed into their dugout and shouted attention.

"All right, all of you, leave's over now, it is time to get down to some serious business of soldiering." He marched up and down on the oil-cloth, leaving muddy boot marks on the polished surface. He glared into each face with a scowl. "Look to your front," he ordered, "this dugout is a disgrace, clean it up immediately."

He walked along looking up into each face, his features barely two inches from the other's nose. In turn each man had to go through the ordeal, breath intermingling with breath, suffering the outburst with forbearance.

"I ask you," Gunn went on, "look around you and see the work that's needed. Your bunks are a disgrace and so are your blankets. They should be folded up neat and square at the head of your beds." He trailed his swagger stick and poked it at the lump of blankets gracing the mattress head. "I ask you, is that right and fair in my judgement? Are you being reasonable with me?" He strode from man to man, glaring into his face with the spit of wrath showering onto the other's skin. "It makes me wonder if I am getting through to you three men.

If I am, I will expect some improvement. If not, I will make you jump like you have never jumped before. That is not a threat, it's a promise, a promise of my temper exceeding yours and making you do as I tell you. Now hear this, clean this dugout out top class within the next day or two, and with it your show of kit must be top whack with every bit of equipment in good condition. That means this dugout must be polished from top to bottom, and I mean from top to bottom. I will be around in the morning to inspect it, I can assure you, now - dismiss." He exited through the sacking door with a loud, "Humph!"

As he went, Smithers gave vent to his feelings with a loud fart.

"I was dying to do that," he said, "anyway, it says what I think of Corporal Gunn; he's not worth a wet fart."

"Yeah, why don't you tell 'im then?" commented Willcox, collapsing on his bunk with a

huge sigh.

"I'm not about to do that, now am I?" said Smithers, sitting on his bed and making a cigarette. "He'll have me shot or something like that for disrespect."

Hartley looked down at the oilcloth floor.

"Look at his footmarks, we've got to clean those off as well. I wish he would scrape the mud off his boots before he comes in."

"That's another thing I wouldn't say," said Willcox, stretching," reminding him to clean his boots off before coming into the dugout. He'll have a fit if you do."

"Don't worry about that, Wilco. I have too much respect for my liberty to go against Corporal Gunn, he'll make it hot for me if I do," commented Hartley.

28

Corporal Gunn was leading his squad of men on a scouting expedition beyond the River Somme and ducked down behind a bush when heard other voices. His squad of five men copied his example and sank into the leaves and fibres of the twisting bushes.

Gunn pushed his rifle ahead of him and gently clicked a round into the breech with hardly a sound. He breathed in with soft breaths, hoping the sound hadn't been overheard. He watched the pot-shaped helmets of the Germans appear behind an outcrop of small plants.

A light rain ran down the black helmets and soaked the field uniforms of the Huns. They could not have been expecting any trouble because their rifles were pointing downwards, dripping rain.

Gunn hugged the ground and tried to keep his gun dry. The other men just behind him were concealed too, hiding their steel helmets from view behind the enveloping leaves that completely concealed them from the passing Huns.

The squad was about five miles from the British lines, under orders to do nothing to hide their real intention of finding the main source of petrol for their lorries and cars. Little by little they let the other Hun troops go by and as they followed them with their eyes, saw the last man vanish into the thick wood. Gunn gathered his squad around him.

"Where's that map, Brophy?" he whispered.

A big man stepped forwards and, unbuttoning a pocket, produced a pencilled map. He stood in the centre of the men and outlined the plan that showed a group of low cast buildings with a cross indicating where the petrol was stored.

"Here's us," he said softly, "here is the petrol, this cross. It's about three miles from here, so we have a bit of hiking to do. I couldn't show you before 'cause it is hush-hush."

"Couldn't we have got it by force with the rest of the company?"

"What, and give them a warning we are coming? Use your sense, man," Gunn exploded quietly.

To allow the Huns time to put some distance between them they took a different route through the wood and presently found themselves at the edge of it looking out from a thick gorse bush. Several pairs of eyes gazed at a narrow dirt track that seemed to go to a farm one way then into more track the other.

"We'll take the one away from the farmyard," hissed Gunn, stepping onto the track and hitching up his ammunition belt before leading the way forward.

The small band of men filed out onto the dirt track and followed Gunn. He pinpointed the farm and the track running away from it and, looking at the map, followed the route with his mind's eye, noting all the directions that pointed to the proposed petrol dump.

The rain slackened off and a watery sun bathed the atmosphere with its feeble rays. They watched for German troops at the small intersection and, at Gunn's direction, turned left. The track got a little firmer as they marched from the farm, and the puddles of water were more spaced out. They slung their rifles on their shoulders and as the rain stopped filed along the road together.

The time went by and every time they came to a crossroads they looked carefully for any sign of enemy soldiers. They met no one. The countryside was deserted of any other person and any buildings were either shell-torn or empty. A mile ahead a group of huts was beginning to emerge on the skyline, and as the day waned and fell into gloom a couple of lights indicated it was their destination.

Gunn formed a tight circle.

"This is it, all we have to do is set the dump alight. Just roll over a couple of petrol drums and loosen the corks. We have got to go past the barbed wire fence and anyone we meet we kill, the rest is up to us. We start the blaze and get away before they know what's hit them, get it?"

They nodded and separated.

Lance Corporal Derek Cobden spun the pliers around his thumb and cut an imaginary strand of barbed wire. He was the next assistant to Corporal Gunn and, after him, was the next in command. He was not a stickler for authority like Gunn, and treated his mates as his equal. He had a lone stripe on his arm, but did not attract any attention to it like the full corporal. He always stood near the squad of troops rather than away from it. He was only newly promoted, but he was a NCO, and the lads knew it.

Gunn had sensed this state of affairs and did not fully let him into his confidence about everything. He only treated him as a lance corporal with two feet in both camps.

As they waited for nightfall at the edge of the petrol dump, Gunn was conscious of being completely alone; a direct result of his observance to duty.

"Wait for it," he hissed to the lance corporal as he stepped forwards to the wire. "Watch for the sentry, he might see you. Wait until it's dark."

A watery moon washed through thin clouds and every time it did so, a sequence of events opened up. The clouds hid the moon then were submerged - first the moon then the clouds. On and off they went until a particularly dense cloud blotted the moon out all together and darkened the atmosphere.

"*Now*," snarled Gunn, his whisper coming on the slight breeze and hissing into their ears.

He stepped into the shadows, quickly followed by Cobden, who grabbed the barbed wire and cut it with one snip of the pliers. The quietness held and matched their combined breathing. They stopped as Gunn stepped through the barbed wire gap, listening. They stooped down low, hugging the shadows provided by a huge pile of iron drums.

The moon passed into shadow and they changed positions nearer to the big petrol dump. With Cobden in front they snaked through the first line of drums and waited there, ever watchful. The sentry was absent. They walked around the drums on the other side. The drums were heavy and on their side, piled on top of each other.

With outdrawn breaths pumping in the moonlight they heaved the nearest drum on its side, every so often stopping, listening for any alien sound. If the sentry was around he was making no sound as they succeeded in righting the petrol drum. One by one they tried to unscrew the metal bung, but it was beyond them.

Gunn produced his bayonet and held it over the drum edge, listening. It was so quiet, not even the sentry stirred. Gunn hit the bayonet with the flat of his hand - nothing. He took off his steel helmet and gave it a hard tap. The bayonet sank into the tin with hardly a sound. The acrid smell of petrol was all around them as it wafted up from the drum. With heaving chests they fought to tip the drum on its side, but found it too heavy. Gunn stood back from the drum as it evaded their efforts. He dug the bayonet into the hard earth, placed the steel helmet under the fulcrum of the lever and jumped on it. The drum tilted and poured several gallons of petrol onto the ground, covering their boots with the gas.

"That's got it, out you go now," Gunn loudly whispered to the men.

As they hared for the fence, he dropped a lit match onto the pool of petrol. As the burning petrol whooshed upwards, a shout rent the air as the sentry realised what was happening. Gunn was just wriggling through the fence when three sentries showed up.

A right royal battle ensued between the opposing forces as they faced each other with bayonets bared. Shadows of the fighting men were cast on the bushes where they whirled in a dance of death by the light of the burning petrol dump.

A tremendous explosion had blazing petrol drums flying through the air then the rest of the pile caught fire and rained down on the sentries inside the wire. For a few seconds the flames leapt higher then the main stack of petrol drums added to the holocaust by going up with one huge blast. This big explosion had the effect of driving the fighting soldiers apart, and Gunn's men dived into the bushes one after the other.

The flames lit up the countryside and as they scattered for cover, the blaze illuminated the forest around them. As they ran their shadows leapt ahead of them, dancing in the night like nightmarish figures enhanced by the light of the distant fire.

Gunn, out of breath, stopped at a large oak tree and gasped out an order to the others. The woods had closed in around them and the distant flames were now just a flash in the sky.

29

LANCE CORPORAL COBDEN DID a body count and found one man missing.

"It's Private Stan Smith," said a trooper. "He got it when a Hun soldier hit him with the butt of his gun. He went down after tripping on a flaming petrol drum lid."

"Just one, that's all we lost, just one man," said Cobden to Gunn when he asked.

They were retracing their footsteps back to the British camp when they came to a halt. They still had the road to contend with after the wood, and to mask their footfalls they tried to find the same track they had used before, keeping to the path. The light from the blazing fuel dump was just a faint glow in the darkness as they stopped, listening for any enemy followers. The wood was deep bush, the only sound to be heard being that of squirrels scampering from their nests after being disturbed.

They rested for a while, leaning their rifles against a tree and dropping down to the roots that were growing outwards. After about half an hour they trailed from the clearing and down a slight hill. They saw a small stream running down the incline and the sight brought on a thirst. Not one of the men had thought about quenching their thirst and the water now had them reaching for their water bottles.

Gunn took his lead at the head of the column and helped himself along by grabbing a bunch of branches. He slipped on the wet ground a couple of times and nearly sat in a big pile of horse dung. He spied the telltale signs of horses' hooves and decided to follow them to the end of the hill. The others had also noticed the hoof marks and followed in his wake to the bottom of the rise.

As they came to a clearing they were able to see the River Somme shining clear in the distance. The battlefield of the Somme was plain as could be and the explosions of bursting shell were heard on the wings of a slight breeze. In the far distance, men could be seen moving around on the battlefield, like little running dots, to avoid the puffs of smoke that were shells exploding.

Gunn indicated he had seen enough, and started to go along the old watercourse to the river. He had managed to retrieve his empty bandolier, and the canvas casing flapped as he walked. The other s followed in his wake, trusting him to lead them to safety. They walked the old course and shortly the river and its full majesty was open to their excited gaze. The little tributary was flowing slowly and as it met the full force of the main river water, it gained momentum and gushed into the river with some impetus.

They had to cross the small river and, as it remained sluggish and easy to ford, they chose the same path they had previously trod get to the petrol dump. At this level the depth of the water was only some three feet or more and easy to cross. The temperature of the water was just above freezing and it struck with coldness at the skin. Lance Corporal Cobden gritted his teeth against the strike of the cold and hitched his gun higher from the sudsy water. His teeth started to chatter with the cold and he shivered as it invaded his groin.

Gunn led the way as usual and stepped into an area just above his waist. He held the rifle above his head and tried to ignore the icy cold water. The small stream was only thirty yards broad and he stepped from it exuding water in small streams. He waited as the other men forded the slow-moving water and stepped from it, dripping wet.

Gunn examined his rifle and wiped a wet spot from the ammunition box with his helmet strap.

"Hurry it up, lads," he said as they waited for the water streaming from their clothes to lessen. "It's only water. It won't harm you," he added.

"No, but it will freeze you," muttered Cobden, gritting his teeth hard against his lower lip.

They marched at a quicker pace to keep warm. Soon, as their uniforms dried on their skin, the weight of their equipment became lighter. The terrain changed from mud to muddy woods. With tall pine trees on each side they trod familiar tracks and made their way to the British trenches and their welcoming dugouts.

Smithers wiped a drip of sweat from his nose and, gripping the handle of the buffer, bore down on the sacking, producing a nice polish. He had been working on the oilcloth for the best part of two hours and was getting fed up with it. He dropped to the wooden bedstead and rolled a thin cigarette. The smoke curled up from the rice paper cigarette and waved in the draught.

At the other end of the dugout Hartley was doing the same, but sweeping the remains of their breakfast off the oilcloth. He had to use the heel of his boot to scrape up a big spot of dried food.

"Someone can't find their mouth from their arse," he complained, sweeping up the small pile. "No wonder the corporal finds a lot of rubbish to clear up with this lot of pigs. They can't even find where their mouth is."

Smithers ignored him and watched the smoke hit the dugout roof.

"Wonder when we go again."

He was talking to Hartley as he was sweeping the pile into a dustpan.

"What are you on about?" enquired Hartley, emptying the dirt into a small tin container.

"What we usually do," said Smithers, blowing smoke rings with his mouth. "I mean you go into action again, I don't know, they don't take me into their confidence."

He headed for the door and the waste bin outside. On returning, he grabbed the buffer and, putting the cigarette out and resting it behind his ear, swung the broom about the room in an arc just as Hartley hastily entered the dugout.

"Here comes the corporal now, he's just been next door and he is heading this way, keep working."

They looked busy and were swinging the buffer for the next few minutes, but Gunn didn't make an appearance. They worked on for a while waiting, but no Gunn; he had decided to give them a miss that morning.

"Well, he would, wouldn't he," cried Smithers. "after all this bullshit and all?" He dropped the buffer and lit up another roll of tobacco. "Well, I'll be jiggered, the bastard has forgotten us," he moaned through his smoke.

Willcox then made an entrance. He breezed through the sacking door just as the work was done. He looked at the brightness of the newly cleaned dugout.

"Good work, you two lads, the dugout looks a lot better now you've had a go at it."

"You missed the cleaning, Wilko, but it will be your turn next time," said Smithers, knowing he was on guard.

The crowds of troops waited in the trench, waiting for the 'off' warning. They had been standing by since the dawn of day and were getting restless. With voices raised in protest at the delay, they were laden with extra equipment, and the weight of the packs was cutting into their muscles.

One particularly heavy private lifted his helmet and wiped the sweat from his shining brow. The bullets from the enemy just kept hammering at the trench wall tops and a bit of clay hit him in the eye.

"Bloody bastards, they caught me one in the eye. I can hardly see out of it now. I want the medical orderly."

The other soldiers around him aped him.

"You'll get more than that when this show is over, fatty."

The whistle blasted into the early morning and the ladders creaked as they scaled them.

Sergeant Cox watched the men climb the ladder and wondered who would have the good fortune to find their way back to the British lines. Not many, he mused. He tried to console himself by saying it was a young man's game and not one for an old man like himself.

He was fifty and often thought of retiring from army life, but had put off the day. All I do is think about it, he thought, that is all. The rest of the NCOs and senior NCOs were older than him; some were in their sixties, but reluctant to retire, citing their pension as a reason.

"Pension, old boy," they said. "If we retire before time we get a reduced pension, almost by as much as one third."

Cox was married in his younger days, so long ago he could not remember when. He could barely recall what she looked like. When he searched his memory he could hardly recollect if she was a blonde or brunette. She was a mousey sort of woman and stood back in the shadows rather than put herself around. Perhaps that is why he had difficulty in remembering what she looked like.

He was brought up by a father who was also in the army. He remembered him with three stripes on his red uniform and a crown in the later years. His mother he remembered even less; he was in his teens when she died of tuberculosis. His was a small family. He had only a sister to confide in and there was very little of that, he recalled. His father encouraged him to join the army, and when he entered as a recruit he was as innocent as the day he was born. He advanced though, and by the age of nineteen he held one stripe. He was as pleased as punch when he won his promotion and could not wait to show it off to his father.

He wore the same ceremonial uniform as his father, and by the time he came to fight in any war, was heading for the trouble in South Africa. He saw service in North Africa, and by the time he got to Cape Town after the trouble there he gained another stripe to accompany the first one.

According to others, he was a strapping man of twenty-seven and completely likeable. The lads, *his lads* as he called them, had a certain respect for him after his encounter with the opposition. He was in the thick of the fighting when called for and stood his ground against any enemy.

At the onset of the Boer War with the Dutch settlers and their friends in South Africa, he distinguished himself with his leadership courage, so that he was made a full sergeant after the Seige of Ladysmith. At the onset of the World War I, he was given the company that he now commanded. The top brass always left it to him to see that his company of solders was fit and capable of service.

This war was different to the last wars in that it was bigger and fought in France. Everything was dissimilar and different. The uniforms had changed from red to khaki; the armaments were exchanged for newer versions. As every man marched away he was carrying a SMLE, an up-to-date rifle called a Short Magazine Lee Enfield, to give it its full title. They still retained the full bayonet and scabbard carried at the side of the soldier.

When Gunn was promoted to his corporal, the job of observing the rules was partially taken from Cox's shoulders by him.

30

THE AERIAL ARM OF the company was taking to the air with a certain degree of confidence today. The three Sopwith Pup fighter planes had been modernised and equipped with a better machine gun. It dealt its blast of leaden slugs with increasing speed and included other bullets that escalated the risk of fire, in other words there was a better chance of catching fire as they hit the target.

The three planes took off in sequence, Pilot officer Sidney Kraft leading the flight with pilots Kell and Dobbs on either side of him. Their mission was primarily to guard the airfield, but to frighten away any enemy planes in the area.

Four German bombers hove into sight over the airfield and proceeded to drop their bombs on the main runway. Kraft pointed to the four bombers and shot away from the others in a tight turn. Kell and Dobbs each followed the leader and dipped down to meet the enemy bombers. Kraft executed a swift back flip and came up under the bombers with his machine gun blazing. Kell and Dobbs turned in tight formation and came out of the grey clouds. They broke off and each tore at the bombers with firing machine guns, which stitched a wide piece of aircraft that fell off in the fusillade.

The leader of the bombers caught the full blast of Kraft's machine gun and began to smoke. Kraft whizzed under the leading bomber and began to circle. The other two Sopwiths came from underneath and raked the bodies of the two remaining German bombers. One aircraft burst into flames and started its gradual descent to earth. The other two planes hurriedly dropped their bombs and started to race away to safety. The planes of Kell and Dobbs caught up with them and gave them a parting fan of armour-piercing bullets that knocked bits off the speeding aircraft as they scattered.

Suddenly, as Dobbs was looking down on the vanishing bombers, three German Fokker aircraft that were shadowing the bombers, shot from behind grey clouds and bore down on him. Kell tried to warn him by indicating them, but Dobbs mistook the signal for a wave and never saw them. One of the Fokkers peeled off and went into a deep glide. The others followed and the three Hun planes attacked Dobbs' plane. Kell tried to help him, but the combined firepower of the three planes was too much for him, and his aircraft burst into red flame.

Kraft, espying the three fighter aircraft, pulled his Pup fighter into a steep glide and rolled over onto the van of the enemy until the last of the three aircraft was in the sights of his machine gun. His Vickers bullets thudded into the plane's underbelly and the volley caused it to smoke. Kraft then ignored the Fokker, and his plane shot up into the path of the second Hun plane. He attacked it from the side and sprayed bullets at it just as Kell downed his adversary in a great big burst of flaming fire.

Kraft waved at Kell and put his aircraft into a dive, following the smoke of the downed Sopwith Pup. It crashed into a small wood and immediately caught fire. He did not see any movement from the British plane, although he flew over the ground twice.

Later on he landed his fighter plane and, hitching a lift in a lorry, was soon at the scene of Dobbs' death and found his partly burned body beside a smoking oak tree. Kraft helped the search party with Dobbs' remains and some time later the body was interred in the heroes' cemetery near the airfield.

Pilot Officer Kell gave his version of the battle in the mess that evening and praised his friend for his devotion to duty.

"Pilot Officer Dobbs was a brave man; he attacked three enemy aircraft knowing he was ringed in by them. He died the same way as he lived; by courage and devotion to duty."

They both had to return to the skies, although the bomb craters in the airfield had to be filled in first. They watched as the ground staff drew up in a lorry and quickly brought the airfield surface back to normality.

The aerial branch of the company of foot, the Ninety-ninth, had another aircraft, a Sopwith Camel. It was an older version, but ready and able to fly. They had been using it to deliver the mail, but it still retained its initial armaments, a Vickers machine gun. Now it would be used to train novice pilots in the art of flying.

After sitting in the seat and trying the controls, a rookie flyer was listening to an experienced pilot, who was leaning over the side talking to him.

"This stick thing between your knees is the joystick. It controls the plane by lifting and lowering the wing flaps, those things that make the plane go up and down. You have two foot pedals that control the direction of the plane. If you want left you press the appropriate pedal and vice versa. The other things like fuel, height, speed, oil pressure, rate of climb etc., are all before you on the instrument board."

The recruit tried the various instruments and watched the results from his seat in the aircraft.

"I can't get into the aircraft 'cause it's a single-seater fighter plane," the pilot said, "but you get the general drift. You'll soon get the knack of handling it after a while. You can go solo if you do."

"You mean go by myself?" said the rookie. "Perhaps I can try now, I've got it all in my head."

"That you won't, you've got to have a lot of training before you can fly," the pilot uttered.

"Yes, I guessed that, but I feel I can handle this plane now that you have shown me how to operate it."

"*Feel* isn't enough. You've got to have the experience and instruction of taking it up in the air."

"But I think I can handle it now-"

"The answer is still no," he pilot retorted. "Perhaps in two or three weeks, but you have no experience now, so you'd just crash or something like that."

"But Dave-"

"No, Derek, you can't."

"Can't I try one of the older planes, Dave?"

"We have only three other aircraft and they are for experienced pilots only. I'm sure they will only say no. Wait until you get some flying hours in."

The recruit climbed out of the aircraft and dropped to the grass runway.

"Sorry, Derek," the pilot said, "but it's for your own good, you could get injured or perhaps killed."

Derek just sighed and walked away.

Corporal Gunn turned into the main trench and ducked as a stray bullet struck the main stay of the trench ramparts. A bit of stone hit the tip of his steel helmet and pinged off into oblivion. His head sang for a brief moment and he shook it to clear it.

The way through the trench was only occupied by the sentry who was on watch. He nodded to the soldier on guard and went up to him.

"Tim Caulder, isn't it? All quiet, Private Caulder?"

"Strangely quiet, Corporal Gunn," he replied. "It might be a push from the other side, I'm thinking."

"Yes, well, stranger things have happened," said Gunn, keep a sharp eye out, "you never know."

He turned from the man just as the shelling restarted, and dodged down behind a trench stanchion as a shell flew over and exploded in the rear. The machine guns started again and whizzed over the ramparts of the trench head, hitting the clay with a hard thump as they connected.

Gunn continued his inspection of the trench and gazed at the sandbag defences with a critical eye. Several bags had lost their contents and needed renewing, he decided, and the end way of the trench wanted several more bags to restore a small division that had been swept away by shellfire. He noted it all down on a slip of paper he had produced.

"A little job for the boys," he mumbled, licking the stub of a pencil. "Keep 'em out of trouble for a while. I'll give it to Smithers and Co., they ain't got nothing to do."

A small smirk crossed his face as he thought about the trio of malingerers in the next dugout. His pace increased as he neared the dugout and he whipped the sacking door away from the doorway and went in. The three occupants immediately snapped to attention and stood there stiff as pokers.

"All right, you three bastards, I've got a job for you. Get yourselves a couple of shovels from the store trench and follow me."

They heaved a collective sigh and trailed out behind the corporal. Smithers, at the rear, hitched up his rifle on his shoulder and followed the other two. The store trench, as it was known, had a dozen shovels, two picks, a heavy iron pick bar and a huge pile of sandbags hanging from wooden frames that stretched from side to side.

The corporal ordered three shovels and gave one each to the men.

"Follow me again and I'll show you what is needed." Gunn led the way around to the fighting trench and pointed to the damaged sandbags. "Scrape up enough mud and earth from the ground to fill the damaged bags and replace them in the gap. That will keep you busy till dinner time or just after. I m putting Hartley in charge, so don't push it, that's all - dismiss."

He marched away, swagger stick under his arm, without a glance at them.

"Shovelling shit again," moaned Smithers, lighting up a cigarette from his tobacco tin. "I'm only surprised it's not latrine duty we got today instead of mud."

Willcox held out a partially full sandbag and waited as Smithers scraped up a heap of wet earth. The ground was hard with stamped down soil and they waited as he dug down a little.

"It's as hard as rock," grated Smithers as he lifted up a shovel full of stony grit. He had filled up two bags when he handed the shovel to Willcox and declared, "Your turn, Wilco, it needs a pick to shift the stuff."

Willcox wielded the shovel and got a big lump of wet clay ready to drop into the sandbag opening. Smithers held the bag open and the lump plopped in. For a while the three men worked at the sandbags and soon the first one was ready to lift into place. They were heavy and, with the weight of the earth and it being saturated with water, it took all their combined strength to lift it into place on the trench walls. They did the same with the second and third sandbags, and were lolling against the clay walls for a rest when Gunn swept around the trench corner.

"Just as I thought, malingering again." He then caught sight of the three sandbags and added, "Well, at least you have made a start on them. Carry on the good work the three of you."

With half a smile on his face, he left them standing stiff and erect. Seeing how hard they had worked to fill and erect the three bags, Smithers was gobsmacked for a while.

"Well, I'll be jiggered," he said eventually, "the bastard was just too late to see us working our arses off like we did. That's the worst thing about him; he's always too late to notice us working."

"I know," said Hartley, "but he has the last word in anything and we are just mere labourers, the lowest of the low. The lowest paid the lowest thought of, but the hardest worked, it just don't seem right. One section of the community is worked the hardest and is the poorest paid, it don't seem right."

To make things worse, the rain began to patter down, stream down the walls of the trench and collect in the centre of the walkway. Although they were getting wet, the rain had the effect of softening the soil and the pebbles beneath.

"I'm not working in the rain," complained Smithers, standing up under a sheet of corrugated iron thrusting out from the slope of the trench.

He avoided a drip from a hole in the sheet of iron where a shell splinter had burst through. The perpetual cigarette was dangling from the corner of his mouth and the smoke dribbled from the other end.

While Willcox dug in the slight rain, Hartley joined Smithers beneath the corrugated iron sheet. They watched him dig for a while.

Have a rest, Wilko," said Smithers. "Stand up under the sheet for a while and I'll have a go."

They took it in turns to shovel until the bag count got too great and they knew they would have to go out and lift them into position on the trench walls. To their good fortune it had stopped raining, and another quirk of fate was as it did so Gunn appeared on the scene. He was just in time to see them struggle to put another bag on top of the others and as they heaved he added his weight to it by pushing it into place on the highest level.

"All right, lads, go and get your dinner, it's just coming around the corner."

The Germans bombed the British positions that afternoon as they worked on the wall. The bombs whistled down on the trench fifty yards from the place they were working and the blast knocked another hole in the walls of the trench.

"More work for us to do," moaned Smithers. "Why can't they bomb the fucking battlefield? Now Gunn will get us to repair that little lot."

He was wrong. Gunn got another gang to repair the fresh hole, and the lads were glad to see them doing the same thing they had done. For a while Smithers almost broke into a smile of relief as he saw the hole being repaired by others.

"Jesus Christ, he got others to do the work," he said disbelievingly. "There are others here besides us, mates."

The next morning they had to go again, and found themselves in no-man's-land, hiding behind a wrecked skeleton of a German staff car. The two pals were gazing from between rusty wheels, eyeing the distant barbed wire separating the two factions.

"How are we gonna get through it?" questioned Smithers, when he saw it had no entrance hole. "I ain't got no cutters to get through the coils, have you?"

"I ain't got no cutters either," said Hartley, ducking down so that his steel helmet was touching the wheel spokes.

"You've got a hand grenade, perhaps we might do it with that," commented Smithers, with a downwards wave of his head to avoid a spent round.

Another bullet hit the iron wheel spokes and whanged off into infinity. Hartley picked the hand grenade pin with the corner of is teeth and lobbed it into the barbed wire coil, where it exploded and lifted the wire a few feet higher.

"Has that done it?" questioned Smithers, lifting his head higher.

"I think so," Hartley replied as the smoke cleared.

Smithers edged over to allow Willcox to join him under the wrecked staff car.

"Hello, Wilko, come to join us? We just blew a hole in the wire."

"Where's Corporal Gunn, he was just ahead of me at the outset," questioned Willcox as he wriggled beneath the car.

"Dunno, did he cop one?" said Smithers, coughing on the grenade smoke.

"What, Gunn cop one, did he hell. He'll never get one, not him, he's too lucky, mate."

A shell burst on the ground and splattered them with mud. It rattled on the iron wreck and covered it with blue smoke. The form of Corporal Gunn edged into the shelter of the staff car and slid up beside Smithers.

"I might've known, Smithers and Hartley, malingerers incorporated themselves," said Gunn, his voice echoing under the iron sides of the wreck. "Now you have got a hole in the wire, you have to finish the job and get to the Hun trench. You should've let well enough alone when you had the chance."

"Yeah, I suppose, Corporal Gunn," said Smithers unhappily.

Gunn made his move when the machine gun fire slackened into silence. He wriggled from his spot beneath the staff car and wormed his body to the hole in the wire. He signalled that he was clearing the barbed wire and lifted it to show it was free of encumbrances. Smithers, his face a picture of misery, left his place of safety, slithered over to the wire and wormed his way through the hole, all the while snagging his clothes and pack on the barbs. He held the wire away from his face and waited until the other two had joined him.

"Situation normal," breathed Hartley as he wriggled through the hole in the wire. "Now the worry begins."

They were about fifty yards from the German lines, and the shell holes ended as the Hun trench began. He meant there was no place for them to shelter from the machine gun fire that had dropped lower to dispose of enemy infiltration, such as them. The machine gun was so placed it could only depress a little lower and no more, so they were fortunate in that respect. They had slithering space to cover if they wanted to survive.

The four men negotiated the first of the barbed wire coils and hid behind a rise in the ground as Gunn flung another grenade at the second line. The bomb erupted under the second one and did the same with the wire coils, only this time it blew a wooden post out of the ground as well.

One by one they twisted through the vicious barbs, holding the wire away from each other's pack as it snagged on it. Now the only thing to face was a German sniper, who had spotted them getting nearer the German trench and was aiming slugs at them as they moved.

A bullet ricocheted off a stone just ahead of Smithers and another buried itself into the ground just by Willcox's head as he waited to move. In reply, he shifted to his side to miss another, which splashed into the thick mud close by. This taught them a lesson and moved them farther apart. Farther out in the field the shells pounded the rest of the company and created more shell holes. Nearly one quarter of the men had run into some difficulty or other, being cut down by machine gun fire, shell fire, or both.

The four men were the most successful part of the company and any watcher from the British trench could see that fact. One of those who saw the engagement was the commander in chief of the company. Using the optical viewer, he was looking at the four men in the van of the company, and he saw the distance they had covered compared with the rest of the company in the rear.

"Who are those brave men?" he questioned his junior officers, who were standing on the firing step. "They deserve a medal citation, all four of them."

The officers, junior and senior, agreed with the commanding officer and noted the names of the four soldiers.

"Now the dangerous part comes," muttered Hartley, as he braced himself for the final part of the charge.

He clicked a round up the spout and gathered himself together, ready for Gunn to give the order to move. This Gunn did by raising himself onto two elbows and signalling to the others. Smithers saw the signal out of the corner of his eye and, raising his steel helmet from the mud, prepared to go forwards again. He was directly behind Gunn as he wriggled through the mud and slime. Gunn turned his head around to see him about three feet away from his leather boots. He grinned with an effort and slithered forwards barely fifteen feet from the Hun trenches. He inched forwards and touched the coarse material of a torn sandbag.

They had made it, still alive and in one piece. The four men spread out, looking for a likely fissure to get into the German trench. Willcox, using one of his grenades, yanked the pin out with his teeth and dropped it into a little cleft left by a shell splinter. He yelled to let the others know what he had done and ducked down as the grenade burst. He was covered with an avalanche of mud and obliterated sandbags, and twisted out of them with a shake of his steel helmet. He followed it up with another hand grenade, which he put through the blown gap.

The explosion occurred and created havoc among the German soldiers, who were crouching behind the sandbags. Other explosions burst as the others copied his actions and threw their share of grenades into the German defences.

Behind the trench walls agonising cries were heard as the Hun soldiers were hit by the grenade. It separated into a thousand different sharp spear points that found a home in the soft flesh of the troopers. When they heard this, Gunn and Co. fell through the damaged wall and landed in the middle of several wounded soldiers.

Two or three of the Hun soldiers who were buried by the fall of earth scrambled up, ready to continue the fight. They were disorientated by the grenade blast and were easy meat for the four company men. They disposed of the German soldiers within several minutes and were fighting for their lives as other enemy troopers came and joined the fray.

The van of the next British soldiers arrived just in time to take on the grey-uniformed soldiers, and within minutes were engaged in a life or death struggle for supremacy.

31

On the British side of the battle a monster was stirring. The tank had arrived at the front and was standing in the hill of no-man's-land with its engine running at full tilt. The tank had the full vision of the opposition, who gazed at it with rapt attention.

It was different from the previous tank in that it had thicker armour at the front and larger guns poking out of the four gun ports, with the inclusion of bigger track armour covering the huge metal treads. It emitted a big blast of smoke and hurtled forwards, tracks spinning crazily, the noise echoing over the flat plains of no-man's-land and into the distant countryside. A fusillade of shells struck the front of the tank, but bounced off the heavy vehicle and exploded on the track - ineffectively. The tank had finally arrived and was doing all it should.

In the space of half an hour, the shells kept arriving and did the same thing. They exploded on the front of the protective steel armour, causing only superficial damage. Except for the battle flag flying from the top, which had a dent in the metal mast, it looked the same as before.

With tracks turning on the hard ground, it gouged out the dirt beneath its enormous treads, straddling big shell holes and divides, crossing everything with great ease. The engine roared as the four machine guns played a death-dealing tattoo on the Hun trench, bringing down sandbags that disintegrated before the enemies' eyes. The noise of the thudding engine echoed into the atmosphere, emitting great clouds of grey smoke that hung in the air like some hideous great monster.

The shell response of the Germans pinged like darts on a metal dartboard, just meeting the iron surface and bouncing right out again. In frustration, the Huns continued to shell the metal monster, but with no effect but to shake up the tank crew inside. In reply, the tank hit the walls of the trench with devastating fire, making big holes in the outer defences.

Behind the sandbag walls of the German trench the men of the Ninety-ninth Company of Foot were surrounded by a bigger group of Germans who threatened to hem them in. The thunderous roar of the tank and the damage so disturbed the Germans that they forgot to fight back, and held their hands up in total surrender.

The Tommies were so surprised by the capitulation that they forgot to collect the Huns' weapons. They were further surprised by the nose of the tank as it thrust its snout into the trench and crushed several Huns who were crouching down in terror at the sight of the metal horror. Its four machine guns mowed down dozens of the enemy as they stood there. The hot metal of the guns smote a hail of fire at the Germans and added to their mortal terror.

The tank reversed back into the ravages of the German trench and ground out, taking a big lump of Hun trench with it. The tracks of the tank were covered in blood and other bits of gore, while the bones of the newly dead rolled around the treads until dislodged by the mud of the battlefield.

Thus ended a phase of the Battle of the Somme. The carnage of hundreds of thousands of soldiers on both sides will go down in history as one of the most bloody battles of the war. They were buried in various cemeteries all over the globe. Even men of different spiritual persuasion and colour were left to die on the battlefields of the Somme. They gave up their lives for the British Empire and the monarchy, most living in dire poverty in their own countries. They heard the call to arms and answered in the only way they could - by giving their lives in reply.

The tank returned to the British side and went back to the armourer to get further supplies of ammunition. It was a total success and even now the observers of the battle were planning more tanks.

The crew inspected the sides of the tank with much joy when they saw no damage to the armour. They grinned with relief when they saw the Union Jack flag lying over on its side on top. That was the total impairment out of all the battles, so that is why they were delighted with the outcome. Later on they set out across the reaches of no-man's-land, intent on doing the same thing to the other Hun trenches.

The hearts of the Germans must have been at a low ebb as they heard the noise of the tank in the distance. They tried everything and shot greater shells at the metal monster to try to find its weakness. The only success they had was when the tank got stuck in one of the really deep holes and rainwater got in. The only option was to wait until nightfall, when the recovery crew had to free it from the hole and dry the driver and the four machine-gunners. Their cries of laughter were heard by the enemy.

A hit was scored on one of the helpers by a vigilant sharp shooter from the German trench - the sum total of the German's success that day in no-man's-land. With the tank's success on the battlefield, the roar of delicious success was heaven to the ears of the British troops and they whistled and cried catcalls at the enemy across the dangerous divide.

Across the field the Germans heard the response from the British troops and ground their teeth in Teutonic rage.

The men who had led the attack, the three troopers and NCO Gunn, got safely back across the stretch of no-man's-land and learned they were to receive a medal for bravery in the face of the enemy.

Smithers was cooking the dinner on the stove top, and couldn't believe it when he learned he was to get the medal

"Fuck the medal," he fumed. "I would rather be at home with my mother and father, it's nicer, and more safe too."

"It's something," said Hartley, then added, "here, I wonder if there is any money with the medal?"

Smithers brightened up when he heard the word 'money'.

"You really think so?" he asked, turning around to face Hartley. "I think it is worth more than that, look at all the risk we had crossing the battlefield, fighting the Germans and all, it's worth more than one medal, maybe two at least."

"Oh yeah, imagine them giving you *two* medals. They ain't the ones to risk their lives without end. Crossing the field and jumping in those shell potholes, praying like billy-o that the next one to fall will fall on somebody else. With the machine gun slicing your head open if you so much as show a helmet."

"Yeah, I know the drill, I've been there before, remember?"

Smithers' eyes were watering as he peeled an onion. He cut it into strips and stirred the pieces into the bully beef stew, sloshing the pan from side to side as he did so. He lit the cigarette stub at the corner of his mouth. A whiz-bang shell exploded in the air and covered the trench with shrapnel, donging on the dugout roof, bringing clouds of dust down on the cooking food. Smithers just stirred the lot into the stew, including a bit of fag ash that fell from the end of his cigarette.

Willcox, who was on the end bunk just waking from a doze, got to his feet and joined in the conversation.

"He's right, you know. How many times have we been across that fucking field since we've been here - a dozen or more times? I reckon we've been across that damned crossing twelve times, so by rights we are entitled to a medal every time we did it. That makes twelve medals in all, or a cash reward in lieu of."

"You think we will get some cash instead," insisted Smithers, sloshing the dinner from side to side.

Before they had a chance to answer, he yelled 'dinner up' and tipped the mix into a waiting tin dish.

The Huns shelled the British trenches non-stop until nightfall, then stopped. A light rain was falling, and everything was soaking wet. Everybody was wearing a groundsheet coverall, with rifle tipped down out of the rain.

The nightly sentry was sloshing through pools of stagnant water and at the end of his nightly walk began his session to march to the next sentry. One spoke to the other as they met.

"Nice night for an enemy foray, got all the right things for it like a light rain and a moonless night."

"Don't say that, Reg. I'm on watch. I don't fancy fighting the Hun on a dirty night like this. I want to get in out of the cold rain to my supper. I'm cold and wet, and my gloves are sodden as well."

"I'm with you there," replied Reg, giving a shudder. "I-"

The next remark was lost in the explosion of a shell that hit the trench and brought down the wall. One of the sentries was killed and the other, Reg, was dug out of the explosive burst with hardly a scratch on him. He joined the rescuers to dig out the unfortunate victim and helped them carry him away on the stretcher. He was right in his assumption, and after an interval of an hour or so the enemy launched an attack.

The pals were awakened out of a deep sleep by the cries of fighting men. They immediately rushed out into the trench and met the force of advancing Germans.

The troop of British soldiers attacked the belly of the force and made it retreat into a section of the fighting trench, all the while attacking with a ferocity that forced the enemy backwards.

In the fore, the three men hit the Germans with all their might, and captured several prisoners. With the prisoners in their midst, the company forced the captives into a gaol in the captive trench.

When Freda caught sight of Gunn she almost fainted with surprise. She was outside cleaning the windows of the pub as he turned the corner into view, tiptoed up to her and grabbed her around the waist.

She had to go into the barroom and sit down for a while until she got over the shock.

"Darling, did I startle you? I'm sorry," apologised Gunn, "but I was so glad to see you it somehow got the better of me. It was foolish really."

She put her hand up to her breast.

"I can feel my heart, it's pounding," she fluttered.

He smiled and helped her up from the chair, putting his arms around her as he did so.

"I missed you so much, dear," she whispered in his ear. "All them months of separation and no one to talk to except the young girl. She's my assistant I got. She's a bit young, but I just give her all the little jobs I can't do myself."

"How've you been, Freda?" breezed Gunn, taking her arm. "I missed you too, especially at night. All those hours we spent together before, darling, I miss terribly."

"I missed you too," she muttered into the crook of his neck, "more than you realise, dear."

"When I heard we were getting leave, I decided to make the journey here and see you. It took two days to reach you here in Calais, but it was worth every penny of the train ride and every moment of my leave to be with you."

Freda was just about to open up the pub and welcome the first customer of the day. He was the usual one, and when he caught sight of the corporal, he broke into a smile of recognition.

"Hello, Corporal Gunn, how's tricks? I'm off with the lads to go where you were. We leave tomorrow early."

"You been up there before?" asked Gunn, hitching his rifle higher on his shoulder.

"Yeah, I've been on sick leave, but they said it is healed enough to return."

"Well, good luck, lad, better luck next time."

Freda turned the gramophone on and as the record turned, the dulcet tones of 'I'll be your Sweetheart', echoed through the bar. As the bar opened and came to life Gunn found his favourite stool and sipped the best beer.

"Can I stay here?" whispered Gunn across the counter.

"Course you can, darling," returned Freda, pouring another pint. "How can I refuse you after all you have been through these past days?"

His only answer was a smile across the bar counter.

That night Gunn had a chance to look at her body across the pink counterpane. Her hair merged with the pink pillow slip and curled right down to rag curlers, giving her the image of a young girl. Her lips were red with just the suggestion of rouge on her cheeks.

"She's beautiful," he whispered, gazing at her full breasts and getting a quickening of senses as his eyes drank in the litheness of her body beneath the sheets.

He voiced his desire with a hoarse voice and quickly took her into

his arms with one movement. When the moment came for intercourse he entered her with gentle movements, not rushing into it,
but savouring the entry bit by bit, letting the delicious feeling drift
in slowly and gently. With his full length inside her he sighed with
pleasure and slowly started towards the moment of intense pleasure.
She moaned in delight as he pressed harder into her body and felt the
sexual juices run out and pervade his full being. She quickened her
reflexes and increased the movement in reply to his ardent thrusts.
Her lips were soft and all embracing, tightening in sexual want, her
hips moving in response to his urgent demands. The well of want
gathered up in his loins and with sudden flush overflowed inside her.
He was breathing with deep pushes and as his breath subsided and
slowed, the sweat of his efforts on his body and face, so that it ran
down his brow in wet droves.

"Did you enjoy it?" she breathed, holding him tightly inside her. "I
did."

Several times they made love and each time it was as though it
was for the first time. They fell apart, gasping with breathlessness,
sweat running down their bodies.

"God, I enjoyed that, darling," he breathed. "You are certainly one
good lover and that's no mistake."

"You looked like you did. Your face is all red," she said, laughing at
him and fluffing up her pillow in readiness for sleep.

He followed her example and prodded his pillow with his elbow.

His dreams were not of sex, but of the war in the east. He was back
in the trenches fighting the Germans, so much so that he woke her
from her sleep with his violent movements. Freda had to wake him
from the dreams.

"You were thrashing about in the bed and mumbling something
about damned German bastards."

"I have bad dreams, which I get every time I go to sleep," he
explained.

He returned to sleep and troubled her no more for the rest of the night. She didn't speak of his bad dreams, but put it down to the intense nature of his soldiering. Probably all soldiers get them faced with the danger of their profession, she thought.

Gunn helped Freda to carry a barrel of beer up from the cellar downstairs and plonking it down on its place under the barroom counter. She looked at him breathing heavily and smiled.

"Thanks for doing that, sweetheart, I can't manage it nowadays. I have to get the men to help me carry it. I just can't do it like I did in my younger days."

"Perhaps you had too much sex last night," he said, laughing.

"Shh! Somebody might hear you," she gently chided him.

The young woman just pretended not to hear the soldier's reply and she carried on with her task at the bar.

Time progressed and the solders came into the bar and ended up sitting at one of the tables. Behind the counter Gunn tried his hand at pouring the beer out. He accepted payment for the beer and put it into the tin box that was used as a cash container. The atmosphere was beginning to show signs of cigarette smoke as each man lit up. Gunn was not a heavy smoker and the clouds of tobacco smoke sometimes caused him to cough.

"How do you stick it, dear?" he questioned Freda with a smile. "Don't it make you cough?"

"I hate it, but I stick it 'cause I have to. If the customers can't smoke they go somewhere else where they can. My living is as simple as that."

"I can see why you pretend to like it," said Gunn with a thin smile. "Some day I will marry you and take you away from all this."

"Hasten the day, darling," returned Freda, wiping the table with as damp cloth.

32

ALL TOO SOON GUNN's leave came to an end and he had to say goodbye to Freda. She was tearful and held him close for a while, kissing him tenderly. He heaved up his backpack, hitched up his rifle to his favourite place on his shoulder and said goodbye. She smiled at him as he walked around the corner and headed for the railway station a quarter of a mile away.

His thoughts were mixed up in his mind. He thought about overstaying his leave and going back to his woman, but only for an instant, to be replaced by thoughts of his duty. What would he be losing if he did? Only his pension, and a likely chance of gaining promotion to sergeant, and possibly further promotion to higher ranks. No, he thought, too much to lose for a moment's weakness. He forced the idea from his mind with an inner shrug.

To a man of his calibre and physique a quarter of a mile was as nothing, and very soon the outline of the railway station came into view. He figured the journey would be as before and, if without incident, he would be back in his trench dugout in three or four hours. He sighed and thought of last night's moments of love. Freda had been more loving than usual because she knew he was going away the following day and made the lovemaking more intense, more sensual; the way she knew he liked. His mind's eye savoured the hours of lovemaking and he could still imagine he was near her and kissing her.

With a shrug he shook off the lustful thoughts and concentrated on his journey back to duty. He was aware that the war was on and as usual he would go back to the same way with the same duty to perform. He sighed again and watched the colourful kaleidoscope passing the windows. The bright daylight hopped from one thing to another and the passage from pasture to buildings caused him to nod his head and sleep...

Suddenly he was awake as the distant guns of the western front flashed on the skyline and echoed in the atmosphere of the daytime. He had a pocket watch and he noted the time. He figured he had been napping for several hours.

He was alone in the carriage, so he opened the widow to get some fresh air. A gust of wind entered and a spot of soot did too, landing straight in his eye. He rubbed it and got rid of the itch with his fingernail. The path of the train wound around a bend in the line and as it did so it emitted a light wail. It was nearing a group of buildings and it put on the brakes in a grinding clash of sliding wheels.

"Next stop," he whispered, "and then the long hike to the war zone."

As a result of the nearness of the war, the train had shortened its outward journey and the line ended at the next stop. He did not regret doing the long ride, for it was worth the journey and the hours of being with Freda. As the last part of the ride finally came to an end, he heaved his pack onto his back and dropped down onto the naked track. It was then Shanks's pony for him and his heavy equipment.

The one man porter waited for the soldier to make his exit. The sounds of battle were booming from the front and the horizon was lit up with flashes of distant firing. As Gunn stepped down the porter pressed a nearby bell and the locomotive started to retrace its recent journey.

Gunn swung the packs and his rifle to his back as he heard the train gather speed and clatter away down the rusty line. He stepped out across the lines, through a sagging fence and onto a rough path. He passed shell-torn houses enclosed by deserted and rundown fences. Everything was as silent as the grave. The war had passed that way and left its hideous mask of death and destruction, the backdrop imprinted on the curtain of fire that intermittently flared up with a resounding certainty.

A black and white cat got up from its perch on the fence, stretched and followed him, winding in and out of his legs as he walked. It was thin and half-starved with ribs showing through its fur. He unwrapped the sandwiches Freda had made for him and crumbled one, which the cat devoured without hesitation. He patted the animal, but it was too interested in the food to notice him

Gunn stepped out onto the potholes of the track and headed for the flash of the guns. As he got nearer to the war zone he stepped over shell holes that were in the process of decomposition; recent holes that had been blasted from the earth and filled with rainwater that was slowly drying. He lifted his eyes and saw the red of the poppies in the corn stubble and the encroaching green of the grass stalks.

He was aware that his steel helmet was on the back of his head and the straps were sliding with the sweat drying on his head. His equipment also moved and began to rub his back and shoulder blades. The far explosions danced on the skyline with each step he took.

For an hour he tramped the rough road, dodging the shell holes, stepping over the puddles and even skirting the big indentations he could not jump. Now the explosions and flashes came as one and echoed across the horizon with frequent regularity.

In the distance he saw the start of the holding trench and the lorries grouped around the entrance. He tramped the muddy track and in minutes started down the slope of the holding trench.

33

SMITHERS AND HARTLEY WILL always remember Friday for three reasons. First because it was the day their friend Willcox was killed by a shell. It was payday and a stray bullet hit Hartley in the forearm. Willcox was sheltering in a fox hole and the hideout received a direct hit from a whiz-bang shell. He and others were killed outright and were carried from the battlefield in blankets. Although wounded, Hartley was able to get his pay from the finance officer and salute him with his left hand.

The boys collected Willcox's personal things and put them in his kitbag. His items were so pathetic, occupying a bundle of only one foot square. Willcox had been a private person in himself, but outgoing in everything else. He had taken his turn in the work detail, and the cooking and guard details, but he had jealously guarded his home life and kept only one photo of his parents and sister, Joan. He had received no letters from home, and to their knowledge never received any mail. Pathetically they had to write to his home address and tell his parents he was killed while on active service. Whether they got their letter they never knew, because they never received a reply. The boys took it that the shock of hearing their boy was killed was too great for them to answer the letter.

Corporal Gunn returned to learn Willcox had been killed, and set about getting them a new soulmate. Of course the two pals missed Willcox, if only for the part he had played in sharing the guard duties. He had not been much of a cook and had no imagination for anything but plain meals. Smithers said he was boring, and he was until the day he had bandaged up Smithers' bad finger and made a good job of it. Smithers was pleased with the result because the finger had an abscess and was hurting a lot.

The vacancy in the dugout was filled by one Private Joe Sands, and he readily carried in his kit with a breezy smile that was a contrast to their recent dugout companion, Private Willcox. Sands was a overweight man with podgy arms and legs that pushed the biscuit mattress to a great bulge beneath the bunk bed.

"What was he like?" asked Sands about the recent occupant of the bunk in which he was sleeping.

"All right, a bit of a bore," returned Hartley, nursing his bad arm. "Yes, he stood his duties like guard and did his share of cooking, but all he did was just slice the bully and fry it on the stove. One day he peeled the potatoes and put them in the pan, but that was just a *flash in the pan* and he didn't do it no more."

Like the others, Sands smoked. He had just lit up a cigarette, and let the smoke curl out of his nose.

"Got killed, didn't he? I'm sleeping in his bunk, hope it ain't catching."

Smithers gave a deep sigh.

"We all take our chances, if we get it, we get it, there's no use in denying it. Plenty of our mates get the chop every day. If you get it, it's your unlucky day."

Sands suddenly pointed to the floor and shouted.

"I just saw a big rat run around the uniform shelf. It had a bit of meat in its mouth and it vanished behind the pots and pans shelf."

"That's Silas, he's our pet rat. He always comes out at dinner time," returned Hartley, crossing his injured arm over his chest and resting it on his stomach.

"As long as he sticks to bully and not human flesh," retorted Sands, coughing on his cigarette.

"He's probably had that as well, seeing the amount of bodies out in no-man's-land," said Hartley.

Gunn made his entrance a little while later and pinned up a notice on the notice board, rapping his hand on the paper as he spoke.

"These are your duties, stick to them like shit to a blanket. If you do you'll be my friend, if you don't we'll fall out I can assure you." He turned around to the newest soldier. "You, Private Sands, get your belongings out of sight and stowed away in your locker. If you can read you can see what your duties are. If you can't, the others will explain them to you - dismiss."

The three men relaxed as he went out, and spread themselves on the comfort of their bunks.

"Is he always like this?" asked Sands.

"He can be a right bastard," said Smithers from the corner of the dugout.

"I've come to the wrong dugout," remarked Sands, with a cough.

"He can be a real terror," said Hartley, "especially if you don't do as he says and keep the dugout clean."

"My other corporal was an understanding man and not one to crack the whip with spit and polish."

"Well, Corporal Gunn is exactly the opposite and lays it on thick," said Smithers.

Sands chose to keep silent and blow out a cloud of blue smoke.

Supper time came and went, and the plates had been cleaned of eaten food and placed on the shelf with the rest of the pots and pans. Daylight faded and the three men lay down to rest as, in the shadows, the rat began his search for crumbs on the floor.

The watery sun was a backdrop to the weather – rain again. It had been raining all day and the drips plopped onto the guard patrolling the stretch outside his dugout.

Rules had provided that each man had a section of trench to patrol, and met on the end of his stretch with his opposite number. These rules made it quite clear that each section must be patrolled by a guard at all times. This way the entire trench was under guard at all times and woe betide anyone who did not comply with the regulations; they were up on a charge with any subsequent offence punishable by imprisonment. On one charge one man got the death penalty for desertion, but it was mainly for confinement for a number of years.

Joe Sands stood his guard duty and complied by meeting on the end of his march and returning to his starting point, where he met the other soldier. Usually they reached a point where they could light up and have a smoke. The point of light provided by a lit match was enough to get a good bead on the smoker as he lit up. The optical sight of the watching sharpshooter was always ready and waiting for the target. Mostly they kept the light shielded and out of sight behind the safety of the trench walls, but most casualties happened in the shallow trench that had no sandbag fortifications.

Today one man who popped his head above the slight trench parapet was shot by a waiting sharpshooter and was carried away with a slug in his temple. That was considered a dangerous shallow trench and only the foolhardy lay in it for any length of time. The machine guns were firing all the time - night or day. They only stopped when they ran out of ammunition. On such a day as this the sunlight reflected on the shine of a steel helmet and when the sharpshooter saw the glint he aimed for the target and the man under its steel protection. That is why the sandbag fortifications were kept in tip top condition, and any damage due to shellfire was always replaced with other filled sandbags.

Sands eyed the welter of trench head droppings that showered down from the bullet holes, and stepped over a bit of clay with some big holes in the packed earth. Usually most of the bullets buried themselves deep into the hard soil and in some cases passed through it and ricocheted off any obstacle in the way. Less in number, but more ominous, were the whiz-bangs that flew over the trench head and exploded in mid-air. They made a whizzing noise that ended in a big bang as the shell erupted in the sky overhead. As they exploded they shot out thousands of sharp objects that ripped right through anything that stood in the way. Lately the Germans had included a device that prevented it from exploding, except when it was interfered with or disabled by anyone.

Thus the war marched on. The enemy was trying all sorts of schemes to try and best the result of the conflict. The German command had opened up the possibility that the war was being lost, and in reply they were trying all kinds of dirty tricks to achieve total victory. Now the class of war had turned the corner and was emerging into something else again. Scientists with the benefit of upper class education had entered the fray, trying to tip the scales in favour of the Huns.

It was the same in the British camp. They had opened up the war with the tank, which was proving a complete success. It was currently being duplicated in dozens of factories all over Great Britain and in the Commonwealth.

Private Sands and his mates never wondered why they were patrolling up and down the trench roadway, they only knew they were fighting the enemy of their country and would do their best to defeat the German yolk. Sands' only immediate duty was to protect the

British possessions from the Huns. Britain gave him a gun, pointed to the enemy and said 'go to it'. Sands thought he was a patriot, and willingly got down to fighting the enemy with the gun. The sum total of his fight against the enemy lay in what Britain has, Britain keeps. Of course the whys and wherefores had no place in Sands' mind. He only knew the corporal would make him jump, and make him jump high, if he did not do as he was told. The consequences were too dire to think about, so he deliberately shut it out of his mind.

His total walk was coming to an end and he was looking forward to eating his meal and taking off the backpack, which was chafing his spine.

"The relief will soon be here, Tom," he said, addressing the other man.

He rested his rifle against the clay walls and cupped his hands together, blowing into them. The rain had eased off and other troopers were passing by on their way with diverse orders to perform. Now and again they edged through the various men who threaded their way past the two sentries.

It was near noon and the midday meal was approaching fast. Sands was feeling hungry, and he could feel his stomach growling in protest. A whiz-bang shell weaved away overhead and, as he ducked in compliance, a shell splinter shot over the roundness of the steel helmet and raced away to the opposite trench walls. The shell contact caused him to have a ringing that echoed through his head and stayed with him all day. His deafness was temporary though, and gradually wore off. It did not affect his appetite and he ate his meal in the comfort of his dugout.

The tank crashed and rolled on the scene, rocking with the speed of its run. The tower of the tank was central and the four machine guns depressed. The noise was terrific and the soldier passing by held their hands over their ears to shut out the sound. The tracks churned up the muddy road and the tank left a trail of displaced earth and rainwater in its wake.

Suddenly it stopped and a single figure stepped down from the steel door and dropped to the trail of mud and water on the ground. He showed a sergeant's stripes, and quickly went around to the back of the machine and opened a plate door. For a few moments he turned the engine of the tank, hitting it with a hammer as he did so. He stepped back from the engine and called to another man who had appeared at his side.

The second man was talking as the sergeant looked at the engine.

"It was making a horrible squealing noise," he said, studying the silent engine.

The sergeant scratched his head under the rim of his steel helmet.

"It suddenly conked out; I think it wants a little oil or something. It was making one hell of a racket."

The second man was a one striper, so he respectfully said nothing until the sergeant addressed him.

One by one the gunners of the tank squirmed out of the metal doors and stepped out onto the mud. They were dressed in greasy overalls that contrasted with the metal of the steel helmets they all wore. The sergeant went back to his hammering and cursed in plain English as he hit his hand with the hammer.

"Blast the fucking thing! I just hit my finger with the hammer, it's bleeding."

He ended up by sucking his finger, licking the abrasion with his reddened tongue. The lance corporal eyed him and turned his eyes up to heaven as the curses left his mouth. After a while the sergeant turned back to the engine and started to tinker with the big flywheel that ran the oil inlet gap.

"Aha, I've got it I think! They are starving you of oil, so I was right. The squeaking was caused by lack of oil, no wonder the thing was running hot. It got hot and expanded with the heat, that's what happened, Smithy."

"No wonder indeed, Sergeant, perhaps someone forgot to fill the oil pots when they did the daily inspection."

"Yeah, I'll put it in my report when we get back to headquarters," muttered the sergeant as he surveyed the engine. "Right, all back on board, you lot, and we can try to start the engine."

The men stubbed out their cigarettes and one by one climbed back into the tank. The sergeant crashed the engine door and stood back to view the vehicle with a puzzled look on his face. He shook his head once then followed the other men inside.

Inside the metal hull of the tank he spoke to the gunners; all rankers and new to the job.

"When I say you must depress your guns, I mean exactly that. After use you must depress your guns so that the rainwater doesn't get in. Must I say it again, Archer, you left it to get wet and rusty, didn't you?"

The offending soldier just mumbled to himself and kept his silence.

The sergeant sat in the driving seat and waited as the lance corporal unhitched a starting handle and fitted it on the end of the engine stem. He swung the big starter and it did nothing.

"*Again,*" growled the sergeant as he tickled the accelerator arm with his damaged finger. "Again, but more swings."

The lance corporal received a kickback as he turned the big black starter. He rubbed his shoulder and tried again. The sergeant pumped in fresh oil with a button on the dashboard and nodded to his underling. The man swung the starter and it kicked back again. Lance Corporal Smith fingered his tender shoulder muscles and, standing bestride the engine, gave it an enormous swing with all the force he could muster.

The engine coughed once and started with a growl that shook the entire inside of the tank, filling the whole interior with oily smoke. For a while as the air cleared and daylight returned, they were left in darkness with the smell of burned oil pervading their nostrils. They once again breathed fresh air as the tank ports gushed in a draught of oil-free atmosphere. The four machine-gunners lifted the machine gun ports and pointed them outwards.

The sergeant pulled the cord and made the revolutions turn faster. He had two sliders that controlled the two tracks, and he twitched the two levers, making the tank turn to the right. The war vehicle twisted to the right and climbed the bank by the side of the track. He had a sight hole ahead of him and he saw the countryside go by as he made the tank crawl up the sides of the road and into the heart of the battlefield.

Now they were in the thick of it, and the sides of the British trench receded and were left behind. The guns of the tank spouted hot lead as the German soldiers ran before its onslaught, and in many a case the tank ran over and squashed the occupants of a shell hole as they sheltered from the terrible fire of the four machine guns.

34

Smithers fingered his medal through bully beef covered hands and licked his fingers as they became covered with the meat. It was his turn to do the cooking again, and he wore the medal on a piece of string around his thin neck. He had served his time on guard duties and he had only just come into the dugout knowing that it certainly was his turn to act as cook.

Hartley was doing his stretch of guard duties and the other occupant, Sands, was fast asleep on his bunk. Smithers tried not to wake him, but the noise of the pots and pans on the stove was something he could not avoid.

"Is it guard duty already?" yawned Sands, lifting his hands to stretch his arms out wide.

"Go back to sleep, Hartley is on guard," said Smithers as he wiped the pan free of its coating of grease.

There was a period of quiet as Sands tried to return to sleep, but after a quarter of an hour had elapsed he gave up and sat up in the bunk with his blankets around his shoulders.

"No use me trying," he grumbled. "Once I get disturbed from kip I can't get back to sleep again, no matter how hard I try."

"Sorry," said Smithers, making no pretence of being quiet now he had woken the man up, "but it is my turn to do the cooking and the pan slipped from the stove top and ended up on the floor."

"Not your fault, Smithy, you had to cook the dinner for all of us, so a little noise won't go amiss-"

The end of his observation was drowned in a sudden bang as a shell cracked in the sky overhead. He waited as the inevitable rain of bits and pieces showered down onto the trench outside and rattled on the corrugated roof of the dugout.

"Amiss while I'm asleep, I was going to say before I was rudely interrupted by the noise on the tin roof," Sands continued.

"It wasn't *me*," commented Smithers. "Blame the Germans for the noise, not me."

"Yeah, I know that Smithy, how long will you be with my dinner? I'm half-starved."

"It's this fucking stove; it wants decoking or something, it's not drawing as it should be."

Sands listened to the excuse.

"It's the flue, it wants sweeping."

"How d' yer know what it wants?" retorted Smithers, blowing on the coal embers as he lifted the stove cover.

"I know 'cause I was a chimney sweep in Civvy Street," protested Sands, sitting upright on the bunk.

Smithers sniggered.

"*You*, a chimney sweep? Wait a mo while I get you a brush and you can get started on it right away."

"You can laugh, but it was an honest living anyway; better than signing on the dole all your life. I know it was mucky and you get covered in soot most of the time, but you get used to the blackness in the long run."

"What did the people say to you? Mammy, Mammy, my black Mammy, like Al Jolson the black singer?"

"Sometimes they called you far worse things, and the kids would follow your cart up the road and sing out the words loudly as you carried your black sack and rods, and the sweep on your shoulder." Sands laughed long and loud at his former life. "What was your home life like, Smithy?"

Smithers turned the bully beef over on its side and stirred in a big onion before answering.

"Me? I had a vegetable round going. I had a barrow to start with then I got a horse and cart as the round got bigger. The horse gave up one day and faded away. I was going to get me one of those lorries, but others heard of my success and I was saddled with competition. Glad I didn't though, 'cause I was getting into too much debt."

A shrill whistle screamed through the air and a shell fell farther back in a rear trench, the draught from it causing the sacking door to tremble.

"That was a big one," Smithers said, still cooking on the stove top and stirring up the dinner mess with an old spoon. He emptied it into a greasy mess tin and handed it to the other man. "There's your dinner, Sandy, save the tin for me and Hartley. Hope you like it, if you don't, hard luck, it's someone else's turn to cook the dinner next time."

The sergeant in charge of the tank pulled one of the levers and it responded by turning to the left. He had no means of knowing the petrol consumption, for the gauge had not been fitted. The oil he knew about, and only had to lift the engine housing to find out, by inspecting it at the back. The only way he had of seeing how much petrol was being used was to go outside and dip a stick into the petrol tank. Of course, that was out, as the tank was in no-man's-land and in sight of the enemy trenches. He reckoned the ammunition supply was running low as well, which had to be rectified.

The lance corporal was also thinking along the same lines, for he leaned over and shouted above the roar of the engine and the noise coming from the tracks.

"Time for more juice, Sergeant, we must be running low."

One of the machine gun rankers crawled down the central aisle of the tank and shouted in the sergeant's ear.

"Sergeant, the ammunition has come to an end, what do we do now?"

The sergeant nodded, pulled the lever and the tank turned away, grinding its path to the British lines several hundred yards away shrouded in a light mist.

Gunner Pile was inspecting his machine gun and sliding the mechanism in and out as he did so.

The full bodied Vickers machine gun was sticking a little and he vaguely suspected the cartridge slide, so he slid it forwards several times to test it. He studied the mechanism and tried it again. It definitely is the slide, no mistake, he mused, and for a third time he slid the mechanism with his thumb, ejecting a brass cartridge as he did so. He edged his finger around the metal slide and felt the edge of the plate, his face lined with worry.

It was a misdemeanour to allow his offensive weapons to go into dereliction. If proved, it was punishable by imprisonment, therefore, he was very worried about the sergeant inspecting the gun and finding something wrong, especially on the maintenance side because he would put it down to slackness on his part, and a period of punishment would be looming. He had other things to consider because he was in line for promotion to lance corporal and an increase in pay. Small wonder his face was lined with worry as he feverishly wiped the oily rag over the slide and tested it again.

As he removed the slide from its nest in the mechanism, he inspected it for any damage. He used a spyglass to let his eye trail over the slide and the delicate mechanism. His heart missed a beat as he saw a brass fragment lodged in the corner of the slide housing. He shook his head in astonishment, noting the bit of brass that had escaped his notice previously. He wondered how long the fragment had been there and what damage it had caused by its constant friction.

In one swift movement he pulled the slide away and, with beating heart, inspected the damage. He was lucky the brass fragment had been discovered without any noticeable effect. He took his tweezers and lifted the particle out from the slide housing and, with instant relief, dropped it onto the tank floor. Just before he closed the gun, he tried the slide for ease of movement and it worked without its former grating. His heart leaped when he saw that the action was free of any problems.

"Thank God," he whispered as he looked around.

The other tank gunner had not noticed his long inspection of the machine gun, and when he hung the metal snout of the gun earthwards he did so knowing there was nothing to worry about and his bid for promotion was safe and secure.

The sergeant *did* inspect the guns and saw that Pile's gun was pointing downwards as he had ordered. He inspected the mechanism by working it several times, eyeing the slide and the cartridge extraction with some satisfaction on his face.

"Good work Gunner Pile, keep up the good work and oil it well. It will go on your record when you get your promotion to lance jack in two or three years' time."

Pile gave a nervous smile and closed the gun by jerking it into action mode.

The fuel tanker hitched up to the tank petrol drum and pumped it full of fuel. The armourer entered the tank, supplied each gunner with a metal crate of .303 gauge ammunition and fitted an additional belt to the machine gun for immediate purposes. The tank also received a drum of oil to serve the engine and other metal parts. Now the monster was ready to start the offensive against the Huns and as the men ate their bully beef sandwiches, it began to spin slowly on its axis, making a beeline for the German positions

In the weak, grey-edged sunlight, the tank met the company on the field, and as it roared past the shell hole in which he was sheltering, Smithers fell in line behind the vehicle, letting the iron frame of the metal monster protect him from all Hun fire. He was followed by Hartley and Sands, who crouched down with him, all peeping around the corner of the tank as it fired its four machine guns at the German trenches. The Hun shells flopped ineffectively off the metal track protectors or passed over the tank before exploding far behind in the tank's wake.

The rest of the company had fallen in line behind the protective bulk. At the head of the company, Smithers and the others set a precedent by using the tank as protection from the German fire. The rest of the company gratefully followed their example and used the tank as a shield.

It climbed over the heavy shell-shocked ground, ducking over the many shell holes and diving down to the pits of water-filled depressions with a great splash that immediately emptied each hole. The tank then met the wire coils and smashed a way through the curls, taking with it the barbed wire, the supporting wooden posts and any concrete props that might add to its strength.

Now the way forward was open for the company to storm the Hun lines, and they yelled with excitement that the way to the enemy line was open to assault. The tank ran right up to the enemy trench and stood back there with its engine ticking over, flicking aside the shells as though they were flea bites.

The men of the company fanned out behind the tank's protection, firing as they threw themselves at the trench walls.

35

THE MAN IN CHARGE of the tank, Sergeant William Fox, leaned over to the man at his side, the lance corporal, and shouted above the noise of the engine.

"The right track crawler is acting up, must be that last bunch of shells from the Hun, must've been a big one amongst them this time."

The lance corporal nodded and yelled in the sergeant's ear.

"We will have to wait until we get back to the repair trench this time."

The sergeant nodded and bent down to the track controls, fiddling with the lever handle at his right side. The line of the tank seemed to be off line when he pulled the right lever. It seemed to be off centre and pulling to the right. He gazed at the two lever handles with a deep frown on his face.

"I've got to get out," Fox said, looking at the two levers with worry lines showing on his face. "I've got to get out, or we will be stuck out here in no-man's-land."

"Out here in this hellhole?" the lance corporal replied with a horrified look on his face.

"It's either that or be stuck with this state of affairs, anyway, I've got the protection of the tank between us and the enemy."

"The track problem might sort itself out, Sergeant," said the lance corporal, gazing through the porthole.

"It might not either," returned Fox, easing himself from the metal seat. "Then where will you be?"

The lance corporal unbuckled his seat harness and stood up.

"If you go out, I'll go out too," he said with grim resolve.

"If you do you will risk getting killed or injured," argued the sergeant, making for the metal door

"What will be, will be," said the lance corporal, with determination set on his features.

Between them they undid the flap that opened the tank into the grey of the day, and dropped to the mud outside. The sergeant had manoeuvred the tank so that one of its sides was sheltered from the Hun trench, so they had some shield from danger if the enemy was to continue firing. They crouched down on the mud, keeping the tank between them and the enemy trench. Fox slid his body under the tank shell and gradually eased himself forwards.

The tank received several hits in its silent state and replied by putting up a wall of fire at the enemy, which was designed to keep their heads down. Fox, with the help of the tank carcass, was inching himself, a little at a time, dipping his head as a shell landed nearby then sliding his body forwards, inspecting the track selector for damage to the lever.

Fox and the lance corporal had help in the way of a shallow shell hole, and they used the it by curling their bodies under the tank. The two men rested in the depression using it to see more of the workings of the tank, desperately trying to find the track selector. The lance corporal found the selector housing and together they unscrewed the metal plate that served to protect it from enemy shellfire. Once or twice the tank shuddered as a shell rocked the metal hull, but the majority of hits missed the iron monster.

Both men were soaked to the skin with slimy water and covered in great globs of stinking mud, but they succeeded in lowering the housing to the ground in the watery sludge of the shell hole. Bit by bit, in the gloom underneath the tank, they felt the metal rod and searched for the break in the two arms. They eventually found it and were relieved to see it was two metal rods that had come apart at a set of screw worms. They spent a precious hour screwing the two halves together again and another half an hour bolting the metal box around the two halves once more.

In the rain of fire from the enemy guns, the atrocious conditions and awkwardness of the task, it was hard to imagine how they managed to do the job, but they did, and now it was up to them to worm their way out from under the tank. They did so, and as the machine gun fire rattled and whined on the tank skin, they were let into the tank's interior. They were just in time, as the ammunition of the four gunners was coming to an end and they had no protection from the Hun lead.

The sergeant crossed his fingers and winked. The lance corporal swung the starter handle and the engine started right away. He looked up to heaven with thankful eyes and twiddled the accelerator with his fingers. He gave the lance corporal a look and grasped the track shifter. In one movement he pulled the track shifter and gazed through the porthole with intent eyes.

"It's working!" he yelled, his eyes on the track ahead. "It's bleeding well working, mate, we cracked it."

The two halves were holding together as the tank's head turned around on its axis and made for the friendly side of the division.

The four gunners, unaware of the drama underneath the tank and what the two men had achieved, just treated everything as normal and emptied the guns of their last rounds with a collective sigh. The sergeant and his men with the tank transporting them, stood on the plate steel floor and bumped and banged on the hard surface until they crossed the pockmarked battlefield.

Smithers, in the lee of the German defences, watched them go. He and Sands were in a shallow shell hole, waiting for the opportunity to storm the German lines. He saw the tank and its passage across the wastes and muttered into his emergent beard.

"Those lucky bastards have got it good; protected by a steel coat that can shelter them like a woolly overcoat."

Sands looked up.

"Now they are deserting us for our side trench. Look at 'em go, they are hotfooting it back to safety."

With the rest of the company watching, the tank was making for the British trench and safety. Smithers eyed it with contempt and sniffed in a glob of mucous that was coming from his left nostril. He also had a bit of brown mud on the tip of his nose and sniffed that back up his nose too. With his helmet on his forehead, he eyed the rest of the war zone with a look of nervousness, bringing his rifle up to his chin and feeling the edge of his bayonet.

"Gawd, I'm hungry," he complained. "Me stomach is complaining to me liver that it needs something to fill it."

"You're always complaining about something. You seem to find fault with everything, Smithy."

"Yeah, I've got something to complain about, Sandy, especially that bully beef we get every day." He reflected and added, "When we gonna get something different for a change? Seems we don't get nothing like an egg or a piece of bacon for breakfast, a duck egg like we had in Blighty, or a bit of fresh bread for a change."

"You'll be lucky. Fresh bread, no such thing for us," said Sands, dipping his head as a grenade exploded ten feet away in a watery hole.

The rainwater splashed up into the air in a sudden shower and covered the ground in deep puddles. Sands spat out the dirty water.

"Fresh bread," he continued, "is for officers only. They get it every day in their safe plush quarters."

Smithers pulled a face and shot at a German who had the nerve to expose himself above the ramparts of the Hun trench ditch. He twisted in the shell hole.

"There go the tank boys, back to mother and the workshops in the rear," he snarled as the rain of leaden death came in return. "No danger for them in that tin coffin they call a tank."

Sands was watching for signs of any movement in the Hun trench, and as the company edged towards the enemy positions he quit the fox/shell hole and slid in the greasy mud to the next one. He was immediately followed by Smithers, who copied his action.

Lines of khaki-clad soldiers gathered on the ground, sliding on the sodden earth where they were safest, and hugging the wet soil that gradually changed to slimy brown mud before their eyes. A flight of Sopwith Pup fighters came out of the clouds right above their heads, and as the soldiers cheered them on, they bore down on the Hun trench with machine guns blazing. One after the other, the planes zoomed down on the German troops and raked them with fire.

The company heard the cries of the Huns as they felt the steel of the British Air Force and the Tommies, and laughed uproariously as the bullets danced a fandango on the sandbags and the men behind. One by one, the aircraft dived over the madly scrambling men and showered them with fire from their Vickers machine guns, before climbing for the safety of the open sky.

The men of the company, using the diversion to change their positions, poured along the ooze amongst exploding shell shots, dodging them and the machine gun fire as they charged the German defences. For several minutes they pounded the German soldiers, taking it in turns to bomb and machine gun the enemy trench. Cries of the wounded and dying were heard by the British troops, and they raised a wild cheer as they charged for the enemy and the German positions beyond.

Smithers and Sands were amongst the first wave of British troops, Smithers waving his steel helmet at the dark shapes that zoomed down from the sky and caused such mayhem with the enemy. The sandbags were strewn about as though some giant avalanche had struck, and the trench was laden with huge holes that the English bombs had caused. Some of the sacks were burning, but most were smoking with the ferocity of the aerial attack.

The bombardment was soon over and the aircraft became as specks in the sky that were soon lost amid the low grey clouds.

The company, aided by the fillip the raid had provided, moved forwards across the mud and through the gaps made by the fighters. There were still many of the enemy to deal with. The grey uniform was still in evidence and the soldiers were ready to fight.

36

Smithers and Sands were nearly up to the German trench and as they climbed through the blown gaps in the sandbags, they were ready for action when they saw the grey uniforms. The Huns were all wearing the German steel helmet, the front sporting a skull and crossbones. With the help of the rest of the company, they shot, stabbed, bayoneted and clubbed the soldiers and, in some cases, hit them with their entrenching tools.

Three German troopers wielding rifles and bayonets, barred their way with weapons outstretched. Smithers and Sands fell into the 'on guard' position and confronted the three men, pointing their bayonets at them, also with weapons outstretched. The enemy soldiers were sweating profusely and one skinny man, with a thin moustache to match, was closing his eyes, expecting death to come at any time. His eyes were filled with tears and he held the rifle with hands that trembled as he held the stock to his side. The man at his side was built entirely differently. He was gorilla-like with great fleshy jowls. He was armed with the rifle like it was a toy. It disappeared into his chest and stomach, and was hidden by the coils of muscle so that it almost vanished from sight. He lifted the gun and pointed the bayonet straight at Sands, aiming for the vital organs in his body.

Sands, like a toy soldier compared with the giant, battled with the glowering point of his bayonet and crossed weapons for a minute, looking for an opening. First the big man lunged then Sands saw an opportunity and tried to make a strike. He was immediately blocked by the German, who thought he noticed a mistake by Sands at the same time. It was his last try. It was a feint by Sands and he knocked the giant's bloody bayonet aside to plunge his weapon into the ample belly of his opponent.

The sizeable man was knocked to the far wall of the trench, bleeding profusely from the belly. He tried to recover by seizing his fallen rifle and attempting to spear Sands on the end of the bayonet. He saw his adversary stumble on a piece of fallen clay and he lifted his rifle, ready to strike. This was also a ruse and Sands, hoping the man would fall into his trap, buried his bayonet into him for the second time. Sands struck, and in the time-honoured way of withdrawing the bayonet from the victim, twisted the weapon in the body of the man and pulled it out. He brought with it a sizeable portion of the German's innards that, with the gush of gleaming blood, were left on the blade of the bloody bayonet.

Smithers was just as busy with others, having just killed his man with the stock edge of his rifle.

The long fighting trench of the Huns was filled with struggling men, all trying desperately to kill their opponents by any means whatsoever. Some of the men of the company were leaning on their adversaries, trying to choke the life out of the man. Others were using rocks and stones, trying to batter the life out of the antagonists. In one case a swarthy company man was stamping on a Hun with his boots. He was deliberately using the sharp edge of his steel tips to create damage.

Swarms of company men infiltrated the German trench and mixed with their German opponents. The fight was just going well with the company men on top of the enemy when the recall whistle sounded - the signal for the company men to retreat. As if by magic, the Britishers stood back from their foe then began to file out of the German trench through the sandbagged holes dug in the sides.

The dead and dying were lying in haphazard positions, and the screams of the mortally wounded echoed on the wings of the afternoon wind. The Hun defences, blown out of the trench by the tank guns across disintegrated clay pits, were scattered like the blowing wind down the hill and slope towards the British enforcements, which further added to the agony. With them went Smithers and Sands, white faced with anxiety at the recent intercourse of anguish, but relieved now that the fighting was over for the period.

The fight was indeed over. The Ninety-ninth ran down the hill, and for once the German guns were stilled of their power and the machine guns of their deadly chattering. For a time the men had the luxury of running without dodging shot and shell. They streamed across the panels of no-man's-land with not a single iota of steel to deter them from their journey, in many cases a laugh flowing from their lips as with relief they streaked away.

The men grinned at the emergence of the tank as it came into view, dipping and diving on the holes and other depressions when it crossed them on its way to the distant German trench. The sergeant in charge of the tank noted the way the men were going and stopped it on the rim of a big hole, where it teetered on the edge, revving its engine into a high roar. The company swarmed around the sides of the tank and, in some cases, knocked their rifle butts against the hard casing with echoing thumps. The sergeant waved to them as they passed and even called to them through the main ports of the tank.

For a while as the Germans recovered from the battle, the company had little opposition and the men got off without any loss to their complement. The enemy was quick to recover and within the space of half an hour gunfire was coming from their positions once more.

The war was on again and as they brought up reinforcements, it was just as perilous as before.

The boys were in their dugout enjoying a meal that Hartley had cooked on the stove.

"Did you have the usual workout?" he asked with a solemn face.

This was Sands' first encounter with the Hun and he was shocked by the outcome of the engagement.

"I never thought I would get the better of the man," he whispered, looking very pale.

"It's always this way when you go into action for the first time," commented Hartley, licking his plate with a red tongue. "Sometimes men are sick with fear, although that is before you go into battle. I can't say what happens after 'cause I ain't suffered from that yet, Sandy."

"Me too," piped up Smithers, coughing on his fag with a hoarse cough. "I don't get nothing after, only before."

The sacking door waved in company of a big shell that cracked in the sky next to the trench and as the explosion came the dust of months fluttered from the shelves and clay ceilings.

The airship made its entrance soon after that. After dropping its load of high explosive bombs, it scuttled for safety into the clouds, followed by a flight of British Sopwith Pups that buzzed about it like a pack of angry bees.

In an attack by the first aircraft the enormous blimp fought back with its own defences and succeeded in raking the aircraft with a fusillade of steel-jacketed slugs that caused the aircraft to quickly catch fire. This victory for the airship was a fillip for the enemy, who aimed at the next aircraft with enthusiasm.

The second plane darted in like a flitting wasp and stung the big balloon of the airship with its Vickers machine gun stinger. The big airship reeled under the ferocity of the attack, bursting into crimson flames, which instantly flared up and engulfed the huge balloon in a puff of flame that enveloped the cabin and the wheelhouse in orange fire. The air was filled with smoke as the airship started to sag and fold. As it fluttered down, the weight of the passenger cabin overrode its carrying capacity and it suddenly plunged earthwards, transporting the screaming men to their gruesome death far below. Additionally, their deaths were assured as its lethal complement of bombs erupted when the skeleton hit the earth with terrific force.

The other planes buzzed around the flaming wreck, inspecting the crash with inquisitive eyes that noted the destruction with satisfaction. The end of the airship was watched by thousands of eyes, especially the three soldiers who were cleaning their equipment.

"So another German experiment comes to an end," cried Sands, gazing up at the sky.

"That's all they are," commented Hartley, coming in from outside. "They can never last with all that air in them, especially carrying all that weight of bombs. They never stood a chance and now it's over for them."

"Yeah, but it's not a nice death," said Smithers, "being burnt alive."

"Being burnt or being blown up by bombs, it was over quick, I can assure you," commented Hartley, lighting a cigarette and inhaling it deep into his lungs.

The next morning thousands of troopers assembled in the fighting trench, waiting for the next tilt at the enemy. The winter was advancing and the white frost lay heavy on the trench walls, and everything had stopped for a while. The rainwater puddles were hard with ice and the breaths of the men showed as vapour plumes.

They were wearing their heavy weather gear and were wrapped up against the cold. Some of the brave ones climbed up the short ladders and had a look at the enemy. One foolhardy man exposed his head and got a bullet in his brain. He fell down onto the timber step and was carried away with his blood staining the white frost to a dark crimson. The men standing on the trench floor made way for him and the medics lifted him onto a waiting stretcher and carried him off to the casualty clearing centre.

"They never learn," a lean corporal retorted at the back of the assembly, his whistle in his lips, ready to sound the 'off'.

The shrill sound of his whistle was drowned by the roar of heavy engines as the tank hove into sight on the clinging mud, standing on the rise of the entry and exit hill and defying the enemy to do anything about it. With faces reflecting glee, the company swarmed up the ladders, secure in the knowledge that a source of security was being offered to them on a plate.

They climbed over the sandbag ramparts of the trench and dropped down behind the tank with alacrity. Scores of Tommies were hidden behind the steel of the tank and as it crawled away they went with it. The men, spear points of breath exuding from collective mouths, followed the steel monster as it clanked over the shell depressions, heading for the enemy and the Huns in the distant mist.

The shells began to fall and the bullets to shower with their intensity, churning up the greasy ground to a watery substance that very quickly changed into mud. To everyone's surprise a second tank clanked onto the battlefield and joined the first, trundling up to its mate and standing aside from it, puffing out great globs of greasy black smoke. The second tank was an exact copy of the first; even the flagpole was identical. The company was jubilant in their welcome of the second tank and readily fell into line behind it. Now the British felt safer behind the wall of steel as they advanced.

The Germans trembled behind their earthen walls and heard the tanks rumbling as they moved past each structure in the battle scene. The British guns, operating a sweeping barrage, crept along the battlefield with their prowling fire that had the opposition continually keeping their heads down with fear.

The long haul between the two factions took the tanks a long time to undertake and the lines of men slowed them down, knowing they were using the tanks to shelter from enemy fire. As the rain began to fall on the advancing troops, the German side was relieved by the turn in the weather, but of course that had no effect on the men in the tank, being inside and dry. They were ready to continue the fight and had the guns to prove it.

The company was soon bogged down and those men who could, had to seek shelter in the conventional way and return to sliding in the clinging quagmire.

———

As usual Smithers was ahead of the advancing company, and Sands and Hartley touched their heads in sympathy and shook their heads; he was a little mad in his estimation of the situation and they knew it.

"Your mate is a little bonkers," Sands said to Hartley, "but he's a brave bastard and not afraid of the enemy."

"You can't tell me about Smithy," said Hartley in the shelter of a burnt out staff car, "he's a good'un is that man. I've been with him since we've been out here and I know him of old."

"I don't think he has a cowardly bone in his body," the other said, hunching his shoulders behind the same car.

"Yeah, he is some bloke, and I know it. It's either that or he's a bloody lunatic," commented Hartley with a wry smile cracking his sallow face. "I think it is lunatic, but I prefer to think of him as a touched hero."

Sands gave him a brief smile.

"I think you are right, Hart," he declared. "He is a bloody hero and a brave one too."

The man in question was just ahead of the main party and finding solace in a lonely shell hole that a single shell had gouged out of the mud with its explosive contents. He looked all around with anxious eyes, searching for his other two mates behind.

Behind him, the two tanks were bogged down in the morass and only just able to extricate themselves from the slimy embrace of the hole-driven landscape, with great difficulty. He thought about waiting for the two tanks to catch up with him, and peeped over the edge of the shell hole with a quick look of consternation. He saw the two tanks battling the mud and obstacles, and at the same time he caught the white face of Sands gazing at him from several yards distant. He was sheltering from the German onslaught in the refuge provided by a rusty and battered German staff car, and as Smithers nodded in greeting the familiar features of Hartley came into view. They were both still all right, and they waved at him with their rifles lifted.

The roaring of the two tanks distracted his attention and as he looked they both topped the enormous depression and surmounted the crater with relief. The fire of the combined tanks beat a rapid tattoo on the Hun trench walls and tore the bags apart, shredding the sacks as they hammered them with the hell fire. The noise of both engines echoed on the terrain and in the stunted trees of a distant bunch of blackened oak trees. As the engine of one tank bawled and the other bellowed in grand alliance, they cleared the depression and, with engines in full cry, headed for the hill and the final attempt at retribution.

Seeing the final assault was in the offing, Smithers and the others jumped out of the safety of their shelter and made for the German trench. Contrary to tradition, the final assault was enacted in silence by the men. The only sound they made was the firing of their rifles as the mad last dash up the slope was accomplished.

37

CORPORAL GUNN HAD MISSED the morning's charge and was busy watching the two tanks as they desperately tried to negotiate the huge depression in the shelled terrain of the battlefield. He heard the scream of the engines as they fought to extricate themselves from the gluey embrace of the shell holes. The mud tried to keep hold of the metal sides of the tanks, and several times it seemed as though it was winning the battle and holding the metal monster in its grip.

Gunn saw the iron treads of the tanks' caterpillars dripping with oily mud falling from the wheels and flailing treads with every turn of the engines' roar. He even faintly thought he heard the shriek of the tanks' engines, screaming in agony as the vicious mud clung to the bottom with hideous ferocity. The morass held firm for a time, but it finally let go of its prey. The tanks had won the battle and were free, the treads waving in the air, churning the noiseless engines in silent protest.

It was the first time Gunn had hoped he could hear the turning engine as it finally tore itself free of the muddy entwines. He shifted his optical viewer, so that he could see what the rest of the company was doing. They were spread out among the shell holes, with their helmets poking out, their rifle butts sticking up like a forest of branchless trees.

Gunn was searching for Smithers as he trained the optical viewer on the various shell holes until he thought he could make out the skinny malingerer. He moved it once more and the faces of the other two troopers came into focus then the familiar face of Smithers was seen and, as if he knew what was happening, Smithers poked out his tongue at the British section, in a deliberate action. Gunn saw the rude gesture and vowed to make him sorry for doing it.

"All right, Smithers," he muttered to himself, "you are king of the castle while you are out there, but just wait until you return, I'll make you hop I will."

Gunn moved the viewer aside and watched the enemy soldiers looking through the trench gaps. They were gazing at the crowds of British soldiers less than fifty yards away and were blazing away at them as they hid behind all sorts of things they could find. Their first line of protection, the barbed wire, was lying in tatters on the ground, squashed and flattened beneath the grinding wheels and treads of the two tanks.

The tanks advanced, one after the other, slithering through the dark deep mud and getting nearer to the German positions. They fired in rotation, first one fired a long burst then the other one, until it seemed the eight machine guns of combined power were keeping up a withering and deadly path of bullets at the Hun trench. To add to this wall of steel, the company kept up its own firepower and rained further slugs at the enemy.

This continual rain of death-dealing bullets was in conjunction with the creeping barrage of shells that were aimed at the German side, and it must have had an adverse effect on the enemy. Gunn mused as he stared at the opposition across the divide. All that presentation of firepower and all directed at the Hun trench.

He brought the sliding tanks into focus and saw the first batch of company men get up in readiness to storm the enemy fortifications.

The forms of the creeping men fell into line behind the two tanks and crouched there with rifles and bayonets bared.

Gunn was not the only one to watch the progress of the company. Sergeant Cox had a telescope and had the battle in his sights for a long time. He was also aware that the three pals were in the front of the company and he saw most of the battle for supremacy.

He was aware that Smithers was the holder of a medal as was Hartley. Cox was also a medal holder and proudly wore his row of medals when and where he was able. He was older now and left the fighting to the young men. He swept the telescope around the field and watched the packed ranks of the company charge forwards, a wall of shining steel reflecting and illustrious in the weak glow of the setting sun.

The reinforcements were in the trench, waiting for the say-so to join the company in no-man's-land. There were upwards of two thousand men in the lee of the trench and they were all ready to face the enemy. The noise of voices was terrific and joined in with the bullets that periodically stitched a line on the rim of the trench head.

Cox gazed at the men beneath the sandbags and wondered how many would be killed in the forthcoming battle that was taking place across the battlefield. How many mums and wives would cry for their brave men sacrificed for the honour of the country? He shook himself and dashed the feeling aside. It was the job of the young man to fight for his country, perhaps to make the ultimate sacrifice and die for king and queen.

It was not for Cox to decide who was to die. In the long run the option would be made by the politicians or the high rankers. It was ever so. They gave the orders and the rank and file carried them out. The politicians have the last say in my future and what they say is good enough for me, regardless, he thought. He sniffed and folded the telescope, adding it to the swagger stick he carried at his side.

He moved down the lines of khaki-clad, acknowledging calls of good luck, which he exchanged with his own greeting to each individual.

"Good luck," he sang out to all, and smiled to each man in turn.

"Good luck to you, Sergeant," they chorused, making way for him.

The NCO in charge held the whistle to his lips and shrilled a blast, sending the men aloft on the ladders. Cox was then alone as each man climbed the rungs to possible perdition. The silence is the most depressing, he thought, eyeing the last rung of the ladder as it still shook with the passage of the last soldier. He thought he heard the voice of the man, but it was just an echo on the dying wind.

A voice sounded along the trench walls, rebounding on the sandbags with finality.

"Good afternoon, Sergeant Cox, has the last man gone?"

Gunn was staring at him with slit eyes that asked him to answer.

"Yes, Coporal Gunn, all away on the blow of the whistle. I wonder how many will make it back?" sighed Cox, holding the telescope at his side.

"I think that guess will be as good as mine," returned Gunn, hitting his own swagger stick on his thigh.

"I think so too, Corporal Gunn, I only know they are a brave bunch of men, the Ninety-ninth of Foot."

Corporal Gunn laughed.

"Don't say that, Sergeant Cox, they might want a promotion or a pay rise!"

Cox echoed his laugh.

"For some that might not be so bad. I have seen a lot of courage displayed today, by someone from whom I least expected it."

"You must mean Smithers. Yes, he has turned out to be something I hadn't expected."

"I do mean Smithers, he has no equal when it comes to guts. I'm recommending him for a special medal."

"What about Hartley?" said Gunn, "he has a lot of guts too."

"Him too, they are both in line for a citation," replied Cox. "I'll see that they both get it."

When the men finally returned to the dugout, the welcome they received was unexpected and surprising. They both entered to see the commanding officer standing upright and ready to receive them.

Resplendent in their new uniforms and gold braid, the group of officers waited for the two men to enter. As they saluted, the two troopers stood to attention and heard the commanding officer congratulate them on their courage and devotion to duty.

"Their selfless courage," the CO was saying, "was due to the efforts of their senior NCO, Sergeant Cox. These men because of their courage and humanity undertook to storm the enemy, and with members of the company of foot, the glorious Ninety-ninth, they distinguished themselves with their courageous, fearless and heroic behaviour. They, and almost alone, fought and won against a far bigger number of German soldiers, and in recognition of these facts we will award the medals for this mark of bravery." He ended his speech by announcing, "The men involved will finish duty immediately and then be transported to the barracks in Calais where they will be presented with their medals. From there they will go on one month's leave to see their respective parents. I only hope your brave example will encourage others to copy your actions."

The officers ended by shaking Smithers and Hartley by the hand.

One month later, Smithers and Hartley arrived home.

Smithers surprised his parents by opening the front door and saying:

"Hello, Mum and Dad, I'm home."